REFORMING REGULATION:

Processes and Problems

D1275737

Lawrence J. White
New York University

PRENTICE-HALL, INC., Englewood Cliffs, N.J. 07632

Library of Congress Cataloging in Publication Data

WHITE, LAWRENCE J. (date)
   Reforming regulation.

   Includes bibliographical references and index.
   1. Trade regulation—United States—Cost effective-
ness. 2. Administrative procedure—United States—
Cost effectiveness. 3. United States. Council of
Economic Advisers. I. Title.
HD3616.U47W45   353.09'1   80-24930
ISBN 0–13–770115-2
ISBN 0–13–770107-1 (pbk.)

Editorial/production supervision
and interior design by Richard C. Laveglia
Cover design by Miriam Recio
Manufacturing buyer: Gordon Osbourne

Printed in the United States of America

10 9 8 7 6 5 4 3 2 1

Prentice-Hall International, Inc., *London*
Prentice-Hall of Australia Pty. Limited, *Sydney*
Prentice-Hall of Canada, Ltd., *Toronto*
Prentice-Hall of India Private Limited, *New Delhi*
Prentice-Hall of Japan, Inc., *Tokyo*
Prentice-Hall of Southeast Asia Pte. Ltd., *Singapore*
Whitehall Books Limited, *Wellington, New Zealand*

To my mother, who has always wanted the greatest good for the greatest number.

Contents

Preface

The hours are long, the pace is brutal, the pressures are killing, and the disappointments are frequent. But, for an economist, a senior staff position with the Council of Economic Advisers probably represents the best job in the federal government (short of being a council member one's self). The opportunity to deal with a wide range of real issues and the ability to help shape federal policy presents an exciting and challenging experience. As a colleague at New York University (and former CEA staff member) remarked, "You are one ear away from the President. You have Charlie Schultze's ear, and he has the President's ear."

During the 1978–1979 academic year I took leave from the N.Y.U. Graduate School of Business Administration to serve as a senior staff economist with the CEA. My responsibilities were microeconomic issues, primarily regulatory matters. This book is about the main issues, mostly regulatory, that were my responsibility during those 11 months. It is offered both as a description of how microeconomics is actually practiced in the executive branch of the U.S. government and as an effort to provide insights into the regulatory process and the way it is being managed and reformed.

I owe debts of gratitude to various parties. The Sloan Foundation, through a grant to N.Y.U. to encourage research on applied microeconomies, provided partial support while this book was written. A number of friends and colleagues read early drafts of the manuscript and provided helpful suggestions and comments: Ernest Bloch, Joanne Czete, Stephen Kohlhagen, Robert Litan, Robert Lurie, William Nordhaus, and William Silber. Penny Stone, Marilyn Eichelberger, and Elise Morris and her typing pool typed and retyped a number of drafts of the manuscript.

Lawrence J. White

part I

INTRODUCTION

chapter 1

Introduction

Over the past century governmental regulation of various kinds has become a pervasive force in the American economy. It is difficult to think of a good, a service, or a workplace that is not affected directly or indirectly by regulation. Some of this regulation is well intentioned but ill conceived; some offers the potential for large social benefits but, if poorly managed, also offers the potential for large social costs. A growing recognition of these problems with regulation has led the American political system increasingly to focus on reforming and managing regulation.

This author served as a senior staff economist with the Council of Economic Advisers (CEA) from September 1978 through July 1979, with responsibility for microeconomic issues, primarily regulatory matters. This book is about some of the major regulatory issues that arose during those 11 months. It is offered both as a description of how microeconomics is actually practiced in the executive branch of the U.S. Government and as an effort to provide insights into the regulatory process and the way in which it is being managed and reformed.

This book is about the *whats* and the *hows* of regulation and of the Carter administration's regulatory reform effort. It will try to explain *what* a number of regulatory programs are designed to achieve and *how* the regulations are established and are carried out. The distinction between old-style economic regulation (control over prices and entry) and new-style health–safety–environment regulation (control over products and processes) will be delineated and explained; the failure to make this distinction has muddied much of the current discussion of regulation. It will describe *what* the goals of the regulatory reform effort have been and *how* the reform procedures have operated. The bulk of this book is focused on 12 case studies of some of the more important regulatory issues that arose during this author's year at CEA. These 12 issues do not, of course, encompass the full range of federal regulatory efforts, but they do provide a fairly broad perspective on regulatory issues, problems, and procedures. Each case study includes the background to the particular regulatory issue, an analysis of the issue itself and of the conflicting positions that were taken on it, the steps in the decision process, the outcome, and some concluding comments. The case studies are preceded by two chapters that give a background on CEA and on regulatory procedures and issues in general, including an economist's general approach to regulatory problems. The book concludes with a summary of the lessons that can be learned from these case studies, a review of the strengths and weaknesses of the regulatory reform effort, and a number of recommendations for improvements in public policy.

Proper reform and management of the regulatory process has been an important goal of the Carter administration. This has not been an easy task, especially on health–safety–environment regulatory issues. There is a deep division in sentiment on these issues that extends across the public, the Congress, and many of the leading figures in the departments and agencies within the Carter administration itself. One group believes that yet more of this health–safety–environment regulation is needed, pointing to continuing instances of the landscape's being despoiled, workers being maimed, and consumers being bilked. The other argues that the world can never be completely safe or completely clean, that the social costs of pushing regulation too hard in these areas can easily outweigh the social gains that are supposed to be achieved. The differences between the two groups are grounded partly in philosophy or ideology, partly in the perceived distributional consequences of the regulation, and partly in the perceived "facts" of the aggregate costs and benefits of regulation.

It is important to realize that there has been an important shift in the center ground of this dispute over the past decade. As recently as the early 1970s, there seemed to be widespread sentiment that the goals toward which these regulations were aimed were important and that the fast-growing American economy could easily accommodate the costs. The dissenters were few. The middle ground was clearly in the area of more regulation. But, as the growth of the American economy slowed, as inflation became more serious and endemic, and as the costs became more apparent, opponents of increased regulation grew in numbers and vocal power. The midpoint of sentiment had clearly shifted.

The Carter administration has tried to find the middle ground in the dispute. It has tried to establish processes and procedures that will lead to sensible, cost-effective regulation. It has tried to provide centralized management of the regulatory process, to establish the terms of the trade-offs among multiple social goals (e.g., cleaner air, greater safety, reduced inflationary pressures, reduced dependence on foreign petroleum) that inevitably come into conflict in regulatory proceedings. Congress has left a vacuum in this area, which the Carter administration has tried to fill. Charles L. Schultze, Chairman of CEA, was one of the main architects of this effort in regulatory reform. Many of these reform procedures were just being put into place or being tested in 1978 and 1979.

Presidential administrations are never wholly unified organizations. There are always differences of opinion and philosophy and conflicts over means and ends. It could not be otherwise in an organization with such diverse functions, responsibilities, and constituencies.[1] (The view that one all too often hears expressed in public, of "the Government" as a monolith that rolls ever onward for good or evil, would quickly disappear after a week's exposure to the processes of government.) These conflicts are usually resolved through compromise or, ultimately, by decisions at the top. Since many of the regulatory reform procedures were new and since there were serious philosophical and political differences of opinion within the administration itself as to the wisdom of these procedures and the outcomes that they generated, conflicts naturally arose within the administration on these issues. Some of these conflicts and their resolution will be described in the case studies in this book.

A number of themes and lessons emerge from this book. They will receive greater attention in the concluding chapter, but they are worth mentioning at the beginning, so that the reader can take note of them as they arise in the case studies. First, the distinction between old-style economic regulation and new-style health–safety–environment regulation is crucial for understanding how various forms of regulation operate, what their costs and consequences are, what the possibilities and meanings of reform are, and what role the executive branch of the federal government can play. This book will focus heavily on new-style regulation, but a few of the chapters do deal with old-style regulatory issues. Second, with respect to health–safety–environment regulation, there is a very strong tendency for the Congress and for regulators to think and act in terms of an overly simplified, dichotomous world: the air is healthy or unhealthy; chemicals are safe or unsafe; the necessary new technology to meet a proposed regulation will or will not be available at a specified future date. They are reluctant to think in terms of degrees of potency, of the varying risks of unfortunate occurrences, of the probabilities of technological events not occurring, or of the varying extra costs that might be incurred to hasten technological development and feasibility. There is a deep irony here. Economists are frequently accused of using oversimplified models in their efforts to predict and evaluate the consequences of governmental actions. Yet, in actuality, it is the lawyers in Congress and the regulatory agencies who legislate and make decisions on the basis of their overly simplified dichotomous model of the world, whereas it is the economists in and out of government who have stressed the continuity and the complexity of the phenomena and processes at issue.

Third, although Congress and the regulatory agencies are acquiring an improved appreciation of the costs of regulation, there are still too many instances in which costs are disregarded, seriously underestimated, or treated in inappropriate ways. For example, the ability of industry to afford (in some vaguely specified sense) the costs of regulation is frequently the sole cost criterion that is used. Fourth, just as lawyers are an important part of the regulatory process itself, they are an important part of the regulatory reform effort. Economists may be able to devise more cost-effective procedures and illuminate the costs and benefits of alternative levels of stringency of regulations. But they need the support of lawyers to convince the lawyers of the regulatory agencies that possible changes in procedures or in stringency levels are within the legal mandate of the legislation under which the regulators are operating. An economist who tries to convince an unsympathetic regulatory lawyer of these same things is doomed to fail.

Finally, there are time and expertise limits on how much can be achieved by CEA and other relatively small agencies within the Executive Office of the President in their efforts to reform regulation. They can help structure regulatory problems and encourage cost-effectiveness. But on many regulatory issues, which often hinge on questions of the costs and consequences of alternative levels of regulatory stringency, they are unlikely to have the detailed expertise that would argue for one level of stringency over another; they are likely to be "out-gunned" by determined regulators.

At the beginning, a number of disclaimers are in order. First, this book does not focus on the *whys* of regulation. It will not try to offer a general theory of regulation or of the regulatory process.[2] The entire area is too diffuse, too complex, and too multifaceted to permit useful theorizing. Further, it will not dwell on the *whys* of the particular outcomes in the case studies; this author was not the decision maker in any of these instances and was not privy to many of the discussions surrounding the decisions. Nevertheless, even in the absence of these *whys*, a book that focuses on the *whats* and *hows* of regulation and of the reform effort should be useful in illustrating a number of the regulatory processes, highlighting their tensions and problems, and indicating generally how microeconomics is actually used to deal with practical, real-world problems of government policy making.

Second, the regulatory issues, their analyses, and the events are all described here by an economist who was located at the center, within the Executive Office of the President. Someone located in the regulatory agencies might well have written a very different book describing the same regulatory issues.[3]

Finally, this book is not about the three issues that gained the most public attention in 1978–1979: the wage–price guidelines that were developed to try to slow inflation, the efforts to maintain the international value of the dollar, and the many energy–oil issues that arose during the year. Since these were not within this author's area of responsibility, few insights can be offered beyond those that might be gleaned from the pages of *The New York Times* or *The Washington Post*. This omission may be disappointing to some readers, since these were the three really "big" issues of the year and, some might say, the most important. But the way in which policies are set and precedents established on the group of "smaller" issues discussed in this book may well have equally important consequences in the longer run. Unless public sentiment and congressional policies change radically, much of the regulation described in the book is likely to continue and, if anything, grow more pervasive.

This book is organized as follows: Chapter 2 describes the Council of Economic Advisers, the role of CEA staff, the general efforts of the Executive Office of the President to manage the regulatory process, and the important role of rulemaking by the regulatory agencies. Chapter 3 offers a brief primer of an economist's view of the proper role of regulation. The important distinction between old-style economic (prices–entry) regulation and new-style social (health–safety–environment) regulation is delineated. This chapter should serve as an important point of reference for the case studies that follow.

Chapters 4 through 7 describe regulatory issues concerning provisions of the Clean Air Act. Chapter 4 focuses on the determination of the ambient air quality standard for ozone (photochemical oxidants). Chapter 5 describes an effort to invoke a provision to require that Ohio electric utilities burn only Ohio coal. Chapter 6 focuses on the control of hydrocarbon and carbon monoxide exhaust emission from heavy-duty trucks. Chapter 7 is about the control of particulate exhaust emissions from diesel automobiles.

Chapters 8 through 11 cover four other new-style social regulatory issues. Chapter 8 is about the fuel economy standards for automobiles for the 1980s. Chapter 9 describes efforts to require extensive information from chemical manufacturers before they begin the manufacture of chemicals. Chapter 10 is about the administration's development of a bill to deal with spills of hazardous substances and with abandoned dumps containing hazardous substances. Chapter 11 focuses on efforts to protect the snail darter fish and not build the Tellico Dam in Tennessee.

Chapters 12 through 15 deal with four old-style economic regulatory issues. Chapter 12 describes the efforts by the administration to develop a regulatory policy toward the U.S. maritime industry. Chapter 13 focuses on the administration's decision concerning the U.S. Postal Service's role in electronic mail. Chapter 14 describes a Department of Energy rulemaking concerning profit margins for gasoline retailers. Chapter 15 concerns conglomerate mergers.

Finally, Chapter 16 offers some lessons and conclusions from these case studies.

The use of initials for agencies, programs, and concepts is endemic to Washington. To a newcomer, it is initially baffling and frustrating. But it has its purpose in saving time and space when these agencies or programs are mentioned repeatedly. For better or worse, I have found the practice useful in this book also. To help the reader, the following is a guide to the frequently used abbreviations:

CAB	Civil Aeronautics Board
CEA	Council of Economic Advisers
CEQ	Council on Environmental Quality
CO	Carbon monoxide
COWPS	Council on Wage and Price Stability
DOE	Department of Energy
DOI	Department of the Interior
DOJ	Department of Justice
DPS	Domestic Policy Staff
EMSS	Electronic message switching system
EOP	Executive Office of the President
EPA	Environmental Protection Agency
FMC	Federal Maritime Commission
FTC	Federal Trade Commission
GM	General Motors
HC	Hydrocarbon
ICC	Interstate Commerce Commission
I&M	Inspection and maintenance program
MARAD	Maritime Administration
NAAQS	National ambient air quality standard
NAS	National Academy of Sciences
NHTSA	National Highway Traffic Safety Administration

NOAA	National Oceanic and Atmospheric Administration
NO$_x$	Nitrogen oxide
NPRM	Notice of proposed rulemaking
NSPS	New source performance standard
NTIA	National Telecommunications and Information Administration
OMB	Office of Management and Budget
OSHA	Occupational Safety and Health Administration
OSTP	Office of Science and Technology Policy
RARG	Regulatory Analysis Review Group
SIP	State implementation plan
SO$_2$	Sulfur dioxide
TVA	Tennessee Valley Authority
UAW	United Automobile Workers
UNCTAD	United Nations Conference on Trade and Development
USPS	U.S. Postal Service
VMT	Vehicle miles traveled
VW	Volkswagen

NOTES TO CHAPTER 1

[1]For a further discussion and description of this phenomenon, see G. P. Schultz and K. W. Dam, *Economic Policy Beyond the Headlines* (New York: Norton, 1977), especially Chapter 1.

[2]For efforts along these lines, see G. J. Stigler, "The Theory of Economic Regulation," *Bell Journal of Economics and Management Science*, 2 (Spring 1971): 2–21; R. A. Posner, "Taxation by Regulation, *Bell Journal of Economics and Management Science*, 2 (Spring 1971) 22–50; R. A. Posner, "Theories of Economic Regulation," *Bell Journal of Economics and Management Science*, 5 (Autumn 1974); 335–358; W. A. Jordan, "Producer Protection, Prior Market Structure and the Effects of Government Regulation," *Journal of Law and Economics*, 15 (April 1972): 151–176; and S. Peltzman, "Toward a More General Theory of Regulation," *Journal of Law and Economics*, 19 (August 1976): 211–240.

[3]For this perspective on an earlier set of issues, see J. Quarles, *Cleaning Up America: An Insider's View of the Environmental Protection Agency* (Boston: Houghton Mifflin, 1976).

part II

BACKGROUND

chapter 2

The Council of Economic Advisers and Regulatory Management

COUNCIL OF ECONOMIC ADVISERS

On federal government organization charts the Council of Economic Advisers is located within the Executive Office of the President. Established by the Employment Act of 1946, CEA has the responsibility for advising the President on economic issues. In January of every year, the short *Economic Report of the President* is accompanied by the longer CEA *Annual Report*. The two reports provide a review of the economy for the past year and a statement of the hopes and plans of the current administration for the coming year. It is a widely distributed document that requires many person-months of long hours and intensive effort in preparation. Indeed, it is the impression of many economists in other parts of the federal government and outside government that the compilation of the *Annual Report* constitutes the sole activity of CEA. But, as part of the continuous process of advising the President, CEA members and staff are constantly gathering information, analyzing data, making projections, and interacting with their counterparts in other parts of the federal government. CEA members and staff frequently take part in interagency task forces to deal with new or troublesome issues. In sum, CEA plays an active role in the day-to-day management of the economy and in the development of longer-range economic policies.

CEA has mostly been identified with macroeconomic policies (inflation, unemployment, growth) and to a lesser extent with international economic policies (trade balance, foreign investment, value of the dollar).[1] Although microeconomic policies (the workings of individual markets, regulatory policies) have also been within the purview of CEA, until recently they did not gain much public attention. Indeed, the *Annual Report,* which gets the most public attention, has been primarily macroeconomics oriented. Nevertheless, CEA has always played an important role within the federal government in helping to shape microeconomic policies.

The Carter administration decided that management of the regulatory process and regulatory reform were high priorities, and CEA played a prominent role in developing policy in this area.[2] The CEA chairman and the member responsible for microeconomics devoted sizable fractions of their time to regulatory matters. During 1978–1979, three professional staff economists devoted virtually all their time to regulatory matters. This area was clearly seen as quite important.

Despite its large responsibilities, CEA is a tiny agency. It is one of the smallest organizations within the federal government and surely the smallest in relation to its responsibilities. CEA has a chairman and two members. During 1978–1979 the chairman was Charles L. Schultze, who had been at the Brookings Institution and had earlier been director of the Bureau of the Budget (now Office of Management and Budget) under President Lyndon Johnson. The member primarily responsible for macroeconomic policy was Lyle E. Gramley, who had been research director at the Federal Reserve. The member primarily responsible for microeconomic policy was William D. Nordhaus, who had been an economics professor at Yale University. All three had come into office with the Carter administration in early 1977. In early 1979 Nordhaus returned to Yale and was replaced by George C. Eads, who had been an economist at the Rand Corporation.

Supporting the three CEA principals are a staff of 12 professional economists,[3] 5 junior staff economists (usually doctoral economics candidates at major universities who have decided to take a year off before completing their degrees), a statistician who keeps track of the reams of data that become grist for CEA's analytic mill, and a special assistant to the chairman. This small staff (plus an occasional consultant) is expected to deal with the entire economy! The professional staff is largely temporary, with most taking one- or two-year leaves of absence from universities, research institutions, or other governmental agencies to serve at CEA.

The small size of the staff means heavy responsibility and long hours, but it also engenders a special *esprit de corps* that can rarely be found anywhere else in the federal government. The average quality of the staff is quite high, and, when conflicts with other governmental agencies arise, a David vs. Goliath attitude often emerges: "We few against their hundreds (or thousands)." Because the staff is short-term, there are costs in the loss of institutional memory and the need to acquaint new staff members with issues, procedures, and contacts, but there are gains in the inflow of fresh ideas and (perhaps most important of all, given the hours and responsibilities) fresh energies.

The general responsibilities of the CEA staff are information processing: gaining data and information about economic issues, analyzing and interpreting it, and conveying it to the chairman and members in oral or memo form. The small size of the staff and its wide scope of responsibility mean that the staff is largely engaged in "fire fighting": dealing with issues in a short-term context as they arise. There simply is not the personnel to undertake long-term studies. Also, because CEA is so small, there is no administrative hierarchy above or below the profes-

15

sional staff—the 12 professional staff economists all report directly to the chairman and the members—and hence the staff has no administrative or management responsibilities.

The information gathering of the microeconomic staff occurs through meetings with the staff members of other agencies and with nongovernment parties and, most important, through telephone conversations and the subsequent sending of documents. Proper use of the telephone, identifying the right people (sometimes through chains of four or five referrals) within agencies who have the necessary information, is a key part of the job.[4]

Although CEA is frequently in conflict with the regulatory agencies—criticizing agency actions and pressing for different policies—cooperation from the staff at these agencies is almost always complete. Documents are always forwarded; information is always made available. This pattern of conflict and cooperation, with cooperation almost always prevailing, may appear a bit surprising. A priori, one might expect more agency hostility to CEA's critical stances. But keeping the lines of communication open, keeping the processes of conflict resolution working, is considered important at all levels.

In more detail, the responsibilities of a professional staff microeconomist at CEA are roughly as follows:[5]

1. Serve as the staff-level person on interagency committees and task forces. Frequently, interagency committees are formed when new issues arise and the administration has to reach a common position and resolve any conflicts among government agencies. These issues can encompass anything from "What should be our policy toward the maritime industry?" (a topic discussed in Chapter 12) to "What is the best way to collect foreign trade statistics?" Although cabinet secretaries (and the CEA chairman) are usually the nominal members of these task forces, virtually all meetings and discussions take place at the staff level. The CEA staff members' role here is to represent CEA's position and keep the chairman and members informed of any progress made.

2. Serve as primary contact with the Office of Management and Budget. Among the many functions of OMB, an important one is the coordination of executive branch positions on various issues. For example, if a department wants to have a new piece of legislation introduced in Congress, OMB will first circulate it among the other relevant departments and agencies to make sure that there are no serious problems or objections. Similarly, if executive branch agencies have been asked to testify on particular issues, their testimony will be circulated for the same purpose. The general reason for this practice

is to try, on most issues, to have a uniform administration position, to prevent the appearance (or actuality) of a chaotic administration that is publicly saying inconsistent things. In a similar fashion, after a bill has been passed by Congress and awaits presidential action, OMB will ask the relevant agencies for their opinions as to whether the President should sign or veto the bill and why.

In all these situations, the CEA staff person receives the request from OMB, familiarizes himself or herself with the background and details, and, if it is important that CEA take a position, prepares a memo for the chairman on the issue, including a suggested letter from the chairman to OMB.[6]

3. Occasionally write speeches or prepare congressional testimony for the chairman or members.

4. Deal with rulemakings on regulatory issues by executive branch agencies. To explain this particular activity further, it is necessary to explain the role of rulemakings in the regulatory process and the evolving role of the Executive Office of the President in dealing with rulemakings.

RULEMAKINGS

When Congress passes a law on regulatory matters, the full details are rarely spelled out. Rather, the details are relegated to the relevant agency to establish. For example, in the case of diesel particulates (discussed in Chapter 7), the relevant passage from the Clean Air Act reads as follows: "The Administrator [of the Environmental Protection Agency] shall prescribe regulations . . . applicable to emissions of particulate matter from classes or categories of vehicles manufactured during and after model year 1981. . . ." It is thus EPA's responsibility to fill in the details: what will be counted as particulate matter; what categories of vehicles will be covered; how much particulate matter will be allowed to be emitted; and what the measurement and testing procedures will be. EPA does this through a proceeding known as an "informal" rulemaking.

The procedure in an informal rulemaking is as follows:[7] EPA's (for example) scientists, engineers, economists, and lawyers spend considerable time trying to develop a set of standards or regulations that the agency believes will meet the requirements of the relevant law. When these have finally been developed, they are published in the *Federal Register* (the publication for all official federal government notices) as a "notice of proposed rulemaking" (NPRM).[8] The regulation will be offered as a *proposed* set of standards. The NPRM contains a preamble, explaining the regulations, their purpose, and how and why they operate, as well as the proposed text of the detailed regulations themselves. It invites public comment on the proposed regulations and in some cases may invite comment on particular aspects of or assumptions in the regulations.

There will then be a public comment period of (usually) 60 or 90 days, during which any individual or organization (including other government agencies) can file written comments with the agency. The agency will also hold public hearings on the proposal, during which any individual or organization can testify. The written comments and the oral testimony become part of the public record for the agency on that rulemaking. At the end of the public comment period, the record is closed, and agency officials are not supposed to have any further outside (*ex parte*) contacts with respect to the proposed rule. The notion here is that the public comment period provides the opportunity for the interplay of ideas and the challenging and rebutting of arguments by the various interested parties. This exchange must stop at some point, and any outsider who conveys information to agency officials after the public comment period has ended would thereby gain an unfair advantage.

The agency then reviews the public record that has been compiled and issues the final regulations. The regulations are supposed to be based on the record developed during the rulemaking. Again, these are published in the *Federal Register* and, again, the notice contains a preamble (this time also answering any important comments or objections that have been raised during the public comment period) and the detailed regulations. The regulations now have the force of law (subject to appeal to the courts).

The rulemaking process just described can be divided conceptually into three distinct sections:[9] the pre-NPRM formulation, culminating in the NPRM publication; the public comment period; and the post-comment period review and final rule publication. This trichotomy will prove useful in the following discussion.

REGULATORY MANAGEMENT AND REFORM

An early goal of the Carter administration was regulatory reform. There was a growing public awareness in the mid-1970s that government regulation was increasing in scope and perhaps becoming excessively burdensome. A frequently cited statistic was the growth in the pages of the *Federal Register:* In 1955, the annual volume of the *Federal Register* ran to 10,000 pages; in 1970, it was 20,000 pages; by 1975, it was up to 60,000 pages.

The Carter administration's strategy was twofold: In the area of traditional economic regulation (see Chapter 3), the administration decided largely on deregulation. Most of this regulation was (and is) lodged outside of the executive branch, in independent commissions (e.g., the Interstate Commerce Commission). Many economists had long argued that most of the commissions had served to impede competition by allowing their regulatees to fix prices and prevent new entry. The commissions were largely protecting the current producers. The consuming public was being ill served by such regulation, and the best solution was the abolition of the commissions, or at least a drastic reduction in their powers. These arguments had slowly percolated through to lawyers generally and to federal government officials in both the legislative and executive branches. Pressured by the Justice Department's Antitrust Division, the Securities and Exchange Commission in the early 1970s gradually removed its sanction for the collusive setting of brokerage fees by the securities industry; by May 1975, brokerage rates were wholly deregulated. The Congress and the executive branch laid the groundwork for airline deregulation during the Ford administration. The Carter administration decided to pursue airline deregulation further by supporting legislation that would reduce and eventually abolish the Civil Aeronautics Board's powers to regulate the airline industry. This legislation was passed by Congress and signed by President Carter in October 1978. The Carter administration has subsequently pursued deregulation legislation in surface transportation (trucking and rail) and telecommunications. (The regulation of the international maritime industry is another story, however, that will be told in Chapter 12). In the spring of 1980 the Congress passed and the president signed a law providing for the substantial deregulation of interest rates that banks and savings institutions can pay their depositors. And in the summer a bill that partially deregulated trucking was passed and signed.

In the area of social (health–safety–environment) regulation, the decision was not to seek legislation that would substantively reduce the amount of regulation in this area. Rather, the administration decided that the executive branch, and, more specifically, the Executive Office of the President, would try to manage this regulation in a more effective and efficient manner. Most of this regulation is the responsibility of executive branch agencies and hence comes under the purview of the President. There was far from a consensus within the administration that the laws required changes, and, even if there had been a consensus, the political costs of a direct legislative assault on the laws authorizing this regulation were probably too great. Appearing to oppose cleaner air and water, safer workplaces, and safer consumer products is a difficult political posture, even if the social costs of achieving these goals are quite high. Better management of this regulation, reducing its costs, was a politically more attractive position.

In this regulatory management effort[10] the primary agencies within the Executive Office have been CEA, the Council on Wage and Price Stability (COWPS), the Office of Management and Budget (OMB), and the Domestic Policy Staff (DPS). COWPS was established in August 1974, primarily to monitor the activities of the private sector that might add to the rate of inflation. COWPS also has a Government Programs and Regulations division that examines government programs and activities. This division issues reports and makes filings on the public record of regulatory agencies (both executive branch agencies and independents) during rulemakings, pointing out weaknesses in the agencies' analyses and offering suggestions on how their regulations could be made more cost effective (i.e., how the ultimate goals of the regulation could be achieved at a lower cost).[11] As part of the regulatory management effort, this section was upgraded and expanded.

OMB was formerly called the Bureau of the Budget. As the addition of the word "management" to its title indicates, it has management responsibilities with respect to the executive branch departments and agencies. It has a Regulatory Policy and Reports Management division that participates in a number of regulatory policy discussions. In addition, the budget specialists within OMB are usually familiar with the regulatory issues that involve the agencies whose budgets they monitor, and the specialists frequently become involved in the discussions and disputes surrounding the issues.

DPS has the responsibility for advising the President on domestic policy issues. It is expected to be sensitive to the political considerations involved in policy decisions. In many instances, DPS has served as an "honest broker" in trying to mediate disputes between executive branch agencies or in defining the issues that must ultimately be referred to the President for resolution. DPS has been quite active in helping shape the regulatory reform program and is usually involved in most of the disputed regulatory issues.

In late 1977 the Regulatory Analysis Review Group (RARG) was formed. This is an interagency group, chaired by CEA and administered by COWPS. Its members consist of all of the executive branch departments except State and Defense, plus the Environmental Protection Agency and the major Executive Office agencies. RARG's function is to review the analyses that accompany major rulemakings by executive branch regulatory agencies. COWPS and CEA staff are the authors of the first drafts of these reviews, which are then circulated among RARG members (including the agency issuing the regulations being reviewed) for comments, revised, and finally filed on the public record of the rulemaking agency during its public comment period. RARG reviews have become, in essence, reports on the proposed regulations themselves.

In the spring of 1978, President Carter issued Executive Order 12044, which requires all executive branch regulatory agencies to provide a regulatory analysis to accompany all major regulations.[12] The agencies' regulatory analyses are supposed to include the consideration of alternatives to the actual regulations chosen, the consideration of the consequences of the alternatives, and a justification for the agency's choice among the alternatives. This requirement fits nicely with the creation of RARG and its functions. OMB has the responsibility for enforcing E.O. 12044.

In October 1978, the appointment of Alfred E. Kahn as Chairman of COWPS and chief presidential adviser on inflation provided greater strength for the regulatory reform effort. Kahn had just served as Chairman of the Civil Aeronautics Board and had been the key figure within the CAB pushing for deregulation of the airline industry. He had been influential in achieving greater (largely downward) fare flexibility within the industry even before Congress passed the deregulation legislation. He enjoyed a high reputation in Washington, and he was genuinely interested in regulatory reform and better regulatory management. The personal staff that he assembled (separate from, but well coordinated with, the COWPS division that examined government programs) took an active interest in regulatory matters.

Also in October 1978 the President created the Regulatory Council.[13] The Council is composed of all the executive branch regulatory agencies plus a number of the independent agencies. It is charged with creating a governmentwide calendar of forthcoming significant regulatory proposals and actions. This calendar provides a means of examining overall and sectoral regulatory impacts. The Regulatory Council is also charged with addressing problems of duplication and conflicts among

21

regulations and regulatory agencies and of examining the special impacts of regulation on particular industries or sectors. Unlike RARG, which is solely a floating interagency task force, the Regulatory Council has a permanent staff and director.

Finally, during 1978 the principle of presidential review of proposed executive branch regulation and Executive Office communications with the executive branch regulatory agencies during the post-comment period were clearly established within the administration. Ultimately, the President is responsible for executive branch regulatory decisions, and his ability to review and make decisions (within the constraints of the applicable laws and the record developed in the particular regulatory proceeding) is an important part of the management process, as is the ability of his personal advisers within the Executive Office to communicate with the agencies during the post-comment period in rulemaking.[14]

In terms of the trichotomy established earlier in this chapter, the Regulatory Council operates primarily during the pre-NPRM stage of regulations; COWPS and RARG reviews and filings occur during the public comment period; and Executive Office communication and possible ultimate presidential review take place during the postcomment period. The basic notion is that through these requirements on the agencies to conduct analyses, consider alternatives, and defend choices and through the reviews imposed at various stages the agencies themselves will be motivated (or forced) to develop better, more cost-effective regulations. And ultimate responsibility for management, for policy development, and for the balancing of conflicting interests and goals must rest with the President and his advisers.

CEA has played an active role throughout this regulatory review and management process. CEA staff members have helped to draft RARG and COWPS filings[15] and have gathered the information for and generally helped shape the decisions of the Executive Office on these regulatory issues. CEA Chairman Schultze was one of the original architects of the program and has continued to take an active part in its development and in a number of the important decisions that have been made on regulatory issues.

Although the various organizations within the EOP have generally been in complete agreement on the principles of the regulatory reform and management program, there have been disagreements on particular regulatory issues. CEA and COWPS have tended to take a harder line; they have been more sensitive to the costs of regulatory proposals and more willing to oppose the regulatory agencies. This has stemmed largely from their attachment to the microeconomics paradigm, which gives great importance to examining the costs and benefits of regulation, discovering the marginal consequences for costs and benefits of changes in regulations, and also, for any given set of benefits, finding the least costly way of achieving them. The two agencies' judgments on regulatory issues tend to be heavily shaped by these cost and benefit considerations, with less weight given to distributional and political consequences. The other organizations within the EOP, especially the Domestic Policy Staff, have generally been more conciliatory, more conscious of distributional considerations, more sensitive to the political pressures that could be brought to bear, and more ready to compromise.

The development of these regulatory reform procedures has constituted a new and almost revolutionary approach to executive branch regulatory decision making. As late as 1975, two leading practitioners of administrative law claimed that "as a practical matter, the inside [executive branch] agencies are no more subject to presidential directives on specific policy issues than the independent agencies. At least as to decision making on a record, it would probably be regarded as a gross breach of the principle of independence for the President to order or even to suggest that one of the agencies decide a particular issue in a particular way."[16] This last statement is something of an exaggeration, at least as applied to the executive branch agencies. There have been clear instances in which the President or his advisers have influenced executive branch regulatory decisions;[17] the Nixon administration set up a special procedure, the Quality of Life Review, to review the regulations of the Environmental Protection Agency;[18] and the Ford administration had tried to require "inflation impact statements" for all major regulatory proposals.[19] But these previous efforts had not been sustained or systematically applied to all executive branch regulatory agencies.

These review procedures have not gone unchallenged. The environmental community and the labor unions, fearing that EOP intervention and influence over executive branch regulatory agencies will mean a relaxation of health–safety–environment regulations, have brought a number of suits challenging the legality of EOP intervention after the close of the public comment period in rulemakings. Their legal argument (as interpreted by an economist) is roughly as follows: The public comment period is the time during a rulemaking in which a regulatory agency is supposed to receive information and arguments from all the interested parties. Once the public comment period ends, the decision maker within the regulatory agency is not supposed to receive any new information from any outside pleaders. Other government agencies, even the President and his advisers, are simply another set of outside *(ex parte)* pleaders. If General Motors or the Environmental Defense Fund cannot talk with the decision maker after the public comment period has ended, neither can anyone from another government agency.

The contrary argument runs as follows: There is no question that the decision maker can talk with his or her staff off the record during the post-comment period and that the staff can provide him or her with analyses (but neither the decision maker nor his or her staff is supposed to receive new *information* from anywhere). Individuals from other government agencies (or, if not from all other government agencies, then certainly from the Executive Office of the President) should be considered to be just like the staff of the decision maker. This might be considered the "one big happy family" theory of the executive branch of the federal government. (It is, of course, true that the executive branch agencies are not actually "one big happy family" but frequently represent a diverse set of competing interests. But it is also frequently the case that even within the regulatory agency itself there are seriously competing interests and viewpoints. The difference is one of degree.)

As a further extension of this last argument, recall that Congress established the regulatory agencies in question within the executive branch, where officials serve at the pleasure of the President and the President is responsible for the decisions of his administration, rather than as independent agencies, where officials are appointed for fixed terms and the policies developed are not subject to presidential control. It is true that the regulatory decisions are supposed to be based on the record developed during the rulemaking, and, if one believes that the law and the record will always point to one, and only one, regulatory outcome, then Executive Office intervention in the final decision is unwise, unwarranted, and probably illegal. But, if one believes that the law and the record will usually point only to a range of outcomes and that regulatory officials have a fairly wide range of discretion, then Executive Office intervention is legitimate. In the latter case, this wide discretion means that the regulatory decision maker is in effect making policy rather than just being narrowly guided by the record. And within the executive branch, policy should ultimately be guided by the President and his advisers. If the President has the power to fire the administrator of EPA, then surely he and his advisers have the power to communicate with him during a rulemaking. If Congress had wanted it otherwise, it should have placed these regulatory functions outside of the executive branch and in an independent agency, as it occasionally has chosen to do (e.g., the Consumer Product Safety Commission).

Even if one believes in the legitimacy of post-comment period contacts between the EOP and the regulatory agencies, there are still two practical issues that need to be resolved. First, should the content of these contacts be off the record (as are discussions within the agency) or on the record? Keeping these contacts off the record encourages the free expression of opinions and exchange of ideas; keeping them on the record provides a clearer picture (e.g., for judicial review) of what may have influenced the final decision. The case for off-the-record discussions within the agency is clear; it would appear to carry over to post-comment period discussions with other agencies. Second, how can the regulatory agency (or the President) avoid having the ultimate decision tainted by true *ex parte* contacts? To deal with this problem the EOP in 1978–1979 developed a set of procedures that said, in effect, if the EOP were going to communicate with the regulatory decision maker, the EOP would have to live by the same rules as did he and his staff. Thus, EOP personnel involved in regulatory issues now keep logs of contacts with outside parties during the public comment periods on proposed rules and avoid outside contacts that would generate new information once the public comment period has ended. Also, the filings and reports by RARG and COWPS on the public record of the regulatory agencies are clearly an important part of this effort to avoid *ex parte* problems; the EOP thereby places its information and arguments on the public record, and the information then can be the basis for the post-comment period discussions.

The practice and extent of this post-comment period activity is still an open legal question. A number of suits filed after the announcement of regulatory decisions have challenged the legitimacy of post-comment period activity by the EOP.

NOTES TO CHAPTER 2

[1]For a description of CEA that stresses this macroeconomics aspect, see E. S. Flash, Jr., *Economic Advice and Presidential Leadership: The Council of Economic Advisers* (New York: Columbia U.P., 1965).

[2]Other major agencies within the EOP that have played a role in the regulatory issues discussed in this book are the Domestic Policy Staff, the Council on Wage and Price

Stability, the Office of Management and Budget, the Office of Science and Technology Policy, and the Council on Environmental Quality.

[3]CEA makes a technical distinction between the senior staff economists, who have doctorate degrees in economics, and staff economists, who have advanced training in economics but have some other kind of advanced degree.

[4]I quickly discovered that by identifying myself over the telephone as a member of the staff at "the *President's* Council of Economic Advisers" I could get the staff at any agency in the federal government to provide key information that I needed; if I did not include the word "President's," secretaries and staff at other agencies and private companies, particularly outside Washington, tended to confuse CEA with the Committee for Economic Development, the Council on Economic Priorities, or other private organizations that might have "Economic" in their titles.

[5]The macroeconomics and international trade professional staff have somewhat different responsibilities and functions.

[6]A friend described this practice as one of "Never write what you sign; never sign what you write."

[7]The distinction in administrative law is primarily between adjudications, which are much closer to judicial proceedings, with formal hearing procedures, and these "informal" rulemakings. See H. H. Bruff, "Presidential Power and Administrative Rulemaking," *Yale Law Journal,* 88 (January 1979): 453.

[8]Sometimes these are preceded by an advance notice of proposed rulemaking, which is purely for the purpose of inviting comments.

[9]My colleague at CEA, Robert Litan, suggested this trichotomy to me.

[10]See also S. J. Tolchin, "Presidential Power and the Politics of RARG," *Regulation* 3 (July–August 1979): 44–49; and C. C. DeMuth, "Constraining Regulatory Costs. Part I: The White House Review Programs," *Regulation,* 4 (January–February 1980): 13–26.

[11]For a compilation of some of the COWPS efforts, see J. C. Miller, III, and B. Yandle, eds., *Benefit–Cost Analyses of Social Regulation: Case Studies from the Council on Wage and Price Stability* (Washington, D.C.: American Enterprise Institute, 1979).

[12]*Federal Register,* March 24, 1978, p. 12661. A major regulation is defined as one that imposed over $100 million in costs annually on the economy or otherwise had a major effect. The requirement applies to regulations that impose costs on other levels of government (e.g., environmental regulations that apply to municipal waste treatment facilities or drinking water supplies) as well as on the private sector.

[13]The idea for the Regulatory Council came from the regulatory agencies themselves, in response to pressure from the Executive Office that they should try better to coordinate their activities.

[14]This point is currently under litigation.

[15]CEA does not have the authority to make its own filings on the public record of regulatory agencies.

[16]L. N. Cutler and D. R. Johnson, "Regulation and the Political Process," *Yale Law Journal,* 84 (June 1975): 1404.

[17]See Bruff, op. cit., pp. 465–466.

[18]Ibid., p. 464, and J. Quarles, *Cleaning Up America: An Insider's View of the Environmental Protection Agency* (Boston: Houghton Mifflin, 1976), pp. 117–142.

[19]E. O. 11821, November 27, 1974. See U. S. Congress, Senate, 95th Congress, 2nd session, Committee on Governmental Affairs, *Study on Federal Regulation,* 6 (December 1978), 78–80.

chapter 3

An Economist's Primer
on Regulation

REGULATION IN THEORY

Why have regulation in the first place? To some, the answer may be obvious: to protect the public interest. To most economists, this is not a sufficient answer. In an economy based on private initiative (private enterprise), there is a presumption that the workings of the competitive marketplace will properly satisfy consumer demands and maximize the well-being that can be obtained from the nation's resources.

Why, then, have regulation? Economists have generally recognized four arguments that *might* justify government intervention in the marketplace:[1]

Monopoly–Oligopoly. If the technology of an industry and the size of its market are such that only one or a very few firms can produce efficiently (and there are few or no potential entrants into the industry), monopoly or oligopoly pricing may occur, and the desirable efficient properties of a competitive market system may not be achieved. Prices will be too high, and output will be too low. There may be an inadequate variety of types and qualities of goods, and the development of new products and new technologies may suffer.

Externalities. If the production activities of some firms or the consumption actions of some consumers affect the welfare of others in a nonmarket context, again the efficiency properties of a competitive system may not be achieved. Economists have given the word "externality" to this phenomenon. In the case of negative externalities, firms or individuals are imposing uncompensated costs on others through their own actions. They are not paying the full social costs implied by their activities. Hence, too low a price will be charged for the output, and too much will be produced or consumed. And the uncompensated costs are being imposed. Air pollution, water pollution, and excessive noise are familiar examples of negative externalities. In the case of positive externalities, firms or individuals convey uncompensated benefits to others, and thus too little output will be produced and consumed. A lumber company's planting trees upstream, which prevents erosion, silting, and flooding of others' residences downstream, is an example of a positive externality.

Public Goods. For situations in which positive externalities in an activity are so pervasive that there are zero extra costs to providing benefits to an individual (and usually, but not always, it is difficult to exclude extra beneficiaries from an activity), economists have coined the phrase "public good." Private initiative may not provide the activity or output at all (if one cannot exclude a beneficiary, one cannot charge him to help cover one's costs) or may provide it in socially inappropriate amounts. National defense, mosquito eradication programs, and knowledge or information (once it is in existence) are all examples of public goods.

Income Distribution. If the income distribution arising from private activities is deemed socially nonoptimal, public intervention in a market that also improves the distribution of income may be justified, though most economists would prefer the first best policy of trying to affect income directly through taxes and grants rather than the second best policy of trying to do it indirectly through market intervention.

An important caveat to the four arguments just listed should be entered immediately. It is easy to find imperfections in markets. Few markets match the economists' textbook examples of perfect competition; externalities of one kind or another are pervasive. But the discovery of a private market imperfection only raises the *possibility* that government intervention could improve matters. Governments, as do all other organizations, lack complete knowledge and perfect foresight, have diverse and frequently ill-defined goals, and make mistakes. In our real world, then, one has to make pragmatic and factual judgments in individual cases as to whether economic efficiency and overall welfare are in fact improved when imperfect governments intervene in imperfect private markets.

REGULATION IN PRACTICE—
"OLD-STYLE" ECONOMIC REGULATION

Efforts to characterize all regulation in the American economy must necessarily be overly broad and imprecise. Nevertheless, economists find it useful to place most regulation into either of two categories: old-style economic regulation and new-style social regulation.

Old-style economic regulation has a number of distinguishing characteristics: It is concerned primarily with the prices charged in individual industries and with entry by new producers into those industries (e.g., airlines, trucking, rail, ocean shipping, telecommunications, banking, securities, electric and gas utilities). At the federal level these regulatory activities are largely the responsibility of independent commissions (with five or more commissioners), most of which are outside of the executive branch (e.g., the Civil Aeronautics Board, the Interstate Commerce Commission, the Federal Maritime Commission, the Federal Communications Commission, the Federal Reserve Board, and the Securities and Exchange Commission). The major exceptions within the executive branch are the Department of Agriculture's setting of agricultural prices and quantity restrictions, the Department of Energy's control over petroleum prices, and the Comptroller of the Currency's control over new entry of national banks. Table 3-1 provides a list of the major federal agencies and their location, year of establishment, and functions. At the state level, regulation of electric, gas, water, and local telephone utilities is usually lodged in state public utility commissions.

The arguments advanced to justify this kind of economic regulation usually cite a mixture of the monopoly–oligopoly and income distribution problems discussed earlier. Local electric, gas, water, and telephone utilities are usually natural monopolies and probably do require some regulatory constraint. In the other areas, where multiple producers and potential entrants are often present, the defenders of regulation usually first raise the specter of monopoly: Unfettered competition is alleged to lead to predatory behavior and the eventual survival of only one or a very few firms, with consequent monopoly–oligopoly problems; regulation is alleged to be necessary to prevent this outcome. The defenders of regulation frequently also offer an income distribution argument that hinges on the phenomenon of cross-subsidy: excess profits are alleged to be earned in some markets (e.g., large-volume transportation markets between major economic centers) that are then used to subsidize losses (and thus keep prices low) in other markets (e.g., low-volume rural markets); unfettered entry and competition would drive down prices in the former markets, eliminate the excess profits ("skim the cream"), and thus eliminate the basis for the cross-subsidy; prices would have to rise in the latter markets to eliminate the losses, and consumers in those markets would suffer "unfairly;" again, regulation is necessary to prevent this.

Many economists have long argued that the monopoly–oligopoly problem was much exaggerated, particularly in transportation, securities, banking, and (in the 1970s) telecommunications. Economies of scale were not as great as believed; there were lots of potential entrants, and predatory behavior was not a likely or serious problem. As for cross-subsidy, nonprice competition in some industries (e.g., scheduling rivalry in airlines) had probably eliminated most or all of the potential excess profits; consequently, there was little cross-subsidy, the alleged losses on rural routes were mostly fictitious, and hence there was little danger that prices in rural areas would skyrocket or service disappear subsequent to deregulation. And, in any event, if there were some national social purpose to be served by keeping rural rates below the costs of service, this goal was most efficiently and equitably achieved through subsidies from general (national) tax revenues rather than by taxing one class of users to subsidize another class.

This message has slowly permeated Washington thinking. In the early 1970s the Securities and Exchange Commission gradually withdrew its sanction for the collusive price fixing of brokerage commissions by the members of the stock exchanges. By May 1975 the last vestiges of sanctioned collusion had disappeared. At the same time, the Congress and the Ford administration were laying the groundwork for deregulation of the domestic airline industry. Pushed further by substantial deregulation efforts on the part of the Civil Aeronautics Board itself (under Alfred Kahn's leadership), this effort came to fruition in October 1978 with the passage and signing of the Airline Deregulation bill that effectively decontrolled prices and entry and phased the CAB out of existence. In the spring of 1980 the Congress passed and the President signed a law that promised the gradual deregulation of the interest rates that banks and savings institutions pay their depositors. In the summer a law that loosened the regulation of the trucking industry was passed and signed. As of this writing, the Carter administration has endorsed bills that would substantially deregulate railroads and portions of telecommunications. The economists' case against economic regulation does seem to be slowly winning.

REGULATION IN PRACTICE—
"NEW-STYLE" SOCIAL REGULATION

New-style social regulation also has a number of distinguishing characteristics. It usually cuts across several sectors of the economy. It focuses on matters such as environmental pollution by industry (and by governmental bodies such as municipal incinerators and sewage plants), worker health and safety in the workplace, and consumer protection in the safety and reliability of the goods and services that consumers buy. The regulatory agencies are, for the most part, within the executive

Table 3-1

"Old-Style" Economic Regulatory Agencies

Agency	Location	Year Established[1]	Regulatory Responsibility
Civil Aeronautics Board (CAB)	Independent	1938	Prices and entry into the airline industry
Federal Communications Commission (FCC)	Independent	1934	Entry into broadcasting, prices and entry into the interstate telecommunications industry
Federal Home Loan Bank Board (FHLBB)	Independent	1932	Interest rates and entry into the savings and loan industry
Federal Maritime Commission (FMC)	Independent	1936	Enforcement of international shipping agreements.
Federal Reserve System (FRS)	Independent	1913	Interest rates and reserve requirements for national banks, approval of mergers; bank holding company acquisitions.
International Trade Commission (ITC)	Independent	1916	International dumping, industry relief
Interstate Commerce Commission (ICC)	Independent	1887	Prices and entry in rail, trucking, buses, and inland and coastal waterways

Agency	Type	Year	Function
Postal Rate Commission (PRC)	Independent	1970	Recommendation of prices to U.S. Postal Service, review of post office closure decisions
Agricultural Stabilization and Conservation Service (ASCS); Commodity Credit Corporation (CCC); Agricultural Marketing Service (AMS)	Executive branch (Department of Agriculture)	1961, 1933, 1937	Prices of farm commodities and acreage allotments, marketing quotas, market orders
Comptroller of the Currency	Executive branch (Department of the Treasury)	1862	Entry, mergers, branching for national banks
Economic Regulatory Administration (ERA)	Executive branch (Department of Energy)	1974	Prices for petroleum and petroleum products, product allocations
Federal Energy Regulatory Commission (formerly Federal Power Commission) (FERC)	Independent but nominally located in the executive branch (Department of Energy)	1930	Prices for natural gas, interstate electricity, oil by pipeline

¹In some cases, prior to the year of establishment some of an agency's functions were carried out by another agency.

branch: for example, the Environmental Protection Agency, the Occupational Safety and Health Administration (within the Department of Labor), the Office of Surface Mining (within the Department of the Interior), the Food and Drug Administration (within the Department of Health and Human Services), and the National Highway Traffic Safety Administration and the Federal Aviation Administration (both within the Department of Transportation). The major exceptions established as independent agencies are the Consumer Product Safety Commission, the Federal Trade Commission, and the Securities and Exchange Commission. Table 3-2 provides a list of the major social regulation agencies, their location, and function. The major form of regulation is the setting of standards—of maximum permissible emissions of pollutants, of permissible worker exposures to hazards, and of permissible goods and services to be made available to consumers.

The economic justification for this type of regulation encompasses a mixture of the externality, public good, and income distribution arguments. Environmental pollution constitutes an externality that may well require some kind of governmental corrective action. Information has the properties of a public good, since, once the information is created, the marginal costs to extra people using it are low or zero and excluding additional users is frequently difficult. Hence, charging a price for information that covers the costs of its creation may be socially inappropriate or difficult or both, and there is no assurance that the private sector will generate the appropriate amount of information to accompany goods and services. The requirement that certain kinds of information be provided or that certain kinds of goods or services or work environments not be provided could be one way of dealing with the problem. Also, poor people may have the most difficulties in acquiring and assessing information about goods, services, and work environments, so information alone may not be enough if one wants to help the poor; direct restrictions on the goods, services, and work environments may be necessary.

The preceding paragraph summarizes the case that an economist might make for social regulation. In practice, the popular case is broader and more moral in tone: Environmental pollution is simply bad, and there should be none or as little of it as possible. Workers simply should not be exposed to hazards. Consumers simply should not be exposed to unsafe or defective goods and services. This last argument, in particular, frequently takes a paternalistic tone: Society knows better than consumers what is good for them; consumers should be protected from themselves.

While acknowledging that some governmental action is required in some areas, many economists disagree with the scope and methods of this new regulation. Their uneasiness with current approaches to social regulation encompasses a number of points. First, a great deal of current regulation focuses too much on the benefits to be achieved—a cleaner environment, safer workplaces, safer products—and not enough on the costs of achieving them. As with lunch, a cleaner environment, safer work places, and safer products are not free. Although these goals are laudable and the benefits in many cases large, they are costly.[2] Some enthusiasts may fondly hope that these costs will be borne solely by the rich through reductions in business profits. However, in most cases the rich are unlikely to be the only or even the major bearers of the costs. Instead, the extra costs of pollution controls, safer workplace equipment, and safer production will ultimately be reflected in a combination of higher prices for the goods and services involved and of lower returns to the providers of inputs—land, labor, and capital.[3] Thus, participants in the economy ultimately pay for these benefits, either in their role as consumers (paying higher prices) or as suppliers of inputs (receiving lower returns). In many cases, this result may well be appropriate and the social benefits may well exceed the social costs, but one should not fool oneself into thinking that achieving these goals is costless or that somehow only the rich will pay.

Second, much regulation does not recognize that there are limits. A completely pollution-free and risk-free environment is simply not possible. It is too costly to eliminate all pollution and all risks, and, as we try to eliminate more of them, the incremental costs become progressively higher. Consequently, lines have to be drawn, balances have to be struck, and trade-offs have to be made. The social benefits of regulatory action have to be compared with their social costs, and at some point society has to say "enough."

One objection to this last line of reasoning is that the saving of lives and improvements in health cannot be valued. Hence, the benefits of regulatory actions cannot be properly evaluated, and the benefit–cost calculations cannot be done. This objection, though, has less force than may first appear. Society is always putting an implicit value on saving lives (or, in brutal reality, extending lives or delaying deaths) or avoiding injuries or illnesses. For example, when a national speed limit of 55 miles per hour was imposed in the aftermath of the 1973 oil embargo, the country pleasantly discovered that not only did this speed limit save fuel but it also meant fewer automobile-related deaths. We could clearly have yet fewer automobile-related deaths if we lowered the speed limit

Table 3-2

"New-Style" Social Regulatory Agencies

Agency	Location	Year Established[1]	Regulatory Responsibility
Commodity Futures Trading Commission (CFTC)	Independent	1975	Information and trading conditions of commodity futures
Consumer Product Safety Commission (CPSC)	Independent	1972	Safety of consumer products
Environmental Protection Agency (EPA)	Executive branch	1970	Air, water, land environmental protection
Equal Employment Opportunity Commission (EEOC)	Independent	1964	Ending discrimination in employment
Federal Trade Commission (FTC)	Independent	1914	Consumer information, advertising, business practices
National Labor Relations Board (NLRB)	Independent	1935	Labor contracts, negotiations
Nuclear Regulatory Commission (NRC)	Independent	1975	Licensing and regulation of companies to build and operate nuclear reactors
Securities and Exchange Commission (SEC)	Independent	1934	Information and trading conditions of securities

Agency	Branch	Year	Function
Agricultural Marketing Service (AMS), Animal and Plant Health Inspection Service (APHIS), Federal Grain Inspection Service (FGIS), Food Safety and Quality Service (FSQS)	Executive branch (Department of Agriculture)	1932 1953 1976 1916	Food inspection, grading, standardization
Bureau of Alcohol, Tobacco, and Firearms (BATF)	Executive branch (Department of the Treasury)	1972	Labeling
Bureau of Land Management (BLM)	Executive branch (Department of the Interior)	1946	Management of public lands
Coast Guard	Executive branch (Department of Transportation)	1915	Ship safety, marine environment protection
Economic Regulatory Administration (ERA)	Executive branch (Department of Energy)	1974	Coal conversion programs, temperature limits for buildings, energy standards for new buildings[2]
Employment Standards Administration (ESA)	Executive branch (Department of Labor)	1913	Minimum wage, overtime hours, ending discrimination in employment, determining prevailing wage rates to be paid on government contracts and subcontracts

Table 3-2 (Continued)

"New-Style" Social Regulatory Agencies

Agency	Location	Year Established[1]	Regulatory Responsibility
Federal Aviation Administration (FAA)	Executive branch (Department of Transportation)	1948	Airline, airport safety
Federal Deposit Insurance Corporation (FDIC)	Executive branch	1933	Bank safety for depositors
Federal Highway Administration (FHWA)	Executive branch (Department of Transportation)	1966	Truck and bus operator safety
Federal Railroad Administration (FRA)	Executive branch (Department of Transportation)	1970	Rail safety
Fish and Wildlife Service (FWS)	Executive branch (Department of the Interior)	1871	Preservation of fish and wildlife
Food and Drug Administration (FDA)	Executive branch (Department of Health and Human Services)	1931	Safety of food and drugs

Forest Service (FS)	Executive branch (Department of Agriculture)	1905	Management of resource use
Mine Safety and Health Administration (MSHA)	Executive branch (Department of Labor)	1973	Miner safety
National Oceanic and Atmospheric Administration (NOAA)	Executive branch (Department of Commerce)	1970	Management of marine resources, protection of marine mammals
National Highway Traffic Safety Administration (NHTSA)	Executive branch (Department of Transportation)	1970	Motor vehicle safety, fuel economy
Occupational Safety and Health Administration (OSHA)	Executive branch (Department of Labor)	1973	Worker safety
Office of Surface Mining Reclamation and Enforcement (OSM)	Executive branch (Department of the Interior)	1977	Environmental effects of surface mining

[1] In some cases, prior to the year of establishment some of the agency's functions were carried out by another agency.
[2] See also ERA's economic regulation responsibility in Table 3-1.

to 45 mph (or spent more resources enforcing the 55 mph limit). But we, as a society, have chosen not to do so. Why? It must be because we have decided implicitly that it would be too costly to do so. Similarly, we do not build pedestrian underpasses under every busy intersection in urban areas or station an ambulance on every block, even though these actions would clearly reduce the number of traffic-related deaths. Again, society is saying implicitly that the costs are too high.[4]

Thus, through its legislative and administrative processes our society is constantly drawing lines and implicitly putting values on health and safety. The same can be and indeed is being done implicitly in the area of regulation. And many economists would argue that these value decisions should be made explicitly rather than implicitly, so that their full implication can be examined and better and more consistent choices can be made.

Third, some regulation ignores opportunities to minimize social costs. For any given social goal or level of regulatory control, the least-cost means of achieving the goal should be sought. This is the principle of cost-effectiveness. This principle will usually mean that performance standards—the specification of results to be achieved—should be preferred over design standards—the specification of detailed designs, engineering techniques, or process changes. The former standards leave open the normal market incentives of cost minimization and profit maximization by firms to find the least-cost way of achieving the results that are ultimately desired. Since the government regulator may not have any direct incentives to minimize the costs of the regulated firms, the latter standards are likely to lead to excessive rigidity, the freezing of control techniques, and ultimately higher costs.

Further, cost-effectiveness implies that the costs of achieving explicit results in various programs must be compared. Suppose we find that, at the margin, it costs $5,000 to prevent a case of a particular disease in one program and $50,000 per case to prevent a case of the same disease in another program. Then the same number of cases could be prevented at a lower cost by shifting resources out of the latter program and into the former; alternatively, the same amount of money could prevent more cases if the same shift of resources were made. Similarly, if the marginal ton of a particular pollutant dumped into the environment has the same public health consequences regardless of whether it is dumped by company A or company B and it costs the former $100 per ton and the latter $10,000 per ton to reduce emissions by a ton, society's resources are better spent by requiring more emissions reduction by company A and less by company B. Again, it costs less to achieve any overall reduction in emissions, or, alternatively, any given sum of money will achieve a greater reduction in emissions. This must continue to be true until the marginal costs per ton of pollutant controlled are equalized between the two companies.

Fourth, since a pollution-free and risk-free society is not going to be achieved, a moral approach that declares pollution and risks to be absolute evils is likely to interfere with sensible choices, sensible lines being drawn, and sensible public policy generally. Further, one should not think of pollution as the exclusive preserve of the private sector; there are plenty of government incinerators and sewage plants polluting the environment. Nor should one think of polluting behavior as stemming from nasty or venal motives. Rather, the externality problem means that the marketplace is not charging a proper price for the pollution and the resulting costs; it is not providing the right incentives for pollution reduction. In a society largely motivated by personal gain, it is unrealistic to expect consumers voluntarily to pay extra for devices or controls from which they gain little direct benefit. And it is equally unrealistic to expect companies to incur pollution control costs from which they gain little or no direct benefit and that will be passed on in higher prices, when their competitors may not do so. Venality has nothing to do with this problem.

Fifth, the rejection of the morality approach has led most economists (and some lawyers) to a property-rights view of the pollution problem. It is the absence of clearly defined and enforceable private property rights in the air and water that has led to excessive pollution. If somebody dumps garbage on my front lawn and I know who did it, I can use the laws to get that person to stop doing it. My property right in my lawn is clearly defined. As a result, there are usually few problems with people dumping garbage on other people's lawns. But, if somebody dumps garbage into the air I breathe, for example, in the form of pollutants coming out of the tailpipes of automobiles, I have no individual property right in the air I breathe that the law can enforce. Further, I may not be able to determine exactly whose car emitted the pollutants that I am breathing, so I could not enforce my property right even if I had one.

One conceptual solution to the problem posed in this way is to vest the property right with governments at one or another level and give them the power to decide how much pollution will be allowed into the environment and to enforce those decisions. This is in fact what is done now, but the property-rights conceptual approach would likely lead to different kinds of regulatory control measures than now generally prevail.

Sixth, regulatory approaches that rely more on economic incentives should be pursued. As noted, performance standards make use of economic incentives and are to be preferred over design standards. Any regulatory devices that would allow firms to trade off low-cost ways of meeting social goals for high-cost ways should be encouraged. In the context of the property-rights approach to pollution, there are alternatives to the current approach of direct controls and standards. Governments could decide on the proper price for the use of society's property (air and water) and charge the appropriate effluent fee to any and all polluters. Polluters would find it worthwhile to reduce their emissions in the lowest-cost fashion, up to the point at which the marginal costs of eliminating the remaining emissions would equal or exceed the costs of paying the effluent fee. Thus, the cost-effective solution would be automatically achieved. Alternatively, governments could decide how much emissions (how much use of society's property) they were prepared to tolerate and then auction off the rights to emit certain pollutants to the highest bidders.[5] Thus, just as governments auction off (or rent out) other scarce resources (e.g., mineral lands), they would be auctioning off these scarce emissions-rights resources. Again, polluters would be paying for the right to use society's property, and polluters would have the incentive to reduce their pollution to the point at which the marginal costs of control were equal to the costs of buying a pollution right at auction. And, again, the cost-effective solution would automatically be established. Further, under either the effluent fee or the auction approach, firms would have unequivocal incentives to discover lower-cost ways of reducing pollutant emissions; under the current "command and control" system of standards, firms' incentives are much less clear.[6]

This fee (taxation) approach could be extended to other kinds of social regulation. Fee schedules could be used to encourage firms to achieve safer workplaces and safer products.

Finally, it is worth remembering that the costs of regulation are largely borne in the first instance by the private sector (or by other levels of government as in the case of municipal water treatment regulation), and thus they mostly do not show up as budgetary costs of the regulatory agencies.[7] (This is true also of the social costs—the improper prices and lack of competition—imposed by economic regulation.) Thus, budgetary limitation efforts, such as California's Proposition 13 and the national balanced budget movement, are likely to have little or no effect on social regulation; the budgets of the regulatory agencies are simply not the large spending items in government budgets. Indeed, as government budgets become tighter, legislators may try through regulation to have the private sector undertake and finance some of the social activities formerly carried out by government.

This economist's approach to social regulation has made less progress in Washington than has the economist's approach to economic regulation. Environmental, health, and safety regulation are still treated largely as moral issues. Much rhetoric is still given to risk-free, completely safe environments. Cost-effectiveness is still a controversial concept; cost–benefit analysis in the health–safety–environment area, because it does require the valuation of lives and health, is yet more controversial. Effluent fees or effluent-rights auctions are not seriously considered in most policy discussions or actions, though noncompliance fees (a close cousin to an effluent fee) have appeared in the Clean Air Act and a few other pieces of legislation (two important examples will be discussed in Chapters 6 and 8).[8]

As noted in Chapter 2, the approach of the Carter administration has been to avoid major pieces of legislation that would fundamentally alter the social regulatory framework but instead to try to manage the existing framework in a better manner. The Council of Economic Advisers and the Council on Wage and Price Stability have emphasized a number of the approaches described here, particularly performance standards, cost-effectiveness, and the role of economic incentives, in their dealings (and conflicts) with the regulatory agencies. The next chapters will describe some of these efforts in detail.

NOTES TO CHAPTER 3

[1]The standard reference here is F. M. Bator, "The Anatomy of Market Failure," *Quarterly Journal of Economics*, 72 (August 1958): 351–379.

[2]For example, the Council on Environmental Quality estimates that the annual costs of environmental regulations promulgated before the end of 1978 were $19 billion in 1977 and would rise to $52 billion (in constant 1977 dollars) by 1986. Additional scores of billions will be required for regulations that were required by law but had not yet been

promulgated at the time of the study. And these estimates do not include the costs of worker safety or consumer protection. See U.S. Council on Environmental Quality, *Environmental Quality, Ninth Annual Report* (Washington, D.C.: U.S. Government Printing Office, 1978).

[3]The problem of determining how much of regulatory costs is passed forward in higher prices and how much is passed backward in lower returns to providers of inputs is part of the larger general problem of the incidence of taxation. Also, it is worth noting that some of the suppliers of capital inputs are not only the "rich capitalists" but also the not-so-rich workers through the investments of their unions' pension funds.

[4]Also, individuals voluntarily take employment in occupations in which the risks of injury and death are higher than in other occupations, in return for higher wages. For a review, see Martin J. Bailey, *Reducing Risks to Life* (Washington, D.C.: American Enterprise Institute, 1980).

[5]The standard reference here is J. H. Dales, *Pollution, Property, and Prices: An Essay in Policy-Making and Economics* (Toronto: U. of Toronto, 1968).

[6]See L. J. White, "Effluent Charges as a Faster Means of Achieving Pollution Abatement," *Public Policy*, 24 (Winter 1976); 111–125; and E. S. Mills and L. J. White, "Government Policies Toward Automotive Emission Control," in A. F. Friedlaender, ed., *Approaches to Controlling Air Pollution* (Cambridge, Mass.: M.I.T., 1978), pp. 379–385.

[7]Of course, the benefits do not show up in the agencies' budgets either, but this is equally true for normal legislative programs that are carried out directly from an agency's budget.

[8]The sale of emissions rights has appeared, almost inadvertently, as part of the "offset" policy under the Clean Air Act. In areas that are in violation of the national ambient air quality standards for a pollutant (see Chapter 4), any new firm that wishes to establish operations that will generate emissions of that pollutant must somehow arrange for a greater reduction of someone else's emissions. Thus, a market in emissions rights is being established implicitly.

part III

NEW-STYLE
SOCIAL REGULATION

chapter **4**

Photochemical Smog (Ozone)

What should be the national ambient air quality standard for photochemical oxidant (ozone)?

The Clean Air Act is the major legislative foundation for regulation by the Environmental Protection Agency (EPA) to improve air quality. This chapter and the following three illustrate a number of the regulatory problems that have arisen under the act. This chapter demonstrates the problems that arise when Congress imposes a simple dichotomous (safe–unsafe) regulatory framework for determining ambient air quality standards on a world that is probably much more complex.

BACKGROUND

The Clean Air Act of 1970 required EPA to establish primary and secondary national ambient air quality standards (NAAQSs) for air pollutants. EPA subsequently established NAAQSs for five pollutants: carbon monoxide, sulfur oxides, total suspended particulates, nitrogen dioxide, and photochemical oxidants. The NAAQSs are the standards that are supposed to be achieved in the ambient air throughout the United States. Thus, by themselves the NAAQSs carry no direct implementation or enforcement requirements. But the NAAQSs are the required goals for state implementation plans (SIPs), which require reductions in pollutant emissions from existing pollution sources, for standards of performance set by EPA for new stationary sources of pollutants (e.g., new electric generating facilities), and for the pollution controls on motor vehicles (required explicitly in the Clean Air Act). Thus, the NAAQSs carry a great deal of indirect importance, since the more stringent are the NAAQSs, the tighter must be the restrictions on emissions from existing sources, new sources, and motor vehicles. Since these restrictions are costly, the setting of the NAAQSs is ultimately of great economic importance.

The primary NAAQSs are supposed to be set at a level that will "protect the public health . . . allowing an adequate margin of safety."[1] They are the first-line targets for all emission-reduction plans. The secondary NAAQSs are supposed to be set at a level that is "requisite to protect the public welfare from any known or anticipated adverse effects associated with the presence of such air pollutant in the ambient air."[2] They are supposed to represent the ultimate goals of air pollution control policy. Thus far, the secondary standards have had few direct or indirect consequences.

The NAAQS system represents a good example of the safe–unsafe dichotomy with which many policymakers feel most comfortable. It is an effort by Congress to find thresholds below which the public health and welfare will be protected. The NAAQS system allows Congress to claim that all the public is being protected, but it also allows Congress to avoid the disastrous economic consequences of trying to achieve zero pollution. In an actual world in which health consequences may well be continuously present all the way down to zero pollution—in which thresholds are absent—this system is likely to create severe policy problems, as will be demonstrated in the following paragraphs.

Because the concepts of thresholds and continuity are important for understanding the conceptual basis for a good deal of regulatory policy and the problems with it, it is worth explaining these concepts in some detail. Suppose that all individuals have the same adverse health (illness) response pattern to exposure to varying concentrations of an air pollutant. (This is usually called a dose–response pattern.) Figures 4-1a to 4-1c illustrate three possible threshold patterns. For pollution con-

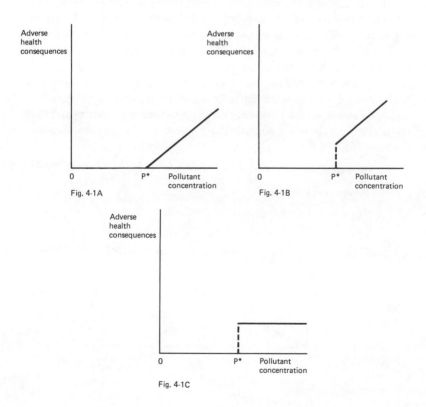

Fig. 4-1A

Fig. 4-1B

Fig. 4-1C

centrations below P*, an individual experiences no health consequences from exposure; it is only at concentrations above P* that health consequences occur.[3] Thus, P* is a threshold representing a safe level of pollution. (Although the dose–response patterns have been drawn as linear—straight lines—beyond the threshold, this is only one among many possible patterns; they could just as well be curved.) By contrast, Figure 4-2 shows a dose–response pattern that is continuous and extends all the way through zero pollution; there are no completely safe pollutant concentrations. (Again, the dose–response curve is drawn as linear, but it could just as well be curved.)

Whether the world actually has thresholds, as in Figures 4-1a to 4-1c, or is continuous through zero pollution, as in Figure 4-2, is an empirical question. There is, however, one further complication. Suppose that the threshold model accurately describes the dose–response patterns of individuals. If different individuals have different thresholds and if some individuals are so sensitive that their thresholds are at or are very close to zero, then the aggregate dose–response curve of the overall population will nevertheless be continuous down to zero pollution; that is, Figure 4-2 will still describe the aggregate health consequences summed over the entire population.

On April 30, 1971, EPA established the primary and secondary NAAQSs for photochemical oxidants at 0.08 parts per million (ppm) for a one-hour average, not to be exceeded more than once per year.[4] Oxidants are strongly oxidizing compounds that are the primary constitu-

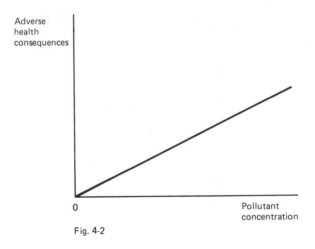

Fig. 4-2

ents of photochemical smog. Ozone is the oxidant found in the largest amounts, and virtually all measurements of photochemical oxidants have been in terms of ozone. Ozone is formed through a complex photochemical reaction between hydrocarbons and nitrogen oxides. Reductions in ozone are achieved through reductions in emissions of these precursors, primarily hydrocarbons, through controls on automobile exhaust, petroleum refinery emissions, dry cleaner emissions, and so on. (This photochemical smog ozone problem should not be confused with the problem of the ozone layer in the stratosphere and its possible depletion because of the use of fluorocarbons in spray cans and refrigerants.)

At relatively high doses of, say, 0.37 ppm and above, ozone causes coughing, wheezing, and chest discomfort, particularly among asthmatics, others with respiratory illnesses, and individuals engaged in vigorous exercise. There does seem to be a considerable range of individual sensitivity to these effects, with more sensitive individuals experiencing effects at lower ozone levels.

The ozone NAAQSs were set at 0.08 ppm because EPA believed that at least one medical study[5] showed that some asthmatics experienced effects at ozone levels of 0.10 ppm. The 0.08 ppm provided the margin of safety. State implementation plans, new source performance standards, and motor vehicle emission control efforts followed during the early and middle 1970s, but as of 1976 all but one of the metropolitan areas in the United States were failing to meet the standard, many of them for 30 or 40 days a year or more.

In December 1976 the American Petroleum Institute petitioned EPA to revise the ozone NAAQS, and in July 1977 the City of Houston offered a similar petition. Among other claims, the petitions argued that EPA had misinterpreted the health evidence and that a less stringent standard was warranted. EPA already had a review effort underway.

On June 22, 1978, EPA proposed (in the form of a notice of proposed rulemaking) a revision to the ozone NAAQSs.[6] Its major provisions were as follows:

1. The primary standard would be changed to a level of 0.10 ppm for a one-hour average, not to be exceeded more than once a year on an expected value basis (using a three-year average of occurrences).
2. The secondary standard would remain at 0.08 ppm.
3. The standard would be explicitly defined in terms of ozone rather than photochemical oxidant.

The NPRM was put out for public comment for 60 days, with the final regulation promised by the end of September.

PRELIMINARY ACTIVITIES

The ozone standard was the first of the NAAQSs to be revised since their initial levels were set in 1971. The proposed revision in the standard was recognized by all—EPA, the Executive Office of the President, and the private industries that would have to restrict hydrocarbon emissions— to be an important regulation.[7] The EOP decided that the proposal was important enough to be the subject of a review by the Regulatory Analysis Review Group (see Chapter 2), and the CEA staff took responsibility for drafting the report that would be filed on the public record in this regulatory proceeding.[8]

The EPA Position

The EPA documentation for the ozone standard was impressive. First, as part of the supporting documentation for any of its NAAQSs, EPA compiles a "criteria document," which is supposed to contain the criteria on which the standard is based. The criteria document is essentially a compilation of everything anyone would ever want to know about the pollutant: its chemical properties, its formation and dissolution, its meteorological properties, its effects on animals, its effects on humans, and so on. The document contains synopses of the relevant scientific studies, plus comments and critiques. The criteria document for photochemical oxidant was a thick, two-volume compilation, citing hundreds of studies of various kinds.

Second, EPA had a description of a particular method that it had tried to use to ascertain the health risks associated with alternative air quality standards for ozone. This effort combined the medical evidence from existing studies, some judgments by a set of experts that EPA had convened, and an estimate of the statistical distribution of meteorological occurrences of ozone in the atmosphere of an urban area.

Finally, EPA had estimates of the annual costs of the hydrocarbon emissions controls implied by alternative ozone standards. The amount of hydrocarbon reductions necessary to meet the alternative ozone standards was estimated for each of the 90 largest urban areas (technically, these were "air quality control regions") using two alternative modeling techniques—a proportional "rollback" method and a non-linear "empirical kinetic modeling approach" (EKMA) method. The annualized costs of these reductions as of 1987 were estimated and then summed for all 90 areas.

From this, EPA had distilled the following justification for its proposed standard of 0.10 ppm, which was part of the preamble to the NPRM: EPA acknowledged that its 1971 interpretation of the evidence for asthmatics had been incorrect. Further, it acknowledged that there probably were no clearly defined thresholds for ozone and that effects were probably continuous in two senses: For any individual there was a continuum of effects that became more serious as ozone concentrations became higher, and across individuals there was a continuum in the sense that there was a wide range of sensitivities and that very sensitive individuals would experience an effect at lower ozone concentrations than would less sensitive individuals.

Nevertheless, EPA had to pick a number. It found one clinical study that allegedly found adverse health effects at an ozone level of 0.15 ppm.[9] There were a number of German and Japanese studies showing effects at lower levels; there appeared to be methodological problems with these studies, but in the thinking of EPA they raised the possibility of effects at lower levels. And a study on animals showed a decreased resistance to bacterial infection at 0.10 ppm. From the scientific studies, EPA considered 0.15 ppm to be the critical number for demonstrating effects. It still, of course, needed the margin of safety that the Clean Air Act called for.

EPA also tried a second strategy for picking the number. It assembled a panel of experts to provide their best judgments as to the ozone concentration level at which health effects would be felt by the most sensitive 1% of the group within the general population that was most likely to be sensitive to the effects of ozone (asthmatics and others with breathing difficulties and individuals engaged in vigorous exercise). Since this latter group was about 5% of the population, this most sensitive 1% constituted 0.05% of the general population. The panel provided median estimates of 0.15–0.18 ppm as the point at which health effects were likely to occur for this 99th percentile individual. The panel also provided a full probability distribution on the likelihood, for the 99th percentile individual, of the health effects occurring at lower or higher ozone levels. Again, 0.15 ppm emerged as a critical number.

Next, EPA characterized the time pattern of ozone concentration occurrences with a particular probability distribution, the Weibull distribution. Using estimates of the parameters of that distribution, EPA could, for alternative ozone standards, determine the probability of the occurrence of ozone concentration at or above any particular level. It could thus determine the probability that a level of 0.15 ppm (the level at which it argued that "health effects are virtually certain"[10]) would be reached or exceeded if alternative ozone air quality standards, which permitted one exceedance (an instance in which the ozone level exceeded the standard) per year, were established. Similarly, it combined the panel health effect estimates with the Weibull distribution of occurrences to obtain a second set of estimates of the probabilities of adverse health effects being experienced if alternative ozone air quality standards were established.

Table 4-1 reproduces the probabilities of adverse health effects being experienced that emerged from EPA's calculation. Column 2 uses EPA's estimate of 0.15 ppm as the critical threshold at which health effects are virtually certain. It indicates, for example, that, if an ozone NAAQS of 0.12 ppm were established, EPA estimated that there was an 8% chance (a 0.08 probability) of adverse health effects being experienced in any given metropolitan area during a year; that is, there was an 8% chance that an ozone level of 0.15 ppm or higher might actually occur (because of meteorological variation). Column 3 uses, as an alternative estimate of the location of the threshold, the complete probability distribution from its panel of experts. Thus, column 3 indicates that, if an ozone standard of 0.12 ppm were set, the summed probabilities of the occurrence of higher ozone levels multiplied by the health experts' estimated probabilities that the threshold might be located at those ozone levels would come to 0.67; that is, if one used the health panel's complete estimates, there appeared to be a greater risk of adverse health effects being experienced than if one simply used 0.15 ppm as the estimated threshold.

Finally, EPA concluded that a standard of 0.10 ppm provided a satisfactorily low risk of health effects being experienced. (An alternative interpretation would be that EPA had concluded that 0.15 ppm was the level at which effects had been demonstrated and 0.10 ppm provided a 0.05 ppm margin of safety, which looked "adequate.")

Almost as an afterthought, EPA proposed leaving the secondary standard at 0.08 ppm because EPA had found evidence of some vegetation damage at higher levels.

EPA acknowledged that the hydrocarbon control costs of meeting the proposed primary ozone standard were substantial. EPA estimated

Table 4-1

EPA's Estimates of the Probabilities of Adverse Health Effects
from Ozone Being Experienced at Different Ozone Standards

| | Probability of Adverse Health Effect Being Experienced if | |
Ozone Air Quality Standard (ppm)	Ozone Level of 0.15 ppm Were Considered to Be the Threshold	Complete Information from EPA's Health Panel Were Used to Determine the Threshold
0.08	Less than 0.01 probability	0.36 probability
0.10	Less than 0.01 probability	0.52 probability
0.12	0.08 probability	0.67 probability
0.14	0.40 probability	0.78–0.80 probability

Source: *Federal Register*, June 22, 1978, pp. 26966–26967

the costs, as of 1987, to be $6.9–9.5 billion *per year* (measured in 1978 dollars). But EPA interpreted the Clean Air Act and its legislative history to require that costs *not* be taken into account in setting the primary standard. The protection of the public health was to be the only criterion. EPA had provided the cost estimates only as a formality to comply with E.O. 12044, which required an assessment of consequences and alternatives.

THE RARG REPORT

The RARG report found weaknesses in EPA's methodology in its interpretation of the medical evidence, in its cost estimates and general lack of interest in costs in setting the standard, and in the off-handed way in which the secondary standard was proposed. The report proposed alternative methodologies and cost estimates. It did not suggest a specific alternative standard,[11] but it did point out that the costs of meeting a 0.16 ppm standard were appreciably lower, while the additional adverse health consequences appeared to be relatively minor.

Methodology

EPA's methodology could be characterized as a "critical person, critical point" methodology. From the acknowledged full continuum of effects over single individuals and across the range of individuals, EPA had picked the "critical point" (the first onset of noticeable health effects) and the "critical person" (the 99th percentile person among the sensitive group). This approach had a number of weaknesses.

First, it effectively ignored the full range of sensitivities among individuals. The remaining 1% of the sensitive population would likely experience adverse health effects at lower ozone concentrations (possibly all the way down to zero) than would the "critical person."[12] Thus, EPA's focus on the risks of the "critical person's" experiencing health effects totally neglected the greater risks (or, indeed, virtual certainty) that yet more sensitive individuals would experience health effects. Also, there were slightly less sensitive individuals than the "critical person" who also were exposed to risks of health effects (albeit lower risks than the "critical person" was exposed to). Again, the focus on the "critical person" ignored these other risks.

Second, EPA's approach ignored the continuum of effects on

given individuals. The "critical person" would be likely to experience yet more severe health effects at ozone concentrations that were higher than the "critical point"; these higher concentrations would have a small but finite possibility of occurring. But the more severe consequences were not entering EPA's calculus of decision. Similarly, the more sensitive 1% were likely to experience more severe health effects at the same ozone level that just induced the "critical point" health effects in the "critical person." Again, these more severe effects were ignored. And, equally, the effects just below the "critical point" were ignored for all individuals. In short, on both these points EPA was trying to impose thresholds where even EPA acknowledged they did not exist.

Third, EPA had not justified its choice of the sensitive group. The group could have been all asthmatics and others with respiratory illnesses, or this group plus those exercising vigorously, or this larger group plus the young and the elderly. Similarly, EPA never justified its choice of the 99th percentile individual as the "critical person." It could easily have chosen the 95th or 90th percentile individual instead. Alternative choices among the size of the sensitive group and which percentile person to choose as the "critical person" would have made only relatively small differences in the absolute number of people exposed to health effects but would have made substantial differences in the choice of the ozone standard. For example, if EPA had retained its same methodology but instead had focused on the 95th or the 90th percentile individual, ozone standards of 0.12 ppm or 0.14 ppm, respectively, would have met the other decision criteria that EPA had established.

The points made thus far can be illustrated in Figure 4-3. Curves a*–f* are dose–response curves for various members of the population. Individual b* is the critical person; H* represents the "critical point" of the first onset of noticeable health effects; the combination of the two yield the threshold ozone level, P*. EPA had ignored the fact that there would still be individuals such as a* who would experience adverse health effects at ozone levels below the critical point; it had ignored the fact that individuals such as c* might (because of meteorological variation) be exposed to ozone levels that would create adverse health effects; it had ignored the more severe effects that a* would experience at ozone level P* (and the more severe effects that b* and c* might experience at higher ozone levels); and it had not justified its choice of individual b* as the "critical person" to whom the "critical point" of adverse health effects would be applied and hence on whom the threshold ozone level was based.

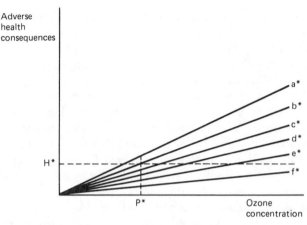

Fig. 4-3

Fourth, EPA did not justify its choice of an acceptable risk. By proposing a standard of 0.10 ppm and rejecting a standard of 0.12 ppm, EPA was implicitly saying that a 0.52 probability of health effects being experienced by the "critical person" (see Table 4-1) was acceptable, whereas a 0.67 probability was not. EPA's only statement on this point was that "the choice of a standard between zero and a level at which health effects are virtually certain (0.15 ppm) is necessarily subjective."[13] This, like the choice of group and the choice of percentile individual, was clearly a policy decision, not a scientific decision, and deserved more justification.

Fifth, EPA's modeling approach essentially assumed that the spatial pattern of ozone concentration levels was uniform within a metropolitan area; that is, that the readings at one monitor site were completely representative of the levels across a given metropolitan area. In fact, however, there was substantial evidence that ozone levels varied considerably within a metropolitan area. (This same problem of geographic variability had arisen a month earlier in CEA's discussions with EPA about the ambient air standard for airborne lead.) Since the monitors were placed in localities that were likely to have the worst (highest) ozone readings, other localities within the same metropolitan area would generally have lower ozone levels. Individuals living in these low-level areas would be protected to a much greater degree than EPA had calculated. Although this overprotection meant extra safety, it was costly. If EPA was aiming at achieving a certain level of protection for the general population, this geographic variability meant that a more lenient ozone standard than 0.10 ppm was the one that would achieve this level of protection.

This problem of geographic variability in pollutant concentration is a general problem for the NAAQS system. The logical extension of the proposition that there are thresholds in the world and that the standard is supposed to be set so as to protect everyone is that the monitors should be placed in the worst localities. If these worst localities can be made to attain the standard, then everyone in other localities will surely be safe. However, if the world does not have thresholds but instead is continuous down to zero pollution, or even if the world has thresholds but is stochastic, so that there is always a risk or probability that the weather or some other set of occurrences will cause a breaching of the threshold, then environmental policy can only aim for a certain level of protection. Ignoring the variability problem while continuing to place the monitors in the worst area must lead to overprotection. Also, there is the problem of where exactly to put the monitor. Especially in the case of pollutants such as sulfur dioxide, particulates, or airborne lead, it clearly makes a big difference as to whether the monitor (which for the purposes of an air quality standard is not measuring total emissions from a facility but is measuring pollutant concentrations in the ambient air) is placed a foot above a factory smokestack, ten yards away, or ten miles away. The NAAQS approach simply has no answer to this dilemma.

Similar to its disregard of geographic variability was EPA's failure to take into account indoor–outdoor differences in ozone levels. Indoor peak concentrations of ozone may reach only 70% of outdoor peak levels. Again, by ignoring this, EPA was setting an ozone standard that was more stringent than was necessary to achieve the desired level of protection. This point did not mean that people should be sent indoors during periods of high ozone concentration but rather that, if a fraction of the population was normally indoors during periods of high ozone concentrations, ignoring this fact meant overprotection.

Medical Evidence

First, all the ozone-related health effects under discussion were short term and reversible. They involved wheezing, coughing, and chest-tightening. They meant temporary discomfort, with complete recovery of an individual's previous state of health shortly after the exposure to ozone ended. Thus far, ozone exposure has not been demonstrated to have long-term debilitating consequences in humans.

(Though the RARG report did not draw the comparison, the contrast with studies of the effects of other pollutants, such as particulates and sulfates, was striking. These other pollutants were almost certainly causing increases in mortality and morbidity.[14] Particulates and sulfates probably killed; ozone appeared to do little more than cause coughing!)

Second, EPA had relied too heavily on the one clinical study in concluding that 0.15 ppm was the level at which "health effects are virtually certain." The DeLucia and Adams study had involved the exposure of six men to ozone levels of 0.15 ppm and 0.30 ppm for one hour, having them exercise vigorously, and studying their consequent lung function and blood biochemistry responses. Significant effects were found at 0.30 ppm, but, as even EPA's criteria document noted, the changes noted at 0.15 ppm were not statistically significant.

Virtually all the other human health studies—clinical and epidemiological—cited by EPA's criteria document found health effects only at ozone levels of 0.25 ppm or above. The exceptions appeared to have substantial methodological flaws.[15] And there had been some studies that had *failed* to find statistically significant health effects in the range of 0.25–0.37 ppm. Thus, a more balanced summary of the evidence appeared to indicate that health effects were virtually certain only at 0.37 ppm or above, that they were less certain in the range of 0.25–0.37 ppm (with less certainty at the lower end of this range but a greater likelihood that asthmatics or others with respiratory illnesses would be affected at the lower end), and that the evidence for effects below 0.25 ppm was quite sparse indeed. There were some animal studies showing decreased resistance to infection and long-term non-reversible effects from relatively low ozone concentrations, but other studies failed to find them, and these effects had not been demonstrated in humans. If there were serious long-term effects, they should have appeared in epidemiological studies—for example, people living in Los Angeles (with consistently high ozone levels) should have been dying faster or have been sicker than people living in other areas (holding other things constant). The epidemiological studies had simply failed to indicate such results. By contrast, epidemiological studies, such as that by Lave and Seskin,[16] had shown that areas with higher concentrations of sulfates and particulates did have higher death rates.

In short, if EPA insisted on specifying a threshold for ozone, it had specified it at too low a level.

Third, the RARG report expressed uneasiness about the small number of experts that EPA had used to determine the critical health effects point for the 99th percentile sensitive individual. Although nine experts were on the panel, EPA had asked questions about four separate health effects, and only three members of the panel had responded to any single question. This was an extremely small sample and raised the possibility of a very large potential variance in the conclusions of the panel. A different panel might well have provided a different set of answers. Ideally, the panel was supposed to reflect accurately the views of experts in the field (and the degree to which there was or was not a consensus of opinion). The larger the panel, the smaller the potential variance in the representation of the views of the entire population of experts. Three seemed far too small.

Costs

The RARG report did not challenge directly EPA's legal interpretation of the Clean Air Act as precluding considerations of cost in the setting of the NAAQS. To do so would have required a substantial input of legal effort and research. But CEA did not (and still does not) have an agency general counsel, and the COWPS general counsel was not particularly active in regulatory matters at that time. (This has since been remedied; see Chapter 5.) Indeed, it was not clear to the individuals involved that a lawyer was needed or that RARG reports were the place for legal arguments.[17] In any event, an economist (or at least this economist) could not make the legal arguments concerning costs.

But the preamble to EPA's NPRM itself provided the opening:

> The Administrator recognizes . . . that controlling ozone to very low levels is a task that will have significant impact on economic and social activity. It is thus important that the standard not be any more stringent than protection of public health demands.[18]

Thus, by implication, costs did matter after all. Otherwise, why not be truly safe and set the standard at zero?

The estimated costs of meeting the standard were substantial. The costs were those resulting from reductions in hydrocarbon emissions. The extent of the necessary reductions (and hence costs) depended on which model, linear or nonlinear, best represented the relationship between hydrocarbon emissions and ozone formation, but in either case the annual costs (as of the late 1980s, when the full set of emission controls would be in place) were large. The left-hand side of Table 4-2

Table 4-2

Estimates of the Annual Costs
of Meeting Alternative Ozone Standards[1]
(billions)

Ozone Standard (ppm)	EPA Estimates				RARC Report Estimates			
	Linear Rollback Model	Marginal Costs	EKMA Model[2]	Marginal Costs	Linear Rollback Model	Marginal Costs	EKMA Model[2]	Marginal Costs
0.08	$8.5	$1.7	$12.1	$3.6	$17.4	$3.1	$23.2	$5.4
0.10	6.9	1.0	9.5	2.0	14.3	1.9	18.8	3.8
0.12	5.9	0.7	7.5	0.8	12.4	1.4	15.0	1.6
0.14	5.2	0.4	6.7	0.7	11.0	0.8	13.4	1.4
0.16	4.8	0.2	6.0	0.4	10.2	0.6	12.0	1.0
0.18	4.6	0.2	5.6	0.3	9.7	0.5	11.0	1.0
0.20	4.4		5.3		9.2		10.1	0.9

[1]All costs are as of 1987, in 1978 dollars.
[2]Environmental kinetic modeling approach.

presents EPA's estimates of the annual costs of alternative standards. For policy purposes, the marginal or incremental costs of moving from one standard to another were the most interesting. EPA had not provided them in the original document, but they were easily calculated.

Substantial as these costs were, they were probably underestimated. Motor vehicles, petroleum refineries and others in the petroleum products distribution chain, and producers and users of solvents and other petroleum-based products were the major sources of hydrocarbon emissions and hence the targets for reductions. The RARG report focused on the underestimates of the costs of motor vehicles emissions control.[19]

First, the estimated costs of the emission controls on new automobiles were too low. Hardware costs were underestimated, and fuel penalties, extra maintenance, and inconvenience costs had been neglected. The RARG report used a National Academy of Sciences study to correct these costs.[20] Second, the costs of emission controls on new trucks and motorcycles (mandated by the Clean Air Act) had been totally neglected. These were estimated and included.

EPA argued that the costs of emission controls on new vehicles were mandated by law and would not change, regardless of the ozone standard chosen; hence, these costs (whatever they were) did not affect marginal costs. It was difficult to assess this argument. One of the reasons that had repeatedly been advanced for the stringent hydrocarbon controls on new vehicles was that they were necessary to allow urban areas to come into compliance with the stringent existing (0.08 ppm) ozone standard. But the report did not pursue the point and thereby conceded it.

Third, EPA had underestimated the costs of inspection and maintenance (I&M) programs for automobiles (and, again, totally neglected these costs for trucks and motorcycles) that would be necessary to reduce hydrocarbon emissions from cars in use. The hardware and engine adjustments on new cars designed to reduce hydrocarbon emissions tend to deteriorate with use; I&M programs were necessary to ensure that they were properly maintained. EPA had included the costs of this program and repair as part of the costs of meeting the ozone standard, but the cost estimates were far too low. A set of EPA-sponsored "restorative maintenance" experiments indicated that the repair costs implied by such programs would be much larger.[21] These costs for all vehicles were reestimated and included in the RARG report. Since the I&M programs were only going to be necessary in areas that could not meet the ozone standard through reductions from other sources, these were marginal costs. The tighter the standard, the more areas that would need I&M programs.

Finally, EPA had included a residual category of unidentified hydrocarbon reductions. After it had identified all the likely sources of hydrocarbon emission reductions, there were still some necessary reductions in some areas (and the tighter the standard, the greater the necessary reductions) that it assumed would somehow occur. It further assumed that the costs of these unidentified reductions would be in the range of $1,000–1,500 per ton of hydrocarbon emissions reduced. These costs had to be too low. The marginal costs of some of the known, identified reductions were already in that range. These were the easy reductions. Surely emission reductions that could not be readily identified had to be more difficult and more expensive. Further, the recalculation of the I&M costs had shown them to be around $2,500 per ton of hydrocarbon reduction. The costs of the unidentified reductions were unlikely to be less than this. Thus, a figure of $2,500 per ton was substituted for EPA's figure. Again, these were marginal costs.

The overall revised cost estimates provided in the RARG report are shown in the right-hand side of Table 4-2. Just the limited changes in costs in the motor vehicle and residual categories had led to estimates of both total and marginal costs that were at least double EPA's estimates. And the report could only hint at the suspicion that other categories of costs in EPA's estimates were similarly understated. For example, EPA argued that in a number of places (particularly refineries) the required controls yielded savings in product recovery that would more than pay for the costs of the controls. This was a favorite EPA argument that appeared in many regulations. But, if the controls were costless and actually benefited the companies, why did they need to be required?

The Secondary Standard

The secondary standard is supposed to be set at a level that will "protect the public welfare." The Clean Air Act elsewhere states that

> All language referring to effects on welfare includes, but is not limited to, effects on soils, water, crops, vegetation, man-made materials, animals, wildlife, weather, visibility, and climate, damage to and deterioration of property, and hazards to transportation, *as well as effects on economic values* and on personal comfort and well-being. (emphasis added)[22]

All parties concerned (including EPA) were prepared to interpret "economic values" as including the costs of pollution control.[23] Accordingly, the RARG report raised this point and called for the explicit balancing of these costs against the benefits in setting the secondary standard, which EPA had not done.

Miscellaneous

Two other points were worth raising. First, natural sources of ozone (primarily incursions of stratospheric ozone) could occasionally lead to ozone concentrations above the standard. EPA promised to disregard these naturally caused ozone "spikes" for purposes of deciding when an area was or was not in compliance with the standard. Second, ozone concentration levels are not random but are serially correlated; that is, a high level in one hour means that there is a strong likelihood of a high level's occurring in the following hour. EPA did not originally take this correlation into account in setting the standard. It promised that it would do so by allowing exceedances of the standard for one day per year (i.e., multiple hours in one day would be allowed) rather than just a single exceedance of only one hour. (These points appeared in the first drafts of the RARG report. But, because EPA readily agreed to the changes and because the report was considered too long anyway, they were cut from the final version.)

In sum, the RARG report was critical of EPA's efforts to impose thresholds where even EPA acknowledged that thresholds probably did not exist, the absence or justification for critical policy choices, the neglect of geographic variability, the interpretation of the medical evidence, the neglect and understatement of costs, and the lack of balancing in the setting of the secondary standard. The report did not propose alternative levels for the primary and secondary standards, but it did point out that the marginal costs were appreciably lower in the area of 0.16 ppm. It also suggested that EPA confront directly the likelihood that thresholds do not exist and change its methodology so as to include the full range of effects for individuals and the full range of sensitivities across individuals. The report provided a suggestive example of such a methodology, which focused on the likely person-hours of unhealthy exposure to ozone that would occur at alternative air quality standards. This kind of methodology did not make the policy choices any easier— indeed, by removing the illusion of threshold levels that would be safe for everyone, it made the choices more difficult—but it at least made the nature of the choices clearer. The report concluded with a four-page explanation of the principles of cost-effectiveness and cost–benefit analysis but without ever using those phrases themselves—they were considered too controversial—and a statement that these principles provided the only way of making sensible public policy choices in a world without safe thresholds.

The RARG report went through four drafts. It was reviewed by CEA and COWPS principals, by the full RARG committee, and by EPA itself. On October 16, 1978, the 31-page (plus appendixes) final RARG report was delivered to EPA to be filed on its public record.

A number of companies and industry groups, fearing the eventual costs of the ozone NPRM, filed critical comments with EPA; a number of local communities did the same. Environmental and public interest groups filed comments supporting the NPRM or urging the continuation of the existing standard of 0.08 ppm.

SUBSEQUENT EVENTS

In early November, EPA produced an internal memo rebutting the RARG report. The memo argued that the RARG report interpreted the medical evidence improperly, that the RARG report had overestimated the costs of hydrocarbon control, and that costs were irrelevant anyway in the determination of the standard. In early December CEA produced an internal memo that answered the EPA rebuttal. It reiterated the points that cost had to be a consideration in a world without thresholds and that the medical evidence was considerably weaker than EPA conceded. Also, it argued that the RARG report had probably underestimated the costs, not overestimated them.

By December, concern within the Executive Office of the President about the proposed ozone standard was rising. Alfred Kahn had joined COWPS as its Chairman and as the President's chief inflation adviser. The costs of government regulations were considered to be one of the contributors to inflation. Kahn became concerned about the ozone standard. Because this was a scientific issue, Frank Press, the President's chief science adviser, became involved, and his staff in the Office of Science and Technology Policy began an intensive review of the medical evidence.

A number of meetings were held between EPA staff and principals and EOP staff and principals. We argued that the costs were substantial, that the health benefits were slight at best, and that the medical evidence was shaky. We compared ozone with sulfates and particulates. We also compared the ozone proposal with a recently promulgated regulation by the Occupational Safety and Health Administration to control worker exposure to lead within factories. That regulation would cost about $500 million per year and promised substantial reductions in the number of birth defects, cases of kidney disorders, and cases of nervous system disorders experienced by workers. By contrast, the ozone standard was going to cost 10 to 30 times as much and promised a little less coughing.

EPA conceded that the medical evidence was not solid but then turned this into an argument for greater caution. EPA steadfastly maintained that it was bound by the Clean Air Act to disregard costs, but for our benefit it pointed out that the costs were not as substantial as we thought (the costs got smaller every time we talked with EPA) and the costs were mostly going to occur in the early and mid-1980s, so there was little or no immediate inflationary impact.

It was clear from these meetings that the number itself, 0.10 ppm, was beginning to take on a life of its own. EPA had proposed that number. Any change (upward) for whatever reason would be a retreat, a political defeat for EPA at the hands of the "antiregulators" within the EOP.

THE OUTCOME

In early January 1979, Douglas Costle, Administrator of EPA, informed the EOP that EPA had decided to set both the primary and secondary NAAQSs for ozone at 0.12 ppm. A last flurry of meetings ensued. EPA held firm. This standard was less stringent than EPA's original proposal of 0.10 ppm and represented a 50% loosening of the existing 0.08 ppm standard. Given the nature of the medical evidence, a 0.12 ppm standard provided an adequate margin of safety but any higher standard would not. As far as the secondary standard was concerned, it would be set at the same level as the primary standard because EPA had not found any significant decrease in the growth or yield of commercial crops or indigenous vegetation at these levels. (Thus EPA was avoiding a balancing cost–benefit calculation even for the secondary standard.) A last-minute EOP suggestion that the 0.12 ppm standard be kept but that four or five exceedances per year be allowed, which would have been statistically the equivalent of a 0.14 ppm standard with one exceedance, fell on deaf ears.

There was serious consideration given to appealing this issue to the President, but in the end it was decided not to do so. This was simply not the right issue or the right time. EPA did, however, promise to mount a major research effort on the effects of ozone and to review the standard again within five years, rather than the maximum ten years required by the Clean Air Act.

On February 8, 1979, EPA published in the *Federal Register* its final regulation embodying the 0.12 ppm standard.[24] EPA was immediately sued by the American Petroleum Institute and by the Natural Resources Defense Council. As of this writing, both suits are pending.

CONCLUDING COMMENTS

The EOP's strength does not lie in engaging the regulatory agencies in pure numbers battles. It lies rather in analyzing programs and proposals, in establishing frameworks for analysis, and in finding more cost-effective ways of achieving goals. The setting of an ambient air quality standard—especially if threshold notions disappear—will involve a direct trade-off of costs and health. It is a pure numbers battle. The EOP may be able to improve the analysis, but, unless political sentiment shifts markedly, the EOP is likely to be at a disadvantage.

One might have hoped that EPA would change its methodology after the dust had settled on the ozone episode. But the preliminary indications are that the NAAQSs for carbon monoxide and nitrogen oxides will be set in the same manner: Evidence will be developed and claims will be made that there are safe thresholds.

Curiously, there is one group within EPA that is pushing in a different direction. The scientists who are working on problems of cancer-causing substances (carcinogens) have adopted a model that assumes that there are no thresholds, that the dose–response curve for carcinogens is continuous and linear all the way down to zero exposure; that is, there is no completely safe level of exposure short of zero. They apparently cannot be shaken from that position. Consequently, if EPA is not prepared to go to zero emissions of these carcinogens (which it is not), it must deal explicitly with risks and decide on appropriate levels of risks for the general population (rather than trying to find "safe" levels). The consequences of this approach are just starting to be seen in EPA's development of water quality standards with respect to toxic pollutants[25] and its development of policy with respect to emissions of airborne carcinogens.[26] Interestingly, in the case of water quality, EPA is making a distinction between carcinogens and other toxic chemicals. In the latter case it is trying to define "safe" levels; in the former, it is only trying to define risk levels. The difference in treatment would probably not be understandable unless one understood the driving scientific forces behind it.

There was a public perception that the EOP won a major victory when EPA moved from the 0.10 ppm standard proposed in the ozone NPRM to the 0.12 ppm standard promulgated in the final rule. It is far from clear that the RARG report or the EOP in fact had any effect. There were many forces within EPA arguing that the medical evidence was weak and could not support the more stringent standard.[27] But, regardless of the reason for the change, the country will save between $1.0 billion and $3.8 billion per year, in perpetuity, starting in the mid-1980s.

NOTES TO CHAPTER 4

[1]Sec. 109 (b)(1) of the Clean Air Act of 1977, 42 U.S.C. 1857.

[2]Sec. 109 (b)(2).

[3]This simplified example ignores the problem of varying exposures over time. It best characterizes a situation in which individuals are exposed to a constant level of pollution over an extended period of time.

[4]*Federal Register*, April 30, 1971, p. 8186.

[5]C. E. Schoettlin and E. Landau, "Air Pollution and Asthmatic Attacks in the Los Angeles Area," *Public Health Reports*, 76 (1961): 545–548.

[6]*Federal Register*, June 22, 1978, pp. 26962–26968.

[7]Curiously, the NPRM almost escaped EOP attention. It was only brought to CEA's attention in mid-July by a friend of another CEA staff member. After this, procedures for reading the *Federal Register* daily were tightened at CEA and COWPS.

[8]I was selected to be the primary author. I was familiar with the economics of the automobile industry and had recently done some writing on the automotive pollution control experience. Hydrocarbon controls, to prevent ozone formation, were a part of that experience, so I was vaguely familiar with the ozone problem. As part of the preparation in writing the report, I collected and read the relevant EPA supporting documents, read some of the underlying scientific (primarily medical and meteorological) articles, and talked with personnel at EPA, CEQ, and OSTP and some of the affected industries.

[9]A. J. Delucia and W. C. Adams, "Effects of O_3 Inhalation during Exercise on Pulmonary Function and Blood Chemistry," *Journal of Applied Physiology*, 43 (1977): 75–81.

[10]*Federal Register*, June 22, 1978, p. 26967.

[11]At the time, the general understanding was that RARG reports technically were reviews of the agency's analysis and not of the regulation itself, so that implicit suggestions for changing the regulations could not be included in the report. That artificial distinction has since been dropped.

[12]EPA had acknowledged this in one of its support documents.

[13]*Federal Register*, June 22, 1978, p. 26967.

[14]See L. B. Lave and E. P. Seskin, *Air Pollution and Human Health* (Baltimore: Johns Hopkins, 1977).

[15]A German clinical study measured ozone differently from the way in which it was measured in the United States, and other pollutants may not have been adequately removed. Japanese epidemiological studies may have had reported symptoms suggested by the subject's knowledge of prevailing ozone levels. And an American study relating athletic performance to ozone levels had correlated performance (this week versus last week) with ozone concentrations *this week*. The proper correlation should have been with relative ozone concentrations (this week versus last week). For this last study, see W. S. Wayne, P. F. Wehrle, and R. E. Carroll, "Pollution and Athletic Performance," *Journal of the American Medical Association*, 199 (March 20, 1967): 901–904.

[16]Lave and Seskin, op. cit., chs. 3–7.

[17]There was another RARG report at about the same time on the Department of Transportation's regulations with respect to the access of the handicapped to public transportation, which was similarly hampered by the absence of legal input.

[18]*Federal Register*, June 22, 1978, p. 26965.

[19]We did not have the time or the expertise to develop independent estimates of the emissions control costs for the other major sectors.

[20]Coordinating Committee on Air Quality Studies, National Academy of Sciences and National Academy of Engineering, *Air Quality and Automobile Emission Control*, Vol. IV, prepared for the U.S. Senate, 93rd Congress, 2nd session, Committee on Public Works, September 1974.

[21]See R. Gafford and R. Carlson, *Evaluation of Restorative Maintenance on 1975 and 1976 Light-Duty Vehicles in Detroit, Michigan* (May 1977); D. R. Liljedahl and J. Terry, *Evaluation of Restorative Maintenance on 1975 and 1976 Light-Duty Vehicles in Chicago, Illinois* (January 1977); L. H. Washington, *Evaluation of Restorative Maintenance on 1975 and 1976 Light-Duty Vehicles in Washington, D.C.* (March 1977); and Automotive Environmental Systems, Inc., *Evaluation of Restorative Maintenance on 1975 and 1976 Light-Duty Vehicles in San Francisco, California* (October 1977). All four are published by Emission Control Technology Division, Office of Air and Waste Management, U.S. Environmental Protection Agency, Washington, D.C.

[22]Sec. 302(h) of the Clean Air Act of 1977, 42 U.S.C. 1857.

[23]Earlier, partly in response to an EOP request, EPA had delayed the close of the public comment period from the original August deadline to the October 16 deadline.

[24]*Federal Register*, February 8, 1979, pp. 8202–8237.

[25]See EPA's NPRM on water quality criteria, *Federal Register*, March 15, 1979, pp. 15926–15931.

[26]See EPA's NPRM on airborne carcinogens, *Federal Register*, October 10, 1979, pp. 58642–58661.

[27]See the comments of Roy Gamse of EPA, quoted in S. J. Tolchin, "Presidential Power and the Politics of RARG," *Regulation*, 3 (July–August 1979): 47.

chapter 5

Ohio Coal

Should EPA prohibit electric utilities in Ohio from buying out-of-state low-sulfur coal?

Environmental policy and the short-run interests of labor often appear to be at odds. Stringent pollution control requirements can be costly, threatening the closure of factories and the local loss of jobs. Section 125 of the Clean Air Act is an exception to this pattern; it tries to preserve local jobs. This chapter provides an example of the policy problems that accompany such job protection efforts.

BACKGROUND

The state implementation plans (SIPs) for meeting the national ambient air quality standard for sulfur dioxide require most coal-burning facilities to reduce their SO_2 emissions. If a facility is burning high-sulfur coal (and intends to continue burning coal), there are two basic ways in which the SO_2 emissions can be reduced: The exhaust gases can be "scrubbed" to eliminate the SO_2, or low-sulfur coal can be burned. (Also, high-sulfur coal can be washed to reduce its sulfur content somewhat, and high- and low-sulfur coal can be blended.) Scrubbers (flue gas desulfurization systems) are expensive, and many potential users consider them unreliable. Low-sulfur coal commands a substantial price premium over high-sulfur coal.

Most of the electric utilities in Ohio have traditionally bought and burned high-sulfur coal, much of it coming from mines in southeastern Ohio. It had long been known that, if and when the Ohio utilities had to reduce their SO_2 emissions, they did not intend to use scrubbers but instead planned to buy low-sulfur coal. Since Ohio had no low-sulfur coal, this meant switching their purchases to out-of-state sources.

As a consequence, during the process of amending the Clean Air Act in 1977, Senator Howard Metzenbaum introduced an amendment that passed and became Section 125 of the Act. Section 125 has three major subsections: Sec. 125(a) allows a governor, EPA, or the President (or his designee) to

> determine that action . . . is necessary to prevent or minimize significant local or regional economic disruption or unemployment which would otherwise result from use by [a major fuel burning stationary] source . . . of coal or coal derivatives other than locally or regionally available coal . . . to comply with the requirements of a state implementation plan.

Section 125(b) then allows the President (or his designee) to prohibit the use of "fuels other than locally or regionally available coal or coal derivatives to comply with implementation plan requirements." In so doing, he "shall take into account the final cost to the consumer of such an action." And Section 125(c) allows EPA, subsequent to a Section 125(b) action, to require the use of regionally available coal and to readjust compliance schedules and timetables.

At the time the amendment passed, it was generally thought that the Ohio utilities intended to buy low-sulfur coal from western states. Senator Jennings Randolph from West Virginia, a state that is a major source of low-sulfur coal, spoke in favor of it on the Senate floor and voted for it. It passed by a vote of 43 to 42.

In early 1978 it became clear that the Ohio utilities intended to buy their low-sulfur coal from Kentucky and West Virginia. The SIP gave them until October 1979 to comply with the SO_2 standard if they chose to burn low-sulfur coal. If they chose the route of high-sulfur coal plus scrubbers, the deadline was extended to April 1980. But, given the very long lead times in ordering, constructing, installing, and breaking in a scrubber, by early 1978 the utilities had passed the point at which the scrubber option was viable.

Fearing the loss of coal sales and jobs, the Ohio Mining and Reclamation Association and the Ohio local of the United Mine Workers petitioned EPA to take action under Sec. 125. Senator Metzenbaum and Governor James Rhodes of Ohio later joined the petitions.

EPA decided to accept the petitions and began the process. This was the first time that any action had been taken under Sec. 125. EPA asked the major Ohio utilities for detailed information on their past and projected coal usage. It retained four engineering and economics consulting firms to analyze the data and predict the likely economic consequences. And in August 1978 it held hearings in Cleveland and in St. Clairesville, Ohio; the latter town is located in the southeastern coal mining area. This was a big political issue in Ohio; not too surprisingly, sentiment was strong in the mining area for preserving the miners' jobs.

PRELIMINARY ACTIONS

In October 1978 EPA informed the EOP that it would probably proceed and make a Sec. 125(a) determination that action was necessary. It was likely that the utilities would be required to buy Ohio coal and that scrubbers would be required in at least some cases. CEA and COWPS took an instant dislike to the proposal. It smacked of protectionism of the worst kind. It tried to protect jobs in the face of change, rather than trying to ease the accommodation to change. It appeared to set an unfortunate precedent. Unions and mine owners in other states might similarly decide that they wanted protection from out-of-state coal, and soon the coal markets of the country would be balkanized. The Ohio utilities were probably making the low-cost choice by buying low-sulfur coal, so any requirements that they buy high-sulfur coal and scrub it probably meant higher costs and ultimately higher prices of electricity to Ohio industries and consumers.

There was only one glimmer of an interesting public policy dilemma in the Ohio coal problem. (As will be clear, to a microeconomist, the issue of the job preservation is not an interesting public policy problem. Labor markets adjust, people move, new job possibilities appear. Public policy can try to facilitate this process, making accommodation to change easier and faster; it should not try to preserve jobs for their own sake.) In recent years, as fuel prices have risen rapidly, many state utility commissions have instituted fuel adjustment clauses that allow electric utilities immediately to raise electricity prices to cover the costs of higher fuel rather than having to petition the commission for permission to raise prices. If new capital equipment is bought, however, the utilities must always gain the commission's permission to include the equipment in the rate base and raise prices accordingly. This can be a slow and tedious process. The low-sulfur-coal option simply involved more expensive fuel; the scrubber option involved capital equipment. It was possible that the Ohio utilities were favoring the former, even though the latter might be a lower-cost option, simply because of the ease of cost recovery permitted by the fuel adjustment clauses. If so, one might have interpreted the Sec. 125 action as an effort to correct with one government policy (Sec. 125) the problem created by another government policy (fuel adjustment clauses). But the cost data did not seem to bear out the point, and it largely dropped from discussion.

CEA took the lead in keeping track of EPA's actions and intentions with respect to Sec. 125.[1] This required us to familiarize ourselves with the economics of coal mining in Ohio and of sulfur emissions control for electric utilities.

There was one possible interpretation of the problem, grounded in textbook economics, that we initially pursued; this interpretation turned out to be incorrect, and it provided a valuable lesson in the dangers of abstract theorizing. The price of coal had roughly quintupled between 1970 and 1978, rising at about the same rate as the price of oil.

The economic theory of land value, developed by David Ricardo over 150 years ago, predicted that the owners of the coal mines should have been the recipients of huge windfalls as a consequence of this price rise. Accordingly, one might have hypothesized, maybe the announcements by the Ohio utilities were all really a bluff, an effort to get the Ohio coal mine owners to drop their prices. After all, if the prices of Ohio high-sulfur coal were low enough, even scrubbers became a viable option. Rather than lose their sales entirely, the Ohio mine owners would be willing to give up some of their windfalls. If no action were taken, surely the Ohio coal prices would fall sufficiently to attract demand back to the Ohio mines. (There was still the problem of the delay in constructing scrubbers, but we were not yet aware of this factor.)

Investigation of coal cost data indicated, however, that this was not the case. Mine owners were not doing badly, but there did not appear to be the huge windfalls that would promise substantial price flexibility. Instead, it appeared that labor costs had risen to absorb most of the windfall. Although output of Ohio coal had been roughly constant from 1970 through 1977, employment had risen by 50%; that is, labor productivity had fallen by a third. (Whether this was due to the need to mine deeper seams, more stringent Department of Labor safety regulations, or tighter union work rules remained an open question.) And labor costs (wages plus benefits) per worker had more than doubled. Windfall gains embedded in owner profits might be flexible; windfall gains embedded in labor costs surely were not. So much for Ricardian land value theories when the United Mine Workers were present!

With that out of the way, two issues loomed as crucial. First, how many tons of coal were going to be shifted out of Ohio (with the consequent loss of jobs)? The answer depended partly on what year was used as a base and, more important, on how the SIPs were enforced: whether a stringent 24-hour or a lenient 30-day averaging period was required for the SO_2 emissions limitations. The sulfur content of coal varies from batch to batch. If a 24-hour averaging period were required, coal with a much lower average sulfur content would be required so as to ensure that the variability from an occasional batch of higher-sulfur content did not lead to a violation. With a 30-day averaging period, there was more room for the low-sulfur batches to offset the high-sulfur batches, and hence a higher average sulfur content coal could be used. EPA was predicting a switch of 15.8 million tons, with the loss of 5,270 mining jobs in Ohio and an overall job loss in Ohio (because of indirect "multiplier" effects) of 13,180–15,300 jobs. But this figure was the sum of the Ohio utility responses, some of which had assumed that a 24-hour averaging period would be required and others of which had assumed a 30-day averaging period. So the 15.8-million-ton figure was not internally consistent. If a 24-hour averaging period were imposed, 20 million tons might be shifted, with a proportionally greater loss of jobs; if a 30-day averaging period were imposed, only 10 million tons might be shifted.

Second, what were the extra costs of requiring the utilities instead to use Ohio coal? The answer depended on predictions as to what would happen to the relative prices of high- and low-sulfur coal, on what exactly EPA would require the utilities to do, and on the costs of scrubber construction, installation, and operation. EPA's consultants had produced a model of long-run coal prices with which we were not entirely comfortable, but we were not really prepared to challenge it. EPA was being vague on exactly what actions it might require. Most important, there were large differences in the estimates of scrubber costs. EPA was claiming that scrubbers would involve little or no extra costs compared with the low-sulfur-coal option. The utilities were claiming that costs would rise as much as 25%. In effect, EPA and its consultants were saying "Scrubbers? Nothing to it!" and the utilities were saying "Scrubbers? You've got to be kidding!"

This difference in the cost estimates of a new and untried technology was a problem that continually arose in regulatory disputes. It frequently hinged on technical disputes between industry engineers and regulatory agency engineers over very detailed points. For economists without engineering expertise who were trying to determine "the truth," these were frustrating disputes indeed. Each side had its ax to grind. The details were often so specific to the companies involved that it was virtually impossible to find "neutral" third parties with the specific expertise who could adjudicate these disputes.

The EPA staff was not wholly comfortable with having to take action under Sec. 125. The staff recognized that protecting jobs was bad policy, and it recognized Sec. 125 to be sloppily written and vague. But the staff felt that EPA was bound by the Act to take action, and it was also genuinely concerned about the possible lack of alternative job possibilities for miners. (And we suspected that the EPA leadership was not all that unhappy about being in a posture of saving jobs; usually it was at odds with labor because environmental regulations threatened the closure of factories.)

In mid-December EPA informed the EOP that it definitely intended to announce a proposed Sec. 125(a) determination that action was necessary. At a last meeting we asked that EPA hold off; EPA declined. On December 28, 1978, EPA published in the *Federal Register* its proposed determination that action was necessary to prevent significant local or regional economic disruption and unemployment in Ohio.[2] It invited public comment by February 26, 1979.

Since this was not yet a rulemaking [if subsequent actions were proposed under Sec. 125(b) and 125(c), those would be rulemakings], a RARG report was not possible. Instead, it was decided that the EOP would get its arguments onto the record through a filing by COWPS. [These kinds of decisions were usually taken at weekly or semiweekly meetings chaired by Alfred (Fred) Kahn, Chairman of COWPS, and attended by representatives of CEA, COWPS, OMB, and DPS. They quickly became known as meetings of "Fred's group," and that name stuck.] Because the CEA staff members were most familiar with the issue, we took responsibility for writing the first draft of the COWPS filing.

EPA'S POSITION

Because this was only a proposed determination that action was necessary, EPA focused only on the shifting of coal purchases and the consequent effects on the local areas in Ohio. EPA did not discuss the details of the possible remedial action that it might require.

Using 1977 as the base year, EPA found that as of 1980 six electric utilities—Cleveland Electric Illuminating, Dayton Power & Light, Cincinnati Gas & Electric, Toledo Edison, Ohio Edison, and Columbus & Southern Ohio Electric—would be shifting 15.8 million tons of coal per year out of Ohio to West Virginia and Kentucky. Half the total was due to Cleveland Electric Illuminating's actions alone. EPA then traced these tons to their county of origin, estimated the split between surface (strip) and deep mines, estimated the mining jobs per ton of coal for each type of mine, and thus arrived at a figure of 5,270 miners' jobs that would be lost; this was 35% of Ohio's total coal mining employment. Four counties that were heavily dependent on coal for their employment accounted for 80% of their losses. EPA then used a mixture of input–output and multiplier analysis to estimate that an additional 7,910 to 10,030 jobs would be lost through indirect "ripple" effects. Thus, a total of 13,180–15,300 jobs, about 0.3% of Ohio's total state employment, would be lost, with much of this loss focused on the four southeastern counties. In those four countries, 7–9% of the labor force would be affected.

Accordingly, EPA concluded that there was significant local or regional economic disruption and unemployment and that action would be necessary to prevent or minimize it.

THE COWPS FILING

We decided to focus on four major points: The low-sulfur coal was still coming from within the region, the unemployment effects were not likely to be nearly as severe as EPA predicted, the remedial actions could well have serious employment and economic consequences elsewhere in Ohio, and finally the remedial actions were bad public policy and created bad precedents.

The Regional Issue

We argued that Ohio by itself was not a distinct coal market. Ohio coal users tended to buy about half of their coal from other states. At the same time, about a quarter of the coal mined in Ohio was shipped to users in other states. Thus, Ohio was far from a self-contained coal market. Instead, it and a group of neighboring states comprised a regional coal market. Five studies of coal markets in the past decade had come to this conclusion. The data we marshalled for 1977 showed this still to be the case. Thus the low-sulfur coal was *still regionally available*, and we questioned whether there was any basis for taking action in the first place.

To lend even more support to this point, we noted that the distances between some of the coal mines *within* Ohio were about the same as the distances between some of the mines in Ohio and some in eastern Kentucky. If the utilities had switched their purchases among the former mines within Ohio, it was unlikely that EPA would have decided that there was significant local or regional disruption. But switches involving equal distance across state boundaries would trigger EPA action. Yet the economic consequences should be the same in either instance. In sum, state boundaries were artificial distinctions that did not reflect coal market boundaries and should not guide economic policies.

Employment Effects

First, we pointed out that the estimate of 15.8 million tons was not an internally consistent figure because of the uncertainty over the required averaging times. Second, at the same time that the 15.8 million tons was being switched out, EPA data indicated that a net 1.4 million tons was going to be added to Ohio coal demand by electric utilities (using scrubbers) in other states. Thus, the net coal loss was 14.4 million tons, with a mining employment loss of 4,880, not the somewhat larger numbers that EPA was using. Third, EPA had neglected the increase in the demand for coal generally that would be occurring because of the federal government's efforts to switch energy users away from petroleum and natural gas and toward coal.

Fourth, EPA was underestimating the resiliency of local economies and the flexibility of the work force. The extreme disruptions that had been predicted for Youngstown, Ohio in 1977 when a major steel mill had closed had not occurred because the local economy was not as static or as brittle as had been thought. And it was important for a growing, changing economy to accommodate itself to such change. Efforts to protect sections of the economy from change would only be counterproductive to long-run growth and welfare and to the anti-inflation efforts of the administration.

Fifth, the rapid increase in coal mining employment in the 1970s probably meant that mostly young workers had been hired. With their lack of seniority, they were the ones likely to be laid off; but younger workers were more flexible, more retrainable, more willing to commute long distances. The picture was not nearly as bleak as EPA painted it.

The Consequences of Subsequent Actions

Because the proposed determination would very likely lead to remedial action, we thought it important to discuss some of the possible dangers of the remedial action.

First, efforts to retain coal mining employment within Ohio would occur largely at the expense of employment in West Virginia and Kentucky coal mines. EPA had not investigated the economic consequences of its action for these latter areas.

Second, although we could not be specific about the extent of the electricity price increases that would occur in the rest of Ohio if EPA required scrubbers, we wanted to raise the possibility that they might

79

be substantial. If they were, the higher electricity prices would add to inflation generally and possibly discourage industrial expansion (or encourage contraction) in central and northern Ohio. Thus, by trying to preserve employment for Ohio miners, EPA might be causing future unemployment (or employment adjustment problems) for factory workers elsewhere in Ohio.

Third, an irony of any remedial actions would be that they would delay the date on which the utilities would reduce their SO_2 emissions. Thus, unlike the usual regulatory action, in which extra costs are imposed but also extra (or prompter) health or safety benefits are achieved, here the regulatory action would not only raise costs but would also *delay* the receipt of any health benefits.

Policy and Precedents

Any remedial action would replace the performance standard implied by the SIP with a specific design and engineering standard. This was inefficient and bad policy.

Finally, we concluded that

. . . to the extent that EPA does require actions under Sections 125(b) and 125(c), this will represent a significant partitioning of coal markets in the United States by regulatory action. For the first time, there will be de facto restrictions on the purchase and shipment of coal crossing state lines, simply because it happens to be crossing state lines. We believe the precedent that may be created by this kind of decision is undesirable. Miners and/or coal companies from other states may petition EPA concerning the economic disruption that is occurring because of the ''import'' of coal from other states. The raising of import barriers at state lines in these United States is not an appealing prospect.

The COWPS filing embodying these ideas went through three drafts and was reviewed by CEA and COWPS principals. It was filed on EPA's public record on February 26, 1979.

SUBSEQUENT ACTIONS

Shortly after EPA's proposed determination was published in the *Federal Register*, the Kentucky and West Virginia coal producers and the Ohio utilities separately went into court to challenge EPA's actions. The former suit was thrown out, but the latter remained as a constant backdrop to the following events. Also, although most political figures from Ohio favored EPA's action under Sec. 125, their counterparts in Kentucky and West Virginia—including Senator Randolph, who had originally voted for the amendment—actively opposed action.

In early January, EPA began negotiations with the Ohio utilities to try to reach side agreements that would eliminate the need to invoke formal actions under Sec. 125(b) and Sec. 125(c). In February, Columbus & Southern agreed to a coal-washing plan that would allow it to continue to burn Ohio coal. This agreement saved 3.5 million tons per year for Ohio. About the same time EPA decided to establish a 24-hour averaging period, but with several allowable exceedances per month, so that the standard was close to the equivalent of a 30-day averaging period. Together, these two actions dropped EPA's estimate of the remaining likely coal switching to 9.5 million tons.

In early April, EPA informed the EOP that it intended to proceed to make a final determination under Sec. 125(a) that action was necessary. And EPA had a suggested plan of action, which involved partial scrubbing at two Cleveland Electric Illuminating power plants, full scrubbing at one Toledo Edison plant, and blending at Ohio Edison.[3] By EPA's estimates this plan would preserve an additional 5.8 million tons for Ohio, saving 2,100 mining jobs and 3,600 other jobs in the state. The scrubbers would take four years to install. In the interim, the utilities could burn a mixture of high- and low-sulfur coal; the air would be a little dirtier than if only low-sulfur coal were burned.

CEA and COWPS were still fundamentally opposed to any Sec. 125 action. Only the President could take action under Sec. 125(b), and he could conceivably decide to forebear. But a Sec. 125(a) determination that *action was necessary* was very forcing; it was unlikely that the President could avoid acting after such a determination had been made by EPA. Accordingly, we argued, because there was a serious difference of opinion within the administration as to whether action by the President should be taken, this was an issue that the President should decide before a Sec. 125(a) determination was made—that is, before his hand was forced.

At the same time the Antitrust Division in the Justice Department indicated that it too was opposed to EPA actions under Sec. 125. It was concerned that limiting Ohio utility coal purchases to Ohio mines meant a decrease in competition that would face the Ohio utilities, with the possibility of higher coal prices charged by coal mine owners.[4]

A number of meetings followed in April and early May. The Domestic Policy Staff acted as honest broker, writing successive drafts of the decision memo for the President, trying to get the two sides to agree to a common statement of the pros and cons of the arguments. EPA maintained its position that the disruption was serious for southeastern Ohio and that the costs of corrective action were modest. CEA–COWPS maintained its position that the effects were not severe and that any action represented bad policy and a bad precedent.[5] (We knew that the state of Illinois was planning to petition EPA under Sec. 125, although EPA claimed it would—and eventually did—reject the Illinois petition.) In addition, we had uncovered employment data that strengthened our case. We discovered that the normal labor turnover among miners was such that, within a period of five years, there would usually be a turnover of 35–40% in the work force. Thus, any protective action was to a large extent protecting job *slots*, not the current individuals in their jobs; we thought this made a difference in how one thought about protective action. Also, the four most seriously affected counties were within 50 miles of 5 major labor markets, 3 of which had 1978 unemployment rates below 6%, an indication of tight labor markets and job possibilities. Thus, the commuting possibilities for laid-off workers were greater than one might have suspected.

Initially, the choices that were to be laid before the President were three: (1) make a determination that significant economic disruption would occur and that action is necessary; require the four power plants to burn regionally available high-sulfur coal; this would be sufficient to force the three companies to buy Ohio coal and to scrub or blend in the manner that EPA had suggested; (2) make a finding of no disruption; no further action would be necessary; (3) make a determination that significant economic disruption would occur and that action is necessary; allow the utilities to phase out the use of high-sulfur coal gradually over a four-year period, after which time they would be allowed to use only low-sulfur coal.

This last option had been suggested by CEA Chairman Schultze and was the CEA–COWPS fallback option. It had the same four years of mixed high- and low-sulfur coal that the scrubber option had, but it had only low-sulfur coal at its end. It gave the affected Ohio mining areas an opportunity to adjust somewhat gradually to the disruption that might be caused, without protecting them indefinitely.

EPA did not like option 3. A transition period might be all right if Ohio jobs were preserved at the end but not if it only allowed time for adjustments. Further, EPA argued that it was illegal, that it could not be done under Sec. 125(c) (which allows EPA to require the use of regionally available coal).

At this point, an important change was taking place at COWPS. A new general counsel and special assistant to the general counsel had been appointed. Both were taking an active interest in regulatory matters (which the COWPS general counsel office had not previously done), and both had attended the series of meetings in which the various drafts of the presidential decision memo were discussed. They were prepared to defend the legality of option 3. Further, they had taken a closer look at EPA's option 1, and they thought *it* was illegal under Sec. 125(c). EPA was only allowed to require the use of regionally available coal, not regionally available high-sulfur coal.

We now had not only a policy disagreement but a legal disagreement within the administration. The latter had to be resolved before the memo could go to the President for a decision. The Office of General Counsel within the Department of Justice offered to serve as legal arbiter. EPA and COWPS prepared short briefs and submitted them to the Department of Justice. The answer soon came back: option 3 was legal; option 1 as it stood was not.

EPA was not happy with the options left open to it. It had conceded that Ohio was not a region, so it could not require the use of only Ohio coal. And, if it could only require regional coal, without specifying the type, the utilities would continue to buy the Kentucky and West Virginia low-sulfur coal, and nothing would have been accomplished.

THE OUTCOME

Always present in the background of the Sec. 125 dispute had been the contention by the Ohio utilities, particularly by Cleveland Electric Illuminating, that the SIPs were unnecessarily stringent and were based on faulty environmental modeling. The actual emissions data, they claimed, showed that high-sulfur Ohio coal could be burned without leading to a violation of the SO_2 air quality standard. But EPA had not been convinced.

In late May EPA became convinced, and it decided to change the SIP for Cleveland Electric. The utility could continue to burn Ohio coal. With the approval of the President, EPA publicly announced this change on June 6. There was also a general understanding that the situations at Ohio Edison and Toledo Edison would be reexamined. All proceedings under Sec. 125 were dropped.

CONCLUDING COMMENTS

In the Sec. 125 dispute, the EOP learned for the first time that it pays to have a good lawyer on one's side in regulatory disputes. The COWPS general counsel's office has since taken an active role in regulatory issues.

The outcome in the Sec. 125 dispute was a victory for sensible policy. Remedial measures to save jobs would have been a bad precedent for other Sec. 125 actions for other states and for other legislation in which these kinds of protectionist measures might be introduced. Public policy should focus on accommodating change and easing adjustment, not in preventing them. With luck, there will be no other Sec. 125 actions.

NOTES TO CHAPTER 5

[1]Robert Lurie, a CEA junior staff member, and I became the primary CEA staff members responsible for the issue. To familiarize ourselves with it, we talked with EPA staff, gathered and read EPA supporting documents, talked with EPA consultants, and talked with the Ohio utilities.

[2]*Federal Register*, December 28, 1978, pp. 60652–60661.

[3]Possible action against Cincinnati Gas & Electric and Dayton Power & Light had been dropped for technical reasons.

[4]We had considered making a somewhat similar argument but had rejected it. Competition even within the Ohio coal mine areas was probably strong enough to prevent collusive price raising by coal mine owners. But limiting purchases to Ohio mines might allow the one clearly established collusive force, Ohio coal miners, to raise their wages above what they otherwise might have been. After considering it, we decided that this was a messy argument that we did not want to touch.

[5]Our argument concerning the regional nature of the coal had been declared to be irrelevant; as long as the coal was nonlocal, that was sufficient.

chapter 6

Heavy-Duty Truck Emissions

What should be the testing and enforcement provisions for heavy-duty truck emissions of hydrocarbons and carbon monoxide?

Most of the publicized disputes over regulatory policy relate to the numerical stringency levels of the regulatory standards; Chapters 4, 7, and 8 provide examples of such disputes. Testing and enforcement procedures, on the other hand, receive much less publicity. They are more technical, more complicated, and less dramatic. But they too are the subject of rulemakings. And in practice the testing and enforcement procedures required by a regulatory agency can be just as important in determining the actual stringency of a standard as the numerical level. As was seen in Chapter 5, when there is variability in the sulfur content of batches of coal, a 24-hour averaging period for an SO_2 emissions standard for coal-burning electric utilities means a much tighter standard (on average, lower-sulfur coal must be burned) than does a 30-day averaging period.

This chapter provides an example of a major rulemaking largely involving testing and enforcement procedures. It shows the issues that can arise in this context. It also demonstrates the value that a COWPS–CEA filing could have as an educational document.

BACKGROUND

The Clean Air Act treats the motor vehicle industry in a very special way. The air pollutant emissions of all other industries are by-products of their *production processes;* for example, coal-fired electric utilities emit sulfur dioxide and particulates as a by-product of producing electricity. Their emissions are either subject to EPA regulations (for new sources) or to state regulations under state implementation plans (for existing sources). All the limitations on emissions have been established through rulemakings.

By contrast, the Clean Air Act devotes an entire title to motor vehicles and places the burden primarily on the motor vehicle manufacturing industry to control the emissions of the new *products* that it sells. Thus, a dry cleaning establishment is responsible for the hydrocarbon emissions from its solvent-using equipment but not for the hydrocarbon emissions of its delivery trucks; the latter are primarily the responsibility of the motor vehicle manufacturer. (This division of responsibility may change with the introduction of inspection and maintenance programs in the 1980s.) Further, rather than leaving the level of emission controls on vehicles to be determined by EPA through rulemakings, the Act specifically established control levels and timetables for the major pollutants (though the original timetable for automobiles specified in the 1970 Act was delayed considerably by the 1977 Amendments). The Act requires that new heavy-duty trucks achieve a 90% reduction (compared with their 1969 levels) in hydrocarbon (HC) and carbon monoxide (CO) emissions by the 1983 model year. Less stringent controls had been required on trucks in the early 1970s, with the requirements gradually tightened in later years.

PRELIMINARY ACTIONS

In December 1978, EPA forwarded to CEA a draft of the preamble and the proposed regulations for 1983 model heavy-duty trucks, along with a regulatory analysis that explained the regulations in greater detail, including EPA's guesses as to the technologies that would be used to meet the standards and their costs. At first glance, one might think that this kind of regulation would be very straightforward: EPA would announce the emission levels equivalent to a 90% reduction, and that would be all. But such regulations are inevitably much more complicated. EPA must try to establish the 1969 baseline from which the 90% reduction is to take place. Further, the testing and enforcement procedures are at least equally important. These can greatly affect the actual level of stringency and level of costs of any nominal set of numerical standards. All these can be and were part of the proposed rulemaking.

On February 17, 1979, the preamble and proposed rules were published, inviting public comment by the end of June.[1] This was clearly not a candidate for a review by the Regulatory Analysis Review Group. The regulations were quite technical and complex, and there were few broad policy issues that could be raised. But the issues were nevertheless important enough to warrant EOP comments; hence a COWPS filing was required. CEA took responsibility for the first draft.

EPA'S POSITION

EPA proposed three specific sets of emission standards for new heavy-duty trucks: the 90% reductions in HC and CO overall, a new standard specifically for idle-mode emissions of HC and CO, and controls on crankcase emissions for diesel trucks, similar to those already required for gasoline-powered trucks.

87

The heart of the proposal, however, was a package of new testing and enforcement procedures:

A New Overall Test. The emission standards are supposed to be enforced through a testing procedure that represents actual on-road use and practice. EPA proposed replacing the existing "steady-state" test with a new "transient" test, arguing that the new test better approximated actual on-road conditions.

Redefinition of the "Useful Life" of the Engine. The testing procedures require that a truck meet the emission standards over the "useful life" of the engine, which had previously been arbitrarily defined as 5 years or 50,000 miles or 1,500 hours of engine operation.[2] EPA proposed lengthening this "lifetime" to the average period of use up to engine retirement or rebuild, whichever comes first.

Revised Durability Testing Requirements. EPA's testing procedures over the "useful life" have been done in two stages: A small set of preuse certification vehicles is tested periodically while they accumulate the full "lifetime" of 1,500 hours or 50,000 miles. These periodic tests are used to establish a deterioration pattern or factor. A larger variety of preuse vehicles is then tested after only a short break-in period, and the deterioration factor is used to project their emissions to 1,500 hours or 50,000 miles. These projected results are then used to determine if the vehicle model type passes or fails.

A similar testing scheme has been used for automobiles. Despite these testing procedures, cars in actual use have been exceeding the relevant HC and CO standards.[3] To prevent this from occurring in trucks, EPA proposed that the deterioration factors be determined from the experience of vehicles in actual use, through procedures to be designed by the manufacturers themselves.

Parameter Adjustments. EPA proposed that the agency itself be allowed to adjust specific engine parameters within the full range of the physical limits of adjustment during testing. This proposal would require the manufacturers to limit the range of settings and thus reduce the likelihood that in-use maladjustments would lead to excessive emissions.

Allowable Maintenance. EPA proposed specific maintenance limitations during the durability testing. It wished to avoid situations in which the manufacturers performed more extensive maintenance to pass the certification test than would likely be performed in actual use.

Pass Rates. EPA proposed a 90% pass rate for the vehicles tested during random audits of actual assembly-line output.[4] The agency's position was that the Clean Air Act requires that *all* production vehicles meet the standards; 90% was a practical approximation to "all." There were no previous pass rates in force for heavy-duty trucks. EPA in 1974 had sought a 90% pass rate for automobiles but subsequently settled for a 60% pass rate, which is currently in force.

EPA considered all these provisions to be a package that could not be split apart. Also, the agency expected (though it did not specifically propose) that inspection and maintenance programs would be instituted in the 1980s, so as to prevent the emissions from in-use vehicles from deteriorating too badly.

EPA expected that the manufacturers would use oxidizing catalysts (similar to those used on most American cars) to meet the standards. The catalysts require the use of unleaded gasoline. The extra cost of the unleaded gasoline, along with the catalysts themselves, constituted the major costs of the regulations. EPA estimated that these costs would come to a total (discounted) of $2.5 billion over the 1983–1987 model years. Expressed in a different manner, the costs per ton of pollutants eliminated were $462 per ton of HC and $16 per ton of CO.

The agency examined two alternatives to its proposals: a more stringent set of emission standards and the continuation of the current "steady-state" emissions test. It decided against them.

Finally, EPA declined to take one action. The Clean Air Act authorized EPA to institute nonconformance penalties for manufacturers whose vehicles failed to meet the standards. These fees would penalize a manufacturer and thus provide an incentive to try to meet the standard, but they would avoid the requirement that EPA close down the manufacturer for failure to meet the standard.[5] In the NPRM, the agency established the principle that, if the fees were ever introduced, they would be based on the marginal costs of compliance. But EPA declared that it believed that the fees were legally required to be instituted only in cases in which there were technological laggards who could not meet the standards. Since EPA was confident that all the truck manufacturers could meet the standards, there was no need to institute the nonconformance penalties.

THE COWPS FILING

Because the catalyst and its required unleaded gasoline were the large cost items in the package, our first effort was to see if there were any ways in which their use might be avoided. Shortages of unleaded gasoline had started to appear in the fall of 1978, and automobile owners were starting to use leaded gas, which would permanently poison the catalysts after three or four tankfulls. The technological package of catalyst and unleaded gas was turning out to be not only costly but possibly too fragile, too easily rendered ineffective. Did EPA's insistence on the transient test make a difference as to whether catalysts were necessary? Could they be avoided if a slightly less stringent set of standards were proposed? We asked these questions of a few truck manufacturers; we were told that catalysts were probably inevitable.

With that route closed, we turned to the testing and enforcement package. Here, we did not have the detailed engineering knowledge to judge the real impact of the proposals. But, equally important, EPA had not provided sufficient information to allow a judgment to be made about the package. Accordingly, the COWPS filing became a critique of EPA's regulatory analysis and thus raised indirect questions about the value of the testing and enforcement package. This kind of methodological pressure on EPA and other regulatory agencies to make cost-effectiveness calculations on individual choices, rather than just to slap together a package on a take-it-or-leave-it basis, was an important part of the EOP regulatory reform effort. A few direct criticisms of some of the pieces of the package were included, along with a critique of the cost analysis. And the nonconformance fee received special attention.

The Absence of Individual Calculations

EPA should have examined separately the costs and emissions consequences of each of its testing and enforcement procedures. Further, where there was room for gradations, such as the pass rate, the costs and consequences of a few alternative levels should have been examined. Only by so doing could EPA find the least-cost way of achieving its goal of a 90% reduction in emissions. If the costs per ton of pollutants removed were appreciably different among the pieces of the package, costs could be minimized by pushing harder on the low-cost pieces and easing the stringency of the high-cost pieces.

EPA argued that the package was a whole, that it could not be pulled apart. But there was simply no support for this claim. Further, to support its claim for the transient test, EPA argued that, "though it is not presently possible to prove a quantifiable increase in air quality by adopting the new procedure, the change is indeed justified."[6] But, because EPA conceded that the new test was more costly, how could it be justified unless one knew about the emissions reduction it would achieve?

Accordingly, we argued that EPA had not satisfied E.O. 12044's requirement that it examine alternative approaches. EPA's cursory examination of the two alternatives was simply not enough.

Specific Questions on the Regulations[7]

The 90% Pass Rate. The motor vehicle manufacturers disagreed strongly with EPA's assertion that the Clean Air Act required that every vehicle meet the standards. They argued that it was the average emissions from vehicles that affected the level of air quality; hence, it was the average that should be subject to regulation. Although the manufacturers had logic on their side (but EPA has rightly pointed out that there are problems with enforcing the warranty provisions of the Act if almost half the vehicles are not expected to meet the standards), it did not seem worthwhile for us to become embroiled in their legal dispute. Instead, we pointed out that the proposed 90% pass rate had some serious consequences. To meet this requirement, the manufacturers would either have to achieve a very low variance (with respect to emissions) in their production line vehicles or they would have to aim for a very low average level of emissions relative to the standard so that the variance would not lead to samples that would exceed the standard. If low variance could not be achieved easily—and that was probably the case—the latter alternative meant that average emissions would be reduced by appreciably more than 90%. Since this apparently was not EPA's intent (EPA had explicitly indicated that it had rejected standards that implied greater reductions than 90%), we suggested that the agency take corrective actions. Either it could lower the pass rate to 60%, consistent with the stringency for automobiles, or it could make some explicit assumptions concerning the variance of production models, infer the average emissions implied by that variance and a 90% pass rate, and set the standards (e.g., at a nominal 80% reduction level) so that the average achieved the 90% reduction.

The Idle Test. EPA did not adequately justify its proposed requirement for a separate idle test. If the overall test was representative of emissions, there was no need for a separate idle test, and constraining the idle mode to a 90% reduction through a separate test could only limit the flexibility of the manufacturers in designing vehicle systems that would pass the overall test. EPA had hinted that there were special problems of excessive CO concentrations in downtown street canyons, but it provided no explicit documentation for these problems, and it had not indicated how the idle test would deal with them. Also, we suspected that the agency might want to use the idle test as the short emissions test that would serve as the basis for future inspection and maintenance programs.[8] But, if that were the case, EPA needed to be more explicit about that justification.

The Role of Inspection and Maintenance. EPA argued that I&M programs were important in keeping truck emissions low (though, again, EPA had not explicitly calculated the costs and consequences). We agreed. As a simple example, many truck users fuel their fleets from their own fuel tanks. There will need to be some kind of check to prevent their using cheaper leaded gasoline, which will poison the catalysts and increase emissions. But EPA had not fully incorporated the I&M programs into its thinking. With I&M programs in place, EPA's proposed restrictions on maintenance and durability procedures during certification testing did not have to be so stringent. The manufacturers would be sensitive to the demands of the truck buyers to provide vehicles that could continue to pass the I&M tests with minimum maintenance. Hence, the market would properly take care of this problem, and EPA's proposed restrictions could prove to be redundant and possibly counterproductive.

Costs

EPA had underestimated the costs of its proposal. First, it had ignored the extra costs of complying with some parts of its package, such as the 90% pass rate or the reduced allowed maintenance. It justified some of these absences with "they pay for themselves, therefore they are costless" arguments. Second, EPA had not included the manufacturer's profit in its calculations of the cost of equipment, justifying their exclusion with the bizarre statement that "the primary purpose of profits is to direct economic resources, and the regulations will assume this role."[9] We pointed out that, although profits do serve this role, they also represent a return on invested capital. A competitive level of profits represents a cost to the motor vehicle industry that is just as real and legitimate as the cost of steel from which the automobiles are made or the cost of the labor that assembles them. The cost of capital could no more be waved away with a regulatory wand than could these other costs. Third, EPA had neglected the fuel consumption penalties that were likely to accompany the use of the catalysts.

The Nonconformance Fee

EPA's refusal to put the nonconformance fee into practice was particularly distressing. The nonconformance fee was a valuable public policy measure. By providing an alternative to shutting down a manufacturer, it provided a relief valve that alleviated these dire (and in practice, unenforceable) consequences of failure to meet the standards. We pointed out that the future was uncertain and that one could easily be far less confident than was EPA that all the manufacturers could meet the standards. It was better to have the relief value in place beforehand rather than have to resort to hasty, last-minute efforts when problems did arise.[10]

Also, the actual determination of marginal costs of compliance (on which the noncompliance fees would be based) would serve as a useful check on EPA's estimate of costs. There is a universal tendency for regulatory agencies' estimates of the costs of compliance to be far below the regulated industry's estimates. The regulatory agencies typically say "it will cost next to nothing," whereas industry says "it will wipe us out." The incentives for each to make these claims is clear. The regulatory agency wants to avoid the implication that it is imposing large costs; industry wants to try to scale down the regulation. There are no internal checks on these claims. A nonconformance fee based on marginal costs of compliance would provide a check. Since the regulatory agencies clearly prefer that the regulated industries comply with the standards rather than avoid them by paying the noncompliance fee, the agencies would have a more direct incentive than is currently the case to develop accurate cost estimates. Also, the marginal cost calculations are vital to marginal cost-effectiveness calculations and thus would be useful in formulating the regulations themselves. These arguments clearly applied in the case of EPA and the heavy-duty truck standards.

Recommendations

We recommended that EPA implement the nonconformance fee; reexamine the individual components of its proposed testing and enforcement package, evaluate the costs and consequences of each component, and use the results to improve the package's cost-effectiveness; reexamine the proposed 90% pass-rate requirement; better justify its proposed idle test; and better integrate the role of I&M into the package.

The COWPS filing embodying these arguments went through three drafts and was reviewed by CEA and COWPS principals. An early draft was also sent to EPA for comments. On June 29, 1979 the final draft of the COWPS filing was delivered to EPA to be placed on its public record.

Most of the truck manufacturers filed comments with EPA that were critical of the proposals.

OUTCOME

In late December 1979 EPA announced the final rules for the heavy-duty truck emission standards.[11] The basic package of testing and enforcement procedures was largely unchanged from the NPRM, but EPA delayed the starting date for the regulations by one year, to give the manufacturers more lead time to develop the necessary procedures.[12] And, in the preamble to the final rules and in the revised regulatory analysis, EPA was much more careful to justify each of the package's provisions. Incremental cost-effectiveness calculations were offered for each provision. (They all appeared to be quite inexpensive in terms of costs per ton of HC and CO removed.) EPA acknowledged that one of the reasons why it wanted the idle test was to permit the idle test's use for inspection and maintenance programs. Finally, although still insisting that it believed that all the truck manufacturers could meet the regulatory requirements, EPA declared its intention to provide nonconformance penalties (to be proposed in a separate NPRM in early 1980) "to provide relief in those rare cases when compliance may not be achieved because of some unforeseen circumstances."[13]

CONCLUDING COMMENTS

Regulatory procedures will likely continue to pose difficult problems for management and reform efforts by the EOP. The issues are technical and unexciting, but they can be important, and they could possibly serve as a "backdoor" means for tightening the actual stringency of regulatory standards without changing the actual standards themselves. There are no easy answers to this problem.

In this rulemaking CEA played a useful role. The final package of procedures was changed only slightly from those in the NPRM, but the process was educational for all concerned. EPA is likely to perform better cost-effectiveness calculations in the future, and in the long-run these better calculations should mean improved regulatory proposals and decisions. Although CEA had not suggested the year's delay in compliance, EPA's decision to grant it indicates its interest in avoiding last-minute compliance confrontations with the industry (see Chapter 7). Finally, EPA's willingness (in the end) to institute the nonconformance penalty is most encouraging of all. As noted, nonconformance fees provide a valuable relief valve to "do it or else . . ." regulations. Wider implementation should bring greater familiarity with the concept and also bring more recognition of its value and place in the nation's regulatory policies.

NOTES TO CHAPTER 6

[1]*Federal Register*, February 13, 1979, pp. 9464–9473.

[2]For diesels, the definitions were 5 years or 100,000 miles or 3,000 hours of engine operation.

[3]Abundant evidence has been accumulating on this point over the past six years. For the latest round of evidence, see Automotive Testing Laboratories, Inc., *A Study of Emissions from Passenger Cars in Six Cities*, prepared for U.S. Environmental Protection Agency, Office of Air, Noise, and Radiation, Office of Mobile Source Air Pollution Control, Emission Control Technology Division, Ann Arbor, Mich., January 1979.

[4]Through a quirk in bureaucratese, this 90% pass rate was labeled by EPA as a "10% acceptable quality level."

[5]For a discussion of the failings of a policy that requires closure as the only alternative to meeting the standard, see the references cited in Chapter 3, note 5.

[6]U.S. Environmental Protection Agency, Office of Mobile Source Air Pollution Control, "Proposed Gaseous Emission Regulations for 1983 and Later Model Year Heavy-Duty Engines: Regulatory Analysis," February 1979, p. 6.

[7]Besides the three points discussed in the following paragraphs, the filing also raised a technical point concerning the calculation of the deterioration factor.

[8]A shorter test is needed for I&M programs because the overall test is much too lengthy and complicated; the latter can only be done in an engineering laboratory, under controlled conditions.

[9]EPA, "Proposed Gaseous Emission Regulations," op. cit., p. 66.

[10]Also, if the standard and the fees were set at the right level, the nonconformance penalty would have most of the favorable properties of an effluent fee.

[11]Federal Register, January 21, 1980, pp. 4135–4227.

[12]The only other major change was that the revision in durability testing requirements—EPA had proposed that deterioration in emissions should be measured on vehicles in actual use—was postponed to allow further study.

[13]Federal Register, January 21, 1980, p. 4143.

chapter 7

Diesel Particulate Emissions

What should be the particulate emission standards for diesel automobiles and light-duty trucks for 1981 and 1983?

Technology forcing is a common strategy of product or process regulation. Regulations are set stringently enough so that the industry being regulated is expected to develop new technology (or bring to production existing, experimental technology) to meet the stringent standards. The industry's "feet" are to be "held to the fire." The strategy runs the risk, however, of choking development entirely or of generating confrontations with the industry if the new technology is not forthcoming.

This chapter provides an example of a regulatory proposal that involved technology forcing. It also provides another example of the CEA–COWPS filings playing an educational role that may have long-run benefits for the regulatory process.

BACKGROUND

Uncontrolled diesel automobiles emit in their exhaust 30 to 100 times as many particulates per mile as do gasoline-powered catalyst-equipped cars. The particulates constitute a direct health problem: The evidence is strong that particulates contribute to increases in mortality and morbidity,[1] and there are national ambient air quality standards for particulates. In addition, diesel particulates are suspected of being carcinogenic. On the other hand, diesels achieve appreciably better fuel economy than do comparable gasoline-powered vehicles (and have other favorable properties discussed later in this chapter). Diesels represent a genuine dilemma for public policy, embodying a clear conflict or trade-off between the national goals of conserving energy and improving the environment.

PRELIMINARY ACTIVITIES

The interest of the Executive Office of the President in diesels first developed in early October 1978 after an article in *The Washington Post*, discussing the possible carcinogenicity problem, caught CEA member Nordhaus's attention. The staffs of CEA and the Office of Science and Technology Policy then took responsibility for keeping abreast of diesel developments. We talked extensively with staff at the National Highway Traffic Safety Administration (which has direct responsibility for regulating the fuel economy standards program, in which diesels may figure heavily), at the Department of Energy (which has a general concern with energy use and efficiency), and at EPA (which regulates the emissions of diesels). The following picture emerged by the end of October:

Diesel particulates were indeed suspected of being carcinogenic. They had been shown to cause mutations in bacteria, which created a strong suspicion (but not conclusive evidence) that they could cause cancer in humans. EPA was conducting a number of animal tests to see if diesel particulates caused cancer in laboratory animals. DOE was planning to undertake research on diesel particulate control technology but had not quite settled its internal bureaucratic turf problem as to which division within DOE would actually do the research.

General Motors was the only domestic manufacturer planning to build diesel automobiles in large numbers, although a number of foreign manufacturers were building diesel autos and exporting them to the United States and Ford and Chrysler might decide to build them if the uncertainty as to their carcinogenicity were eliminated. General Motors considered diesels to be an important component of its efforts to meet the fuel economy standards. It was currently producing a few diesels and was aiming for 15–20% of its production to be diesels by the mid-1980s; it intended to make its major production commitment to diesels in late 1979 or early 1980. EPA hoped to have the results from its animal tests analyzed by that time, so that it could give General Motors guidance as to its likely regulatory posture with respect to the carcinogenicity question.

On a largely separate track, EPA would soon (within the next few months) promulgate a notice of proposed rulemaking that would propose emission standards for diesel particulates for cars and light-duty trucks. The Clean Air Act required that EPA set standards for the 1981 model year. EPA was planning a comparatively modest set of standards for the 1981 model year and a stringent set for the 1983 model year. These standards had little to do with the carcinogenicity question but were simply part of the general effort to reduce particulate loadings in the ambient air and thus help communities to achieve the NAAQSs for particulates.

Diesels promised to be an important regulatory issue. We suggested that the EOP ask for briefings from EPA, DOE, and the three automobile companies to obtain their latest research and thoughts on the subject. We also suggested that the EOP urge DOE to start its research as quickly as possible. These briefings took place over the next few months, and DOE did begin its research.

As discussion of the problem proceeded during October and November, it became clear that a broad public policy study of the diesel problem was needed. All aspects of diesel vehicles, their advantages and disadvantages, needed to be weighed and considered in any regulatory policy toward them. The individual regulatory agencies each tended to have a narrow perspective: its own narrow regulatory mission. A broader perspective was needed. If diesel particulates were carcinogenic, then it was possible that the particulates emitted by home heating furnaces, electric utilities, and any other high-temperature coal or oil combustion source were also carcinogenic. We needed to avoid the knee-jerk public reaction of "It causes cancer? Ban it!" that might occur if (as could well be the case) it were established that diesel particulates were carcinogenic. It was a broad problem; it deserved a broad study.

A model for this kind of study had emerged from the recent experience with saccharine. In 1977, on the basis of animal tests, the Food and Drug Administration had concluded that saccharine was a likely carcinogen. The Delaney clause in the Federal Food, Drug, and Cosmetic Act required that any food additive found to be carcinogenic in humans or animals be banned. In April 1977, FDA proposed the ban of saccharine as a food additive. There was an immediate and sharp public reaction, with many agreeing that anything carcinogenic should be banned and others arguing that saccharine was too important to the diet of too many people to be banned. Congress in November 1977 passed a law delaying the ban and authorizing a National Academy of Sciences study of the problem. The NAS released its first report in November 1978.[2] The report indicated that, yes, saccharine did appear to be a carcinogen, but that it was not a very potent carcinogen and that the real problem probably lay in children's consumption of large quantities of dietetic soft drinks.

This report was useful in shaping the public discussion of the saccharine problem and would have been even more useful had it been available to dampen some of the more extreme reactions at the time the FDA first proposed banning saccharine.

We hoped that a similarly calm, reasoned study could be concluded before the public screaming started on diesels. We did not want or expect a whitewash of the diesel problem; instead, we hoped for a thorough discussion of all its facets. The NAS was again a logical candidate to undertake the study, both because of its high prestige in scientific and political circles and because it had conducted an investigation of automotive emissions regulation (hydrocarbons, carbon monoxide, and nitrogen oxides) five years earlier.

CEA convinced the other EOP agencies that a study would be worthwhile. The Office of Science and Technology Policy (OSTP), in particular, became enthusiastic about the study, and its staff spent a good fraction of the spring convincing EPA, DOE, NHTSA, and NAS of the worth of the study and negotiating with them over the details of the study plan, budgets, and contributions. The NAS study actually got under way in June 1979. It will be an 18-month study, so it, like the saccharine study, will be completed only after the initial regulatory decisions have been made. Nevertheless, it should provide a valuable perspective on the diesel problem and assist the later regulatory decision that will inevitably occur.

EPA's NPRM on particulates was proceeding on a separate track. In December 1978 EPA provided CEA with a draft of the proposed preamble and regulation. EPA was proposing an emission standard of 0.6 grams of particulates per mile for the 1981 model year and 0.2 g/mi for the 1983 model year. We had some fears at the time that the 1981 standard could not be achieved by larger cars (e.g., General Motors' diesel Cutlass) within the short amount of development time remaining; it was now December 1978, and the 1981 model cars would begin their certification testing in September or October 1979 (a year in advance of new model introduction). We had stronger fears that the 1983 standard could be met only by the Volkswagen Rabbit and that, if EPA persisted in its standard, it would eliminate most diesels from the road.

Having seen in the ozone controversy (Chapter 4) the force acquired by specific standards proposed in the NPRM, we urged EPA to soften the standards proposed in the NPRM or to propose a range (inviting comment on the range) rather than the specific point-estimate numbers. EPA (not too surprisingly) declined, but the preamble to the NPRM that eventually appeared was softer in tone and raised more questions for public comment than had the preamble we had been shown in December. Perhaps we did have some effect, though not as much as we would have liked.

On February 1, 1979, EPA published its NPRM on diesel particulates emissions standards for automobiles and light trucks in the *Federal Register*, inviting public comment.[3] The EOP decided that our comments would be put on the record through a COWPS filing rather than through a RARG report. There were two reasons for this decision. First, RARG could only review four regulations from any agency in any year;

we suspected that there might be four bigger, more important, regulations that would emerge from EPA in the next year. Second, OSTP was then engaged in the negotiations with EPA over the NAS study on diesels. It was feared that a highly critical RARG report might attract a lot of public attention and might make those negotiations more difficult, whereas a COWPS report would inevitably attract less public attention and hence, even if highly critical, would be less likely to ruffle EPA feathers. CEA took responsibility for preparing the first draft of the COWPS filing.

THE EPA POSITION

Section 202(a)(3)(A)(iii) of the Clean Air Act reads as follows:

> The Administrator shall prescribe regulations under paragraph (1) of this subsection applicable to emissions of particulate matter from classes or categories of vehicles manufactured during and after model year 1981 (or during any earlier model year, if practicable). Such regulations shall contain standards which reflect the greatest degree of emission reduction achievable through the application of technology which the Administrator determines will be available for the model year to which such standards apply, giving appropriate consideration to the cost of applying such technology within the period of time available to manufacturers and to noise, energy, and safety factors associated with the application of such technology. Such standards shall be promulgated and shall take effect as expeditiously as practicable taking into account the period necessary for compliance.

EPA proposed a standard for automobile and light-duty trucks of 0.6 g/mi of particulates for 1981 and 0.2 g/mi for 1983.[4] EPA expected that average particulate emissions from these vehicles would average 1.1 g/mi in the absence of particulate controls (but with the exhaust gas recirculation that was necessary to control NO_x emissions), though larger cars tended to emit more and smaller cars less. Thus, the proposed standards promised reductions of 45% and 92%, respectively. EPA had an environmental model for particulates that used Kansas City, Missouri as a case study and projected the results to national levels. The model showed why the controls on diesel particulates were important for meeting the NAAQSs for particulates.

EPA predicted that the manufacturers would use turbochargers to reduce particulates so as to meet the 1981 standards and would use trapoxidizers (a device that traps the particulates in the exhaust and periodically burns them off) to meet the 1983 standards.[5] The 1981 standards would raise the cost of new diesel automobiles to consumers by $170. But turbochargers offered fuel economy improvements that were great enough so that the turbochargers more than paid for themselves. Hence, EPA concluded, the 1981 standard was costless (or, strictly speaking, involved a negative cost of $160 per ton of particulates removed). The costs of the 1983 controls were around $150 per vehicle and were estimated to yield marginal costs of $3,200 per ton of particulates removed compared with the 1981 standards. EPA compared these costs with the costs of controlling particulates in other industries and found them reasonable. The agency examined a number of alternative emissions standards for 1981; it only examined the possibility of delay with respect to the 1983 standard.

THE COWPS FILING

The COWPS filing made five major points. First, although diesels involved health hazards, they also had a number of favorable attributes that should not be forgotten. Second, the technology forcing strategy that EPA was pursuing, especially with respect to the 1983 standards, had some serious drawbacks; EPA was probably pushing too far, too fast. Third, the agency had seriously underestimated the costs of the standards. Fourth, EPA's Kansas City environmental model had a number of flaws. Fifth, for any level of stringency in the standard that EPA chose, there was a better way of formulating the standard. The filing concluded with a set of policy recommendations.

The Advantages of Diesels

The fuel economy advantages of diesels were well known: 25–30% fuel savings over comparable gasoline-powered vehicles. Diesels were likely to be an important part of General Motors', and perhaps other manufacturers', strategy in meeting the fuel economy standards for automobiles in the 1980s (see Chapter 8).

A possible counterargument (sometimes heard at EPA) went as follows: Diesels would not decrease the overall fuel usage of the United States, because the automobile manufacturers would try only to meet, but not do better than, the fuel economy standards; diesels, by offering greater fuel economy, would simply allow the manufacturers to offer greater numbers of large cars while still meeting the standards. There was an answer to the counterargument: At that time (prior to the sharp increases in gasoline prices in 1979 and 1980) the ability of the manufacturers to meet the standards of the 1980s, without excessive forcing of the sales mix of cars toward small sizes that consumers might not want, was open to question; diesels could well be an important part of the effort to meet the standards. Also, the comfort and performance of large cars were valued by many consumers, and this consumer satisfaction should count as an advantage of the diesel, even if there were no aggregate effects on fuel consumption. And, if fuel economy did become an overriding national goal, the widespread use of diesels might allow the fuel economy standards to be revised upward; the fuel economy standards were endogenous to the process, not exogenous.

A second well-known advantage to diesel vehicles is their low tailpipe emission of hydrocarbons (HC) and carbon monoxide (CO). Diesels do not require catalysts to achieve low emissions of these pollutants and will probably have lower emissions than the catalyst-equipped gasoline-powered cars that have to meet the tight 1980 and 1981 standards for these pollutants. (Diesels, though, will have more difficulty in meeting the NO_x standard.)

A third, less well-known advantage of diesels is their reduced HC *evaporative* emissions. Diesels have no carburetor and use a much less volatile fuel. There are virtually no HC evaporative emissions in the fuel distribution chain for diesels, from the refinery to the vehicle. By contrast, the current HC evaporative emissions for gasoline-powered vehicles, from refinery to the carburetor, are the equivalent of 1.9 g/mi. Even after EPA has implemented all its planned measures in controlling HC evaporative emissions from all gasoline sources, evaporative emissions will still be in the range of 0.6–0.7 g/mi for the gasoline vehicle "system," as opposed to virtually zero evaporative emissions from the diesel "system." Thus, if a significant number of diesels were to replace gasoline vehicles, HC evaporative emissions would be reduced by this 0.6–0.7 g/mi per diesel.[6] Since the 1980 tailpipe HC emission standards are 0.41 g/mi (and will be achieved for gasoline vehicles only at substantial cost), these reductions in HC evaporative emissions are clearly substantial.[7]

A fourth advantage, even less well known, is the safety of diesels in the event of serious crashes. Since the fuel is much less volatile, the chances of the fuel's igniting in the event of a crash are much lower. This increased safety is reflected in the lower insurance rates for truck fleets using diesel engines rather than gasoline engines; insurance companies typically give a 10% reduction on collision and damage insurance for diesel trucks. Similarly, in the marine field, insurance companies typically give a 10–15% reduction on the hull insurance on diesel boats as compared with gasoline-powered boats.[8]

Technology Forcing and the Feasibility of the Standards

The feasibility of the 1981 standard was in some doubt, especially for larger cars, if EPA did not grant a waiver (permitted by another section of the Clean Air Act) of the stringent NO_x standard for 1981. This waiver was the subject of a separate rulemaking by EPA, but the NO_x and particulate standards were related. Virtually all the evidence showed a clear technological trade-off between lowering particulate emission and lowering NO_x emissions. There were substantial doubts within the industry concerning the effectiveness of turbocharging in reducing particulates, and, as of the spring of 1979, there were less than eight months of lead time before the 1981 models would begin their emissions certificates tests in the fall of 1979. If the manufacturers simultaneously had to meet the strict NO_x standard (i.e., if EPA did not grant the NO_x waiver), there could well be compliance problems for particulates for the larger diesels.

Further, the 1983 standards appeared to be infeasible for all but the Volkswagen diesel Rabbit with its small engine. Trap oxidizers were in a very early stage of development. There had not yet been one—not even a hand-built device, to say nothing of mass-produced oxidizers— that had performed satisfactorily for the 50,000 miles required by the standard. There were only two and a half years until the 1983 models would begin their certification tests in the fall of 1981. This was not a long time to develop, test, and transfer to reliable mass production a new technology that, at the end, had to meet a very stringent and rigid set of requirements.

Also, EPA was proposing that light-duty trucks (pickup trucks and vans) meet the same standards as automobiles. This was contrary to EPA's practice for other pollutant emissions, in which light-duty trucks had separate (more lenient) standards. Larger vehicles (such as light-duty trucks) required larger engines, and the larger engines generally emitted more particulates and would have greater difficulty in achieving any given standard.

The standards represented an effort at technology forcing by EPA—forcing the manufacturers to develop control technology that they otherwise would neglect. Because particulates represented a genuine negative externality, some kind of government action was necessary. But there were dangers to trying to force technology too fast. The rush to meet stringent standards under short deadlines might produce high-cost, inefficient solutions, whereas a less rushed development might lead to lower-cost technologies. Alternatively, if the standards were considered unachievable, development and spread of the basic technology (e.g., diesels) might be discouraged and delayed. Yet another possibility was that there might be last-minute waivers of the standard, with costly uncertainties for all parties concerned. A mixture of all these results had plagued the program of controls on automotive emissions of other pollutants.[9] A repeat of this experience in the area of particulates could not be good public policy.

Further, this seemed to be an especially inappropriate time to be trying to require a stringent and costly standard for 1983. The NAAQS for particulates was under reconsideration by EPA, with final action scheduled for December 1980. If EPA changed the level or the form of the ambient standard, this might change the necessary level or form of the required controls on diesels. Also, more would be known about the carcinogenicity issue in a year to 18 months; EPA's testing results would begin coming in, and the NAS study would be close to completion. Perhaps some control technologies had harmful or beneficial effects with respect to carcinogenicity. And the role of alternative specifications of diesel fuel in the creation of particulates and their carcinogenicity would be better understood within a year to 18 months. Although the emissions standards were not aimed at the carcinogenicity question, the latter could well influence the ultimate controls on diesel emission.

All these points argued for a delay in the imposition of very stringent (and costly) emissions standards. Although the argument can always be made that delay will yield more knowledge, here the case seemed especially strong, because of the specific events that would be occurring in the following 18 months. There seemed to be significant risks that a hasty, costly technological solution to one set of stringent standards might be developed, only to be scrapped in the light of new information or a changed NAAQS. A delay of 18 months in promulgating very stringent standards would mean a delay of 1 or 2 model years in their eventual application; in the interim, whatever standards were established for 1981 would still be in effect, and the manufacturers would be on notice that stringent standards were likely to follow. This modest delay seemed to promise a substantial benefit: a better final set of diesel particulate standards.

The Costs of the Standard

EPA had underestimated the costs of the standards. First, it had probably underestimated the cost of a turbocharger, including the extra labor and components and changes in the engine and drivetrain that would be necessary to accommodate a turbocharger.

Second, EPA had assumed that a turbocharger would last the life of the vehicle. But virtually no engine components last the life of a vehicle. There was no information about turbocharger life directly available. But a call to the Department of Commerce yielded the information that the 1972 *Census of Manufacturers* contained market data for roughly similar parts: fuel pumps and water pumps. The market data indicated that these parts were replaced roughly once during the life of an average car. If this replacement pattern were true also of turbochargers, the cost of the standards would be appreciably higher than EPA had estimated.

Third, EPA had estimated that the cost of fuel in the 1980s would rise by 10% per year in *real* terms (corrected for general inflation); that is, fuel would rise 10% per year faster than the average prices of other consumer items. This seemed much too high, even in the wake of the fuel price rises of 1973–1974 and of early 1979. Although there might be short periods during which fuel prices might rise that rapidly, over a decade or more it was unlikely that fuel prices would maintain annual increases of that magnitude. The Department of Energy was estimating long-term real price increases of 3%. We used 5% to be extra conservative. A lower real price increase for diesel fuel meant less discounted savings from the use of turbochargers and hence a higher net cost of the standard.

We also registered suspicion of the "it pays for itself" argument concerning the fuel saving aspect of turbochargers and noted that, although EPA (properly) discounted future monetary costs and benefits, it did not discount future nonmonetary benefits, that is, future particulate reductions. But the case for discounting the latter is the same:

Presumably, society cares more about reductions in particulates this year than next year.

When these changes in estimated costs were made, the negative $160 per ton of particulates controlled for the 1981 standard (EPA estimate) became instead a positive range of $1,720 to $4,740 per ton; the $3,200 per ton for the 1983 standard (EPA's estimate) became instead a range of $5,500 to $7,760 per ton.

It was possible to compare these costs per ton with the costs of controlling particulates from other sources. EPA had been issuing regulations on new source performance standards (NSPS) for particulates from other industries. The support documents for those regulations could be used in some cases[10] to calculate the marginal costs of control in going from an intermediate level of control to a stringent level, roughly comparable to going from the 1981 diesel standards to the 1983 standards. Table 7-1 provides the compilation of these marginal costs per ton. The particulates from these other sources were also the products of combustion and were likely to be small and highly transportable. Thus, it was possible to view control of the various sources of particulates as alternative ways of achieving particulate reductions. The marginal costs of the stringent diesel particulate standard were appreciably above the marginal costs of control of other particulates. If the other standards represented EPA's implicit notions as to the proper degree of stringency to impose, then the 1983 diesel standards were clearly out of line.

We also tried to determine the costs of other, less obvious ways of controlling particulates in urban areas. Upgrading the fuel oil burned by home heating furnaces was one possibility, but the extra costs of the higher-quality oil turned out to be far too high for the particulate reductions that would occur. An earlier dispute between CEA and the Department of the Interior concerning strip mining, however, had revealed that reentrained "fugitive" dust from roadways was an important source of particulate loadings in the air. And EPA's environmental model of Kansas City indicated that reentrained fugitive dust from streets accounted for 16% of particulate emissions. More frequent street cleanings (especially washings) could probably reduce airborne particulates from that source. Other offices at EPA (not the one involved in the diesel regulations) had investigated this question, and we obtained EPA studies that indicated that the costs of reducing airborne particulates by cleaning the street more frequently were about $120 per ton, or 20 to 50 times cheaper than the costs of diesel particulate control.

An objection to this last line of argument might be that the

Table 7-1

Marginal Costs per Metric Ton of Controlling Particulates
(1978 dollars)

Diesel light-duty vehicles		
1981 standards:	EPA's estimate	–$ 160
	COWPS estimate	1,720
1983 standards:	EPA's estimate	3,200
	COWPS estimate	5,500
Electric utilities[1]		
Eastern Coal, NSPS:	100 MW	1,931
	1,100 MW steam electric	2,203
Medium-sized industrial boilers, NSPS[2]		614–1,199
Sewage incinerators, NSPS[3]		1,335–2,205
Electric arc furnaces, NSPS[3]		2,095
Kraft pulp mills, NSPS:[4]	Recovery furnaces	385–781
	Melt tanks	259–344
Lime kilns, NSPS:[5]	New	3,120
	Retrofit	1,750

[1]PEDCO, "Particulate and Sulfur Dioxide Emission Control Costs for Large Coal-Fired Boilers," Report prepared for U.S. Environmental Protection Agency, Office of Air and Waste Management, Office of Air Quality Planning and Standards, Research Triangle Park, N.C., February 1978.

[2]Industrial Gas Cleaning Institute, "Particulate Emission Control Costs for Intermediate-Sized Boilers," Report prepared for U.S. Environmental Protection Agency, Strategies and Air Standards Division, Economic Analysis Branch, Research Triangle Park, N.C., February 1977.

[3]U.S. Environmental Protection Agency, Office of Air, Noise, and Radiation, Mobile Source Air Pollution Control, "Diesel Particulate Regulations, Draft Regulatory Analysis," December 22,1978, p. 88.

[4]U.S. Environmental Protection Agency, Office of Air and Waste Management, Office of Air Quality Planning and Standards, *Standards Support and Environmental Impact Statement*. Volume I. *Proposed Standards of Performance for Kraft Pulp Mills,* September 1976.

[5]U.S. Environmental Protection Agency, Office of Air and Waste Management, Office of Air Quality Planning and Standards, *Standards Support and Environmental Impact Statement*. Volume I. *Proposed Standards of Performance for Lime Manufacturing Plants,* April 1977.

particulates controlled through street cleaning are different from those controlled from diesels. But, to some extent, the reentrainment involves combustion particles that have fallen on the streets. Also, the EPA studies indicated that 50% of the reentrained street dust particulates were quite small (and hence were respirable and a potential health hazard). And, most important, the NAAQS for particulates at that time did not differentiate among particulate types. EPA was arguing that the diesel standards were aimed at helping communities to meet the NAAQS: More frequent street cleaning offered a far cheaper way of doing it. And, if EPA wanted instead to focus on and differentiate among types of particulates, this was best done by waiting the 18 months until the NAAQS was possibly revised to accommodate this differentiation.

The Environmental Model

EPA's model represented a sophisticated effort to relate diesel ownership, likely particulate emissions, traffic flows, and environmental patterns so as to predict air quality in Kansas City in 1990.[11] But it had a number of flaws. First, it assumed that airborne particulate levels would remain unchanged from their 1974 levels except for the extra diesel particulates. But national particulate emissions from all sources had declined markedly within the past decade, from 22.6 million tons in 1970 to 13.4 million tons in 1974 to 12.4 million tons in 1977.[12] Thus, EPA's starting assumption was clearly incorrect. Admittedly, this reduction could not continue indefinitely, but the increasing coverage of state implementation plans for existing emission sources, the new source performance standards for new emissions sources (many of which would replace existing sources), and the replacement of older cars burning leaded gasoline (and emitting 0.2 g/mi of particulates) with newer catalyst-equipped cars burning unleaded gasoline (and emitting only 0.008 g/mi of particulates) would all mean a continued reduction in particulate emissions and hence in particulate levels in the ambient air.

Second, the model overestimated the national population in 1990 by about a quarter (compared with recent Bureau of the Census estimates) and hence overestimated the likely exposure consequences (in terms of millions of people who would be exposed to specific levels of particulates) from the diesel particulates that were projected from the Kansas City experience.

Third, the model predicted that vehicle miles traveled (VMTs), the proximate source of diesel particulate emissions, would increase in central cities as rapidly as in the suburbs. But it was generally considered true that VMTs in congested downtown areas had risen more slowly in the past decade or two and would continue to rise more slowly than in the suburbs.[13] This meant that the unfavorable effects of diesels in downtown areas, about which EPA was especially concerned, had been overestimated.

Fourth, EPA had made no effort to demonstrate that Kansas City was typical or representative of other cities and hence that the results of the model could properly be projected to the remainder of the country.

Despite these flaws, the results of the model showed the consequences of diesels, even uncontrolled, to be quite modest. The NAAQS for particulates is 75 micrograms per cubic meter ($\mu g/m^3$) for an annual average. Uncontrolled diesel autos and light-duty trucks would add only 0.7–1.9 $\mu g/m^3$ to particulate levels in the ambient air on an annual average basis. Only 1 million people would be exposed to extra loadings as high as 1.4–2.4 $\mu g/m^3$.

EPA argued, however, that at roadside sites the effects would be more substantial: extra particulate loadings of 8.4–21.1 $\mu g/m^3$ on an annual average basis. These extra loadings would cause a significant number of roadside sites to be above the NAAQS. But no one spends all (or even most) of the 24 hours of a day breathing roadside air. These roadside site figures illustrated once again (see the discussion in Chapter 4) the policy problems that follow from the nonuniformity of air quality and the placement of air quality monitors. If a monitor were placed directly behind a diesel vehicle's tailpipe, the recorded particulate levels (and apparent violations of the NAAQS for particulates) would be much higher still! But the information would not be useful for policy purposes.

Also, EPA provided a model of the peak effects of diesels on particulate loadings in any 24-hour period, since there is a separate 24-hour maximum NAAQS for particulates of 260 $\mu g/m^3$. But EPA did not indicate whether or not the diesel particulate peak coincided with the peak from other sources. If not, then diesel particulates would only be filling in the time pattern "valleys" and would be unlikely to cause violations of the 24-hour NAAQS.

In sum, the environmental evidence, even with the flaws in the model, indicated that the environmental consequences of diesels, even uncontrolled, would not be severe. This did not mean that there was no health problem at all. But it did mean that diesel vehicles were not likely to cause an urban health crisis that would justify very severe, costly control measures on diesels. And, as was indicated earlier, there were less expensive ways to control urban particulates if they did become a more serious problem.

Alternative Forms of the Standard

The proposed standard was like that of all EPA emissions standards on vehicles: All model types, large or small, must meet the standard established for the general class of vehicles. This uniform requirement cannot yield an efficient outcome. Different vehicles have different degrees of difficulty, and hence different costs, in meeting any given emissions standard. Generally, smaller vehicles can meet the standards more easily. Congress and EPA had recognized this differential difficulty by establishing separate emissions standards for HC, CO, and NO_x for the broad classes of heavy-duty trucks, light-duty trucks, and automobiles. But within these classes there were still large differences in vehicle size and type.

Unlike EPA's uniform class standards, a system of effluent fees on particulate emission would yield an efficient outcome.[14] Unfortunately, effluent fees were outside the range of policies that could be recommended, since they required congressional legislative action rather than EPA administrative action; also, the chances of the Congress legislating a true effluent fee system appear to be nil. But it was fairly easy to determine the outcome under a system of effluent fees: Vehicles with lower marginal costs of emissions control would have lower emissions and pay lower fees; vehicles with higher marginal costs of emissions control would have higher emissions and pay higher fees. And the way to incorporate that efficient outcome into the EPA method of standard setting was to let the standards apply to each manufacturer (rather than to each model) on a sales–weighted average basis. This scheme would give the manufacturer the flexibility to trade-off extra reductions from vehicles for which the marginal costs of control were low against less reductions for vehicles for which the marginal costs of control were high. Regardless of the level of stringency chosen for the emissions standard, a sales–weighted average approach had to mean lower costs of compliance as compared with EPA's approach. Thus, the sales–weighted average approach had to be more cost effective.

This last proposition is easily demonstrated with the aid of some simple geometry. In Figure 7-1, diesel automobile A would have OA emissions if uncontrolled, with *marginal costs* of control represented by curve AGC; thus, to meet a standard of OX g/mi (or, equivalently, to reduce emissions by AX), diesel A would have marginal costs of XC and total costs of meeting the standard of CAX. Similarly, diesel B (perhaps

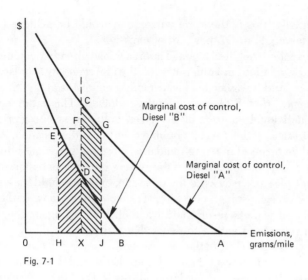

Fig. 7-1

because it is smaller) would have fewer emissions, OB, if uncontrolled, with curve BDE representing its marginal costs of emissions control.

Suppose that EPA concludes that a standard of OX is the proper one for diesels. If each model must meet the standard, diesel A will have total costs of CAX, and diesel B will have total costs of DBX.

Suppose, instead, that the same standard of OX is imposed but that the manufacturer is allowed to meet the standard on a sales–weighted average basis; suppose also, for simplicity, that diesels A and B each represent 50% of the manufacturer's sales.[15] In this case, the manufacturer would find it worthwhile to pursue the following strategy: Reduce diesel B's emissions further, to the level OH, which would cause extra costs equal to the striped area EDXH; at the same time, ease the controls on diesel A so that emissions were OJ, which would save costs equal to the striped area CGJX. The sales–weighted average of OH and OJ emissions would come to OX emissions per vehicle, and thus total emissions would be the same as if the "every model must meet the OX standard" system were in effect. But, as is clear from the diagram, cost savings CGJX are greater than are extra costs EDXH; or, equivalently, the total EBH plus GAJ is less than the total of DBX plus CAX. By allowing the manufacturer the flexibility to expand the low-cost means of control (diesel B) so as to offset the high-cost means of control (diesel A), total costs are reduced, yet emissions are not increased.[16] And, not coincidentally, this is the same outcome as would be achieved by an effluent fee equal to OL per unit of emissions.

This sales–weighted average approach had already been incorporated into regulations in a different area: the fuel economy standards (see Chapter 8). And it was analogous to another control strategy, the "bubble concept," that EPA had recently endorsed. This latter concept allowed individual emitters of any given pollutant at one geographic location to act as if there were a bubble over the entire location. All that mattered (in terms of meeting standards) were the emission reductions from the overall bubble. Thus, if there were multiple emission sources (e.g., multiple smokestacks) at the same site, emitters could trade off the low-cost ways against high-cost ways of reducing emissions. In the same way, a diesel manufacturer could trade off low-cost against high-cost emission reductions within the fleet that was being sold.

Once the principle of the sales–weighted average was clear, it was necessary to incorporate it into a system that would deviate least from EPA's established methods and procedures.[17] The best way seemed to be as follows: After the initial 50,000-mile certification tests by the vehicles, each manufacturer could establish a limited number (say, five to ten, so as to maintain administrative simplicity) subcategories and establish a separate emissions standard for each subcategory. Then, all EPA's usual testing and enforcement procedures would apply to these subcategories. At the end of the sales year, the weighted average of the sales of the subcategories would be used to determine if the manufacturer was above the EPA standard and, hence, in or out of compliance. Since initialization is important in Washington, this proposal was given the title "The Corporate Average Particulate Emissions from Diesels," or CAPED, standard.[18]

One other change in the form of the standard seemed worthwhile. Virtually all of the evidence pointed to a trade-off between particulate control and NO_x control. More of the one pollutant meant less of the other at any stage of development of technology. It seemed sensible for EPA to take this into account in setting the standard, especially since it had the extra flexibility of the NO_x waiver at its disposal. Incorporating the trade-off into the standards would give the manufacturers greater flexibility in meeting the standard, and it would reduce the likelihood that a technology that was especially good at controlling one pollutant would be rejected because it could not quite achieve the standard for the other pollutant. Further, there was a precedent. The emissions standards for heavy-duty trucks for 1979–1982 have a standard for HC emissions and a separate standard for the sum of HC and NO_x emissions; the latter standard obviously allows the trading-off of HC and NO_x emissions (up to the separate HC standard).

Recommendations

1. We recommended that EPA promulgate the proposed 1981 standard of 0.6 g/mi only if it was prepared to grant the NO_x waivers; otherwise some large diesels might not be able to meet the standard. Our informal soundings had led us to believe that, with the waiver, all vehicles could properly meet the standard. Further, the ozone case (Chapter 4) had been a chastening experience. The diesel particulate standard was not the place for the EOP to get into another pure numbers battle with EPA over the stringency of the standard without any strong, impartial engineering expertise on our side.

2. EPA should delay the promulgation of any more stringent standards (e.g., the one considered for 1983) until the likely form of the revisions in the NAAQS were known. Also, by that time information on carcinogenicity and the role of fuels would become available. At most, the effective date of a more stringent standard would be delayed by two model years. In the interim, the 1981 standard would be in effect, and the manufacturers would be on notice. Again, this was not the place to get into a numbers battle over stringency, and there were sound reasons for the delay.

3. The CAPED sales–weighted average setting the standard should be adopted.

4. A separate standard for light-duty trucks should be established.

5. EPA should consider an approach to the NO_x waiver and the particulate standard that would allow explicitly for the trade-off between the two.

The COWPS filing incorporating these ideas went through three drafts and was reviewed by CEA and COWPS principals. It was also reviewed by the COWPS general counsel to make sure that the recommendations (especially the sales–weighted average approach) were not contrary to the Clean Air Act. This was one of the first COWPS or RARG filings to be reviewed by the COWPS general counsel. (It subsequently became standard practice.) An early draft was shown to EPA for comments. On April 19, 1979 the final draft was delivered to EPA to be placed on its public record.

The Department of Energy and the Department of Commerce also filed comments on the NPRM with EPA. Both these agencies argued for delay and less stringency. And most of the motor vehicle manufacturers filed comments critical of the NPRM, urging delay and less stringency. Public interest and environmental groups filed comments supporting the NPRM as proposed.

THE OUTCOME

In February 1980 EPA announced the final regulations for diesel particulate emissions from light-duty vehicles.[19] For automobiles, a standard of 0.6 g/mi was set for the 1982 model year, a year later than had been originally proposed. (By February 1980, the 1981 vehicles were already undergoing certification tests; it was too late to set a standard for that model year). The more stringent standard of 0.2 g/mi was set for the 1985 model year, two years later than had been originally proposed. For light-duty trucks, the 0.6 g/mi standard applied in 1982,[20] but a standard of 0.26 g/mi (somewhat less stringent than the comparable automobile standard) applied in 1985.

EPA declined to establish a sales–weighted averaging scheme for the standards on the grounds that the concept needed more study. At the same time as the final rules were announced, however, the agency also announced the formation of an EPA task force to try to develop an averaging scheme that, if feasible, would be proposed as part of EPA's forthcoming NPRM to control nitrous oxides from heavy-duty trucks.

The regulatory analysis accompanying the final regulations was greatly improved over its earlier version. Cost-effectiveness calculations had been done much more carefully and more sensibly; the environmental modeling had improved.

CONCLUDING REMARKS

Delay was definitely the correct public policy decision. Without the delay, a confrontation in 1981 or 1982 over the diesel regulations was highly likely—a confrontation that would be costly and damaging to all parties concerned. Diesel vehicle development might be discouraged or delayed; EPA would likely lose the confrontation and would have to modify the regulations; its credibility would be damaged; last-minute changes would mean higher costs.

The role of the EOP in achieving this outcome is far from clear. Other agencies, the industry, and many individuals within EPA were urging delay and/or less stringency. And two manufacturers had proposed sales–weighted averaging schemes. For whatever reasons, EPA's final rules for diesel particulates do represent sensible public policy. And, if sales–weighted average approach is eventually adopted by EPA, a policy encouraging flexibility and cost-effectiveness will have been added to EPA's regulatory repertoire.

NOTES TO CHAPTER 7

[1] See L. B. Lave and E. P. Seskin, *Air Pollution and Human Health* (Baltimore: Johns Hopkins, 1977).

[2] National Academy of Sciences, Assembly of Life Sciences, *Saccharine: Technical Assessment of Risks and Benefits* (Washington, D.C.: National Academy of Sciences, November 1978).

[3] *Federal Register*, February 1, 1979, pp. 6650–6657.

[4] EPA had decided to propose standards for heavy-duty trucks for 1983 at a future date.

[5] The exception was the Volkswagen Rabbit, which could meet the 1981 standards without controls and required only a turbocharger to meet the 1983 standard.

[6] If only a few diesels replace gasoline vehicles, only the carburetor and vehicle fueling evaporative losses would be eliminated. But if, say, 20% of the fleet becomes diesels, then 20% fewer storage tanks are needed for gasoline, 20% fewer handlings occur, and so on.

[7] We were led to this argument by a chance remark by a Washington representative of a motor vehicle manufacturer. He mentioned that the company wanted some kind of offset from EPA for the fact that the diesels had no carburetors and therefore had no HC evaporative losses from carburetors. This statement triggered my thinking about evaporative losses throughout the gasoline fuel distribution system, and I remembered that EPA had estimated the HC evaporative losses from the gasoline distribution system as part of the ozone rulemaking (Chapter 4).

[8] This argument was triggered by a friend on the staff of the Office of Science and Technology Policy. When he was told about the reduced HC evaporative emissions, he replied, "I wonder if the less volatile fuel means fewer fires in the event of crashes." A call to the National Highway Traffic Safety Administration indicated that there were no good data on fiery crashes and diesel involvement. But another friend mentioned that he thought diesel boats got a break on insurance. (I had forgotten about insurance rates as a reflection of safety experience!) A few calls to insurance companies confirmed the rate reduction for diesel boats and diesel truck fleets. (And, when I asked why the rates were lower, I was told, "Oh, the fuel is less volatile; there is less chance of a fire if there is a crash.") Inquiries concerning diesel automobiles indicated that insurance reductions had

not yet appeared for these vehicles. Perhaps there was not yet sufficient experience with diesel automobiles.

[9]See L. J. White and E. S. Mills, "Government Policies toward Automotive Emissions Control," in A. F. Friedlaender, ed., *Approaches to Controlling Air Pollution* (Cambridge, Mass.: M.I.T., 1978).

[10]All too often the documents mentioned costs but did not indicate the tons of particulates that would be controlled.

[11]The model was constructed for EPA under contract by a consulting firm. See T. Briggs, I. Throgmorton, and M. Karaffa of PEDCO, *Air Quality Assessment of Particulate Emissions from Diesel-Powered Vehicles*, Report prepared for U.S. Environmental Protection Agency, Office of Air and Waste Management, Office of Air Quality Planning and Standards, Research Triangle Park, N.C., March 1978.

[12]See U.S. Environmental Protection Agency, Office of Air, Noise and Radiation, Office of Air Quality Planning and Standards, *National Air Quality, Monitoring and Emission Trends Report, 1977*, Research Triangle Park, N.C., December 1978.

[13]Although it is the conventional wisdom, this point proved especially hard to document. The Federal Highway Administration does not keep time-series estimates of central city versus suburban VMTs for individual cities. Neither do most cities themselves. But a study obtained from the Washington, D.C., Council of Governments indicated that in the 1968–1975 period VMTs on major arterial roads in the entire metropolitan area rose by 40%, whereas they *fell* 3% within the District of Columbia itself. See Metropolitan Washington Council of Governments, Transportation Planning Board, *Annual Report 1977;* and Metropolitan Washington Council of Governments, *Existing Transportation Systems in the Metropolitan Area: A Findings Report*, June 1972, p. 82.

[14]This is a standard economic result that can be found in any textbook. See, for example, E. Mansfield, *Microeconomics: Theory and Applications*, 2nd ed. (New York: Norton, 1975), pp. 516–518.

[15]The proof of this proposition does not depend on the 50:50 sales weights; it applies generally to multiple categories with any percentages.

[16]The only possible problem that might arise would be if diesel A were used relatively heavily in some areas and diesel B were used heavily in others. Then, the specific areas would get more or less emissions than would occur under a uniform standard. There were no data indicating that this might be a problem for diesel emissions in actual use.

[17]Both General Motors and Volkswagen independently proposed averaging procedures. But neither tried to integrate their proposals with EPA's existing procedures.

[18]We also urged EPA to explore the possibility of using this sales–weighted average approach for the other emissions standards for motor vehicles.

[19]*Federal Register*, March 5, 1980, pp. 14495–14525.

[20]EPA pointed out that light-duty trucks had to meet less stringent NO_x requirements than did automobiles; hence the truck manufacturers had more room to trade off greater NO_x emissions against lower particulate emissions and hence could be expected to meet the 1982 standard even though the trucks had larger engines than did cars.

chapter 8

Fuel Economy Standards

Should the National Highway Traffic Safety
Administration revise the automotive fuel
economy standards for the 1980s?

Disputes between regulators and the industries that they are regulating frequently focus on the cost and feasibility of regulation. These questions, in turn, often hinge on very detailed engineering and scientific interpretations of experiments or guesses about future technological developments. The EOP may be able to help focus the debate and develop a common framework that the disputing parties accept, so that the nature of their differences is clear. This chapter provides an example of cost–benefit analysis serving as that common framework. But the EOP is unlikely to have the detailed expertise that would allow it to adjudicate the dispute, as the example presented in this chapter also indicates.

BACKGROUND

Title V of the Energy Policy and Conservation Act of 1975[1] established a set of fuel economy standards for automobiles for 1978–1980 and 1985. The standards for 1981–1984 were to be filled in by the National Highway Traffic Safety Administration (which is part of the Department of Transportation). They were subsequently established through a NHTSA rulemaking completed in June 1977.[2] The standards are shown in Table 8-1.

The fuel economy of each model car is determined by fuel economy measurements taken during the EPA certification test for pollutant emissions. The fuel economy standards apply to the sales–weighted average of the fuel economy of the entire fleet of automobiles sold by the manufacturer during a model year. Accordingly, whether or not the manufacturer has violated the standards cannot be determined until the end of the sales year. If the manufacturer's fleet average is below the standard, that manufacturer must pay a penalty of $5 per 0.1 miles per gallon (mpg) that the average falls short of the standard, for all the cars sold by that manufacturer during that sales year.[3]

The fuel economy standards thus embody two nice properties. First, they employ the sale–weighted average principle, allowing the manufacturer to trade off more expensive ways of achieving the required fuel economy against less expensive ways. They even allow a one-year carry-forward, carry-back feature, so that a manufacturer's achievements beyond the required standards can be used to offset shortfalls one year earlier or one year later. Second, they contain a noncompliance fee, rather than the "achieve-it-or-else-we-will-close-you-down" provisions of the automotive emissions control portions of the Clean Air Act. But

Table 8-1

Fuel Economy Standards for Automobiles

Year	Miles per Gallon	
1978	18.0[a]	
1979	19.0[a]	
1980	20.0[a]	
1981	22.0[b]	(21.5)[c]
1982	24.0[j]	(23.0)[c]
1983	26.0[b]	(24.5)[c]
1984	27.0[b]	(26.0)[c]
1985	27.5[a]	

[a]Mandated by the Energy Policy and Conservation Act of 1975.
[b]Established by NHTSA rulemaking, June 1977.
[c]Alternative "straight-line" schedule suggested by automobile manufacturers.

the noncompliance fee does have one drawback: Technically, a failure to achieve the fuel economy standard is a violation of the law. Managers of corporations generally do not like to be accused of violating laws.

At the beginning, one has to ask, Why have fuel economy standards? Why have this regulation? Why not let manufacturers and consumers make their own decisions as to fuel economy? If consumers are willing to pay the price, why not let them burn all the fuel they want? There are a number of answers that can be given:

1. Other policies of the federal government have kept the prices of petroleum products below their true opportunity costs: world market prices. Thus, even if manufacturers and consumers do respond properly to the prices that they see in the market price, those prices have been the wrong ones; they have been too low to induce manufacturers to produce and consumers to buy fuel-efficient vehicles. Fuel economy standards are a second best effort to patch up other failures in policy by the federal government.

2. The United States has some market power (monopsony power) in buying petroleum in world markets. If in aggregate it buys less, the price of oil will fall to all consumers (other things held constant); if it buys more, the price of oil will rise to all consumers. Individual consumers will ignore this external effect of their extra consumption. Again, fuel economy standards are a second best remedy. An excise tax on petroleum to take into account the externality would be first best.

3. Extra petroleum bought from abroad (even if its price does not rise) means more imports, a decline in the value of the dollar, and a

121

higher real cost of imports generally (an unfavorable terms-of-trade effect). Again, this argument rests on the United State's having market power in some of the goods that it sells or buys. Alternatively, the higher import prices mean a higher domestic price level and an added inflation–unemployment trade-off burden. Again, extra gasoline purchases involve an externality, and, again, an excise tax on petroleum would be the first best remedy.

4. It is politically unwise to be dependent on foreigners for a large fraction of our energy requirements. The less we buy, the better off we are. But individual consumers will ignore this external effect of their purchases. Again, gasoline purchases involve externalities, and, again, excise taxes are first best.

5. Consumers as individuals do not value the future fuel consumption of their vehicles as highly as does society as a whole (i.e., individual consumers use a higher discount rate). One possible explanation of this difference is that consumers simply have short time horizons. Another is that they are very unsure as to whether their car will maintain its fuel economy performance after three or four years. If, when it comes time to trade it in for a new car, used-car buyers have difficulty ascertaining the true fuel economy of the used car that they are about to purchase, then good fuel economy will count for little. The shortsightedness version of this argument is simply another version of the externality argument, and the excise tax is the proper solution. The imperfect information version is a tougher problem. The proper remedy is more information about the mean and variance of fuel economy for individual used-car models.

6. Even if consumers wanted automobiles with good fuel economy, the manufacturers would not provide them. Even though one could make the argument that the automobile manufacturers were slow in bringing compact and subcompact cars to the American market in the late 1950s and the 1960s,[4] that episode has passed. It seems unlikely that the manufacturers today would not find it profitable to cater to the preferences of a public that wanted greater fuel economy.[5] To claim that the manufacturers would do otherwise is to claim that they do not know their own best interests.

7. Consumers simply do not know their own best interests with respect to fuel economy.

The preference of many economists (including this author) would be to allow gasoline prices to rise to world market levels and, perhaps, add an excise tax to allow for the externalities. Fuel economy standards are a distinctly inferior second best policy. But, in a world in which both the Congress and the executive branch have been most reluctant to allow gasoline prices to rise to world market levels, let alone add an excise tax for externalities, are we better off having fuel economy standards? Here one has to ask, How far away is the price of gasoline from its world market price and hence how distorted are the price signals that manufacturers and consumers are receiving? But also one has to ask, How likely is it that the setting of standards might lead to unexpected inefficiencies or dislocations? It is a close call.

Section 502(a)(3) of the Energy Policy and Conservation Act requires that the Secretary of Transportation set the fuel economy standards by July 1977 for each model year, 1981–1984, at a level that "(A) is the maximum feasible average fuel economy level, and (B) will result in a steady progress toward meeting the average fuel economy standard [27.5 mpg] established by or pursuant to this subsection for model year 1985." Section 502(e) of the Act then specifies that, "in determining maximum feasible average fuel economy, the Secretary shall consider (1) technological feasibility; (2) economic practicability; (3) the effect of other Federal motor vehicle standards on fuel economy; and (4) the need of the Nation to conserve energy."

The fuel economy standards could always be met by the production only of very small cars (e.g., Chevrolet Chevettes or Plymouth Omnis). But that is not what Congress had intended. Rather, Congress apparently hoped to push the automobile manufacturers to develop new technologies that would achieve greater fuel economy without disturbing too greatly the characteristics of the mix of American cars. This was another instance of technology forcing through regulation.

In the rulemaking completed in June 1977, NHTSA had decided that there were a number of inexpensive ways of improving fuel economy without altering the general mix of cars. Accordingly, it established the schedule indicated in Table 8-1. A characteristic of the schedule is that it called for larger annual increases (2.0 mpg) in the early years 1980–1983 and small annual increases (1.0 mpg and 0.5 mpg) in the later years (1983–1985). This characteristic caused the schedule to be described as "front loaded."

The automobile manufacturers protested the rapid pace of this schedule at the time of the rulemaking, but they did not protest very vigorously. Apparently, at that time they were uncertain as to what could or could not be achieved technologically in the 1981–1984 period.

THE MANUFACTURERS' REQUESTS

By late 1978 the automobile manufacturers had become distinctly more pessimistic as to what could be achieved. Ford had come perilously close to failing to meet the standards during the 1978 model year; unexpect-

123

edly strong demand for larger cars with large engines had forced the company to ration the supply of large V-8 engines to dealers, making neither Ford nor its dealers very happy. (The 1978 model year was that blissful year when gasoline was still in the 60¢- to 70¢-per-gallon range—relatively cheap—and many consumers still wanted large cars.)

In December and January, General Motors and Ford began correspondence and discussions with NHTSA about the possibility of modifying the fuel economy standards. The companies' first choice was a lowering of the 1985 fuel economy standard to 26.0 mpg (which NHTSA could accomplish through a rulemaking) and a gradual approach to that target in the intervening years. But, recognizing that this scenario was probably out of the question, they instead focused on a "straight-line" approach to the 27.5 mpg figure in 1985, with 1.5 mpg increments each year rather than on the "front-loaded" schedule that NHTSA had established. Their suggested schedule is in Table 8-1. Their argument was that, although the NHTSA schedule was probably technologically feasible (the General Motors representatives winced a little bit when they said this; the Ford representatives winced a lot) without forcing the mix of car models to change excessively, it would be very expensive to meet that schedule. The technological and cost assumptions that NHTSA had made to support its findings in 1977 were overly optimistic then and were even more so now. The NHTSA schedule called for the rapid application of technology, down-sizing of vehicles, and weight reduction. These rapid actions would be very expensive. The more leisurely pace of the straight-line schedule would avoid some of the more expensive early actions and allow the development of newer technologies, which would take more time to bring to commercial application but which represented far cheaper ways of achieving fuel economy. Thus, the companies argued, the straight-line schedule meant slightly more gasoline consumed by the 1981–1984 model cars, but the manufacturing cost savings (which would be passed on to consumers) would outweigh the costs of the extra gasoline consumed.

The companies were also concerned about the large investment requirements that the down-sizing, redesign, and reengineering of their cars would require. They were concerned that these financial requirements would severely tax their financial capabilities, particularly if there were a serious recession in the early 1980s that would reduce car sales and hence reduce the profits on which they were relying to finance the investments.

Finally, implicit was the companies' fear of what might happen if the standards could not be met through pure technological advances. The companies claimed that they would not violate the standards, even though the penalties were not Draconian. A violation, they claimed, might leave them open to stockholder suits. Hence, to achieve the standards, they might have to force the mix of cars farther toward small cars than they otherwise would have—probably by raising the price of large cars (or otherwise restricting their supply) and lowering the price of small cars. Presumably, this was a less profitable strategy for the manufacturers; otherwise, they would have done it voluntarily. Also, it might not work very well. Consumers might not buy appreciably more small cars and would simply hold their older large cars for a longer period. Alternatively, the potential large-car buyers might switch their purchases to pickup trucks and vans (which enjoyed a boom year in 1978) to get the interior space and power that they wanted. The latter scenario was clearly more favorable to the manufacturers than the former scenario, but it still meant a great deal of uncertainty. Either scenario meant less fuel economy gains than would otherwise be expected, since the older cars that consumers would retain and the trucks and vans that they might buy had lower fuel economy than would be the case for new cars. There were even some scenarios that could be spun out that indicated that, because of this failure to shift the mix, aggregate gasoline consumption might be *greater* under more stringent fuel economy standards than under less stringent ones.

The NHTSA initial position was that the 1977 rulemaking had demonstrated that the standards were feasible and worthwhile; the agency was not convinced that the world had changed sufficiently to throw those conclusions into doubt. NHTSA issued a report to Congress in late January 1979 that updated the 1977 results and argued that the standards were still feasible and worthwhile. As the debate proceeded, however, NHTSA acknowledged that some of its 1977 technological assumptions could no longer be used, and the NHTSA staff began intensive review of the companies' new technological and cost data.

Two other new (since 1977) elements crept into the debate. First, the auto manufacturers argued that the stringent emissions control standards due for 1980 and 1981 were going to cause fuel economy decreases that had not been considered in the 1977 rulemaking. Section 502(e) of the Act indicated that "the effect of the other Federal motor vehicle standards on fuel economy" should be taken into consideration. Second, Section 503(d)(1) of the Act stated that the fuel economy measurements should be based on the testing procedures used by EPA during the 1975 model year "or procedures which yield comparable results." EPA had made a number of changes in the procedures since 1975. The manufacturers claimed that, for their 1979 fleet, these changes meant a decrease in average measures of fuel economy of 0.6–0.8 mpg, so the procedures were not "comparable." (EPA, for its part, claimed that the changed procedures would not have altered the fuel economy results of the 1975 model fleet, so the procedures were "comparable."[6]) Both these points, the manufacturers claimed, argued for more lenient fuel economy standards.

The manufacturers never formally petitioned NHTSA for a change in the standards. NHTSA told the manufacturers that, by keeping the request informal, the discussions and the flow of information would be freer and easier and the decision-making processes smoother. This, then, was not a rulemaking but was an informal request for a rulemaking.

THE CEA ROLE

The companies also contacted EOP officials and pleaded their case in that forum. This appeared to be another possible opportunity for better regulatory management. If the automobile companies were right, there were substantial social gains to be achieved from the modest slackening in the 1981–1984 standards. In early February 1979 CEA took responsibility for gathering the necessary information and analyzing the issues.

We decided to focus mainly on the cost–benefit aspects of the problem; these cost–benefit aspects constituted the true social issue. Further, we focused on the *incremental* question: Did the social gains in *changing* from the NHTSA standard to the companies' alternative straight-line standards outweigh the social cost from that change? The social gains were the value of the resources that would be saved by not having to launch an all-out effort to meet the more stringent NHTSA standards; the social costs were the value of the extra gasoline that would be burned under the companies' alternative standards. We did not pay much attention to the financing and cash flow problems of the automobile companies because these problems were partly a function of their vertical integration strategies. If they chose to buy more input items from suppliers and manufacture fewer inputs themselves, they would incur fewer investment costs themselves (but, of course, incur higher piece costs) and spread the financing problem and the risks more widely.

As of January and early February, the companies and NHTSA were talking past each other. The two sides were using different assumptions and different time periods for their comparisons. It was difficult, if not impossible, to use NHTSA's 1977 analysis for tracking from assumptions to conclusions. If we were going to analyze the problem properly and possibly offer any help in resolving the dispute, we needed to establish a common framework to which all could agree.

One frustrating aspect of the debate was the general yes–no nature of the analysis that both NHTSA and the companies provided. All the analysis was done as if the technologies were certain. Everyone seemed to be looking for a simple yes-or-no answer to the question, "Can the NHTSA standards be achieved?" But there were a host of uncertainties regarding the technologies, their dates of commercial application, the fuel economy improvements they would bring, and their costs.

The proper analysis would have taken each technological event (e.g., better tires, turbochargers, better aerodynamic design) and put a probability distribution on the likely fuel economy improvements it could bring in each year (e.g., there is a 20% chance that better tires will mean a 0.1 mpg improvement, a 40% chance they will mean a 0.2 mpg improvement, etc.). Then, the complete array of technological improvements for any year could be combined and the probabilities compounded. Thus, the complete story would say, for example, that the planned technological changes for 1983 have a 60% probability of just meeting the NHTSA standards, a 10% chance of exceeding them by 0.5 mpg or more, and a 30% chance of falling short by 0.5 mpg or more. And this conclusion could be traced back to the underlying probability distributions of the individual technological events.

These probability distributions would not be easy to calculate, but they would allow a far better appreciation of the risks of policy decisions. Policymakers could then ask if a 30% chance of a shortfall (with the possible disruptions that would follow) was worth taking, rather than fooling themselves into believing that a 70% probability of achieving or exceeding the standards implied complete certainty. Unfortunately, regulatory decision makers (and their staffs) mostly seem to be looking for yes–no answers and not the subtlety of probability distributions. The search for yes–no answers is another example of the regulators' desire to dichotomize the world into simple categories; in this fuel economy dispute, even the automobile companies were going along with this approach.

It was too late to alter this approach for this regulatory problem, but it was suggested to all who would listen that the probability distribution approach was a superior methodology; maybe the next regulatory problem of this kind would be handled better.

General Motors and Ford provided us with the same information that they had provided NHTSA: their detailed product plans and costs for the 1980–1985 model years under the NHTSA standards and under the straight-line alternative. General Motors' plans were especially detailed. We were not in a strong position to assess their accuracy and had to accept them largely at face value. But a few things about General Motors' plans struck us as nonsensical and unlikely, especially a plan (under the NHTSA schedule) to require that motorists replace their emission control catalysts after 25,000 miles on General Motors' 1981–1983 models. General Motors planned to tune the engines so as to achieve an extra 0.3 mpg; but this tuning would cause the catalysts to deteriorate more quickly, requiring a replacement at 25,000 miles. Since most motorists would not voluntarily replace the catalyst, General Motors planned to require the motorist to pay for the catalyst at the time of new car purchase, giving the buyer a certificate entitling him or her to a free replacement; at 25,000 miles, a red flag would appear, covering the odometer (thus causing some inconvenience for the motorist but not interfering with the operation of the car) and reminding the motorist that the free catalyst change was due. Although this replacement procedure was legal (William Ruckelshaus, Administrator of EPA in 1973, had agreed to it), EPA would clearly be very unhappy; it was difficult to believe that General Motors would actually decide to incur EPA's wrath in this way.[7] Also, this replacement procedure was a very expensive ($140) way to achieve an extra 0.3 mpg. (Paying the noncompliance fee of $15 for the same 0.3 mpg would be far cheaper.) It was likely, in a crunch, that General Motors would instead accelerate some other technological means of gaining the extra 0.3 mpg.

The structure of the cost–benefit analysis was fairly straightforward. One could start with the NHTSA schedule. The companies' cost schedules provided the average (annualized) cost saving per car per year that would be achieved for the straight-line alternative; these savings were the incremental benefits of the change. The incremental costs were the extra gallons of gasoline that would be consumed over the lifetimes of the 1981–1984 models because of the straight-line alternative. NHTSA had a schedule of the annual mileage of a typical car in each year of its use, which all parties were prepared to accept. Once the present and future prices of a gallon of gasoline and the discount rate for the future lifetime extra consumption were determined, the costs were easily calculated. Thus, the incremental benefits and costs for a typical car in each model year could be calculated and multiplied by the predicted number of cars that would be sold, and then these figures could be discounted back to a common starting date (e.g., 1980) to determine the net present value (benefits less costs) of the change to the straight-line standard. Throughout this analysis, it was assumed that the model mix would not change appreciably under either schedule.

The value of three variables had to be determined: the discount rate for discounting future costs and benefits, the starting price of gasoline, and the projected rate of price increase for gasoline through 1995. The discount rate for evaluating government projects was specified by OMB to be 10% in real (constant dollar) terms.[8] We used a range of alternative starting gasoline prices and a range of projected real increases in gasoline prices. Further, because the regulations were primarily designed to reduce the country's dependence on foreign oil, we considered the relevant gasoline price to be a pretax price.[9]

(There was one other element that was a backdrop to the calculations and discussion. The Department of Energy had compiled figures showing that actual on-road fuel economy was appreciably worse than the results indicated by the EPA tests for comparable pre-use certification models.[10] The average shortfall was 17% in 1977, and it was worse for more fuel-efficient cars. If the trend continued, the shortfall would be in the range of 20–25% by 1985. The causes of this shortfall have not been satisfactorily explained. These shortfalls did not change any of the conclusions qualitatively, but they were disconcerting.)

The cost–benefit calculations showed that even at a pretax price of gasoline of 80¢/gal (well above the actual pretax price as of late February 1979) and a projected real annual price increase of 5% for gasoline (well above the rate of 3% that seemed most likely at that time), the shift to the straight-line standard made sense. This was true even when the General Motors cost numbers were adjusted to eliminate the catalyst change (and other adjustments were hypothesized to make up the difference). Further, when one also considered the risks of technological failings or of consumers' being unhappy with the smaller and less powerful vehicles that would be available, the case for the more moderate pace became yet more compelling.

By early March 1979 CEA had produced a long internal memo describing the background, the problem, the analysis, and the results. The memo suggested that we not immediately press NHTSA to make the change to the straight-line standards but, rather, that we only urge

NHTSA to reopen the 1977 rulemaking, to issue an open-ended NPRM that would, in effect, say, "the world has changed since 1977; we are not sure if the standards should be changed; here are some possibilities; we invite comment."

The memo was delivered to the EOP principals on Friday, March 2, 1979. That afternoon, a request came from the House Subcommittee on Energy and Power (chaired by Representative John Dingle of Michigan) of the Committee on Interstate and Foreign Commerce, asking CEA Chairman Schultze to testify about the fuel economy standards on March 13. Also asked to testify were representatives from EPA, NHTSA, DOE, and the Federal Trade Commission (the last because the FTC has the power to recommend that the penalties for failure to meet the fuel economy standard be waived if they would have an anticompetitive effect). Schultze was not eager to testify and even less eager at this point to stake out a position in the controversy, so his testimony was deliberately designed to be largely noncontroversial. It said that CEA and COWPS, in cooperation with NHTSA, were analyzing the problem. It pointed out that "the need of the Nation to conserve energy" (specifically mentioned by the Act) was not boundless, that there were limits in the amounts of domestic resources we should spend to conserve energy. Hence, a cost–benefit analysis was necessary. And it laid out the necessary steps in the cost–benefit analysis that should guide the decision.

The hearings were largely uneventful, except for Representative Dingel's sharp criticisms of EPA and DOE. Much to our surprise, CEA's testimony was well received.

SUBSEQUENT EVENTS

In the following weeks, we did a number of variations on the basic analysis. One could turn the problem around and ask, given a projected rate of price increase, How high would the current (pretax) price of gasoline have to be before one would favor the NHTSA standards over the straight-line alternative? The difference between this break-even price and the actual current price indicated the implicit premium that would be paid (in the extra use of domestic resources) under the NHTSA standards to avoid importing one more gallon of gasoline. This implicit premium could be compared with one's notion of a proper premium to be placed on the current price so as to account for all the externalities involved in the increased dependence on foreign sources of petroleum. If the former were larger than the latter, the NHTSA standards would not be worthwhile. Alternatively, from a given starting price for gasoline, one could calculate how fast the annual price rise for gasoline between 1979 and 1995 would have to be before one would favor the NHTSA standards. Again, if the necessary annual increase were faster than one expected would likely occur, the NHTSA standards would not be worthwhile.

These alternative calculations showed (as they had to, since they were simply different ways of making the initial cost–benefit calculation) that the straight-line standards were to be preferred if one believed that the auto company numbers (even as modified) represented the likely state of the world.

All parties to the dispute had been exposed to the lessons of this cost–benefit approach from CEA's testimony before the Dingle subcommittee. (NHTSA was also given a copy of the basic CEA memorandum, which helped.) At least, we all now had a common basis for dialogues.

The suggestion that the rulemaking should be reopened without any prejudgment of the correct standard was made to NHTSA a number of times. The answer was always the same: "We are getting all the available information through the present process. We will not get any new information through a rulemaking. We will not issue a new NPRM unless we are already convinced that there are good grounds for a change." So much for open government!

NHTSA had turned its engineers loose on the General Motors and Ford technological and cost data. Though the cost data passed largely unscathed, the NHTSA engineers questioned a number of the technological assumptions of the companies. By late April, NHTSA's position was becoming clear. The agency's engineers did not believe that the companies would have to take the expensive actions that the latter claimed were necessary under the NHTSA standards (but not necessary under the more gradual approach). There were cheaper technological advances available that would even allow the companies to make up the loss from the emissions standards and the changed testing procedures. Accordingly, NHTSA found that the straight-line alternative did not pass the cost–benefit test.

At this point, the EOP was again caught in the middle, between agency engineers saying one thing and industry engineers saying another. Each group had its ax to grind. There was no neutral third party to whom we could turn. The problems were too specific. Even the Office of Science and Technology Policy could not help.[11] Further, we had to ask ourselves, Were the companies truly prepared to take expensive technological actions to avoid paying the modest penalty (but also to avoid violating the law)? Were they bluffing? Were they sincere but likely to change their minds?

Since NHTSA's decision with respect to the standard was an important one, the EOP insisted that it not be made final and public until the principals in the EOP had been briefed. Because NHTSA wanted more time to be sure of its decision and because of conflicting schedules, these briefings took almost a month to set up.

There was one other complicating factor. In December 1978, Secretary of Transportation Brock Adams had made a speech in Detroit calling for an engineering revolution in automobiles that would allow cars to achieve 50 mpg or more. Through the efforts of OSTP, this vague suggestion was eventually turned into a joint research effort between the automobile industry and the federal government. (Parenthetically, one of the fears of the industry was that new research discoveries from this joint effort would promptly be rammed down its throats through new regulatory requirements for yet greater fuel economy, even before the discoveries were made practicable and commercially feasible.) A meeting between the President and the leading auto industry executives in mid-May formally launched the research program. At that meeting, the President promised that the NHTSA decision would receive EOP review before it was made final.

The NHTSA briefings of the EOP finally occurred and stretched over two sessions. At the end of the second, in late May, NHTSA announced that it was ready to proceed to make a final announcement denying the companies' request to adopt the straight-line schedule. The EOP was still caught uncomfortably between the conflicting stories of the auto industry engineers and the NHTSA engineers. One possible compromise was for NHTSA to allow the auto companies to have a chance to examine and try to refute the NHTSA engineering analysis before the announcement was made. Another was (as had been suggested three months earlier) for NHTSA to reopen the rulemaking, indicate that the standards were open to question but also present its latest conclusions, and invite public comment. Both were conveyed to NHTSA.

At this point, events in the world had definitely turned in NHTSA's favor. By early June, gasoline lines had been in existence in

California for over two months and had started to become a serious phenomenon in Washington, D.C., and other East Coast cities. It was not a propitious time to be pushing for policies, such as the straight-line standards, that would mean greater gasoline consumption (even if that extra consumption would take place in the early 1980s). It would be difficult to sustain an appeal to the President on this issue.

In mid-June, NHTSA decided that it was going to proceed with the announcement. The EOP thought that it had a last-minute compromise worked out, in which the announcement would not convey a sense of finality and would allow the auto companies to review NHTSA's analysis.

THE OUTCOME

On June 20, Secretary of Transportation Brock Adams announced that the fuel economy standards would remain as they had been established in the 1977 rulemaking and issued an NHTSA report justifying the decision. He indicated that the decision was final. This announcement incensed the EOP principals, who believed that their last-minute compromise had been violated, as had the President's commitment to the auto companies. They appealed to the President, who then told Adams and the companies that there would still be EOP review if the companies felt that they had a strong rebuttal case.

As of this writing, nothing further has happened. The higher prices of gasoline that followed the disruptions in Iran in early 1979 and the OPEC price increase in the summer appear to have shifted automobile buying patterns sufficiently toward smaller cars so that any immediate problems in meeting the standards have disappeared. The interesting question for the 1980s, though, is what will happen to the price of gasoline relative to the general price level. The experience following the previous OPEC price hike of 1973–1974 was that the real price of gasoline fell for the following four years. (That is one of the major reasons why the demand for large cars, pickup trucks, and vans was so strong in 1978.) If this same pattern emerges in the early 1980s, consumer demand for larger cars may again grow, and the fuel economy standards may cause strains.

In August 1979, the president of General Motors, E. M. Estes, announced in a speech that General Motors expected to exceed the 1985 standards (and, by implication, the standards in the interim years).[12]

For the moment, the battle over the fuel economy standards for the early 1980s is probably over. But the Carter energy program, announced in July 1979, may lead to new battles over fuel economy standards for the mid- and late 1980s.

CONCLUDING COMMENTS

Once CEA had gotten all the parties to understand and agree to a common form of analysis, our useful role was largely over. We could be a watchdog on the proceedings, to make sure that egregious assumptions or analyses did not slip in. But CEA and more generally the EOP simply did not have the expertise to step authoritatively into the technological dispute. And the EOP never will.

Shortly before the final announcement was made, the NHTSA and COWPS legal staffs exchanged memos on the proper interpretation of the phrases "economic practicability" and "the need of the Nation to conserve energy" contained in the Energy Policy and Conservation Act. The NHTSA lawyers argued that these phrases required NHTSA to impose regulations that pushed the industry as hard as possible, with economic practicability allowing anything that did not cause the financial collapse of the industry. The COWPS lawyers argued that the law was flexible enough to allow cost–benefit considerations and that these considerations should be included in the formulation of the regulations. Since the NHTSA decision was based largely on its findings that the existing standards did pass a cost–benefit test, these arguments were moot at the time. But they may well play a role in the determination of standards for the late 1980s. The NHTSA lawyers' position—that economic considerations refer solely to the financial health of the industry and possible factory closures (i.e., employment effects) and not to efficiency or cost–benefit considerations—is one that is widely held by the regulatory agencies. It is a position that will require an extensive legal and economic counterattack by the EOP in the coming years.

The insistence on yes–no answers (comparable to the regulatory search for safe thresholds in the pollution area) and the lack of interest in probability distributions are disturbing revelations from the fuel economy standards dispute. As noted, they are part of the general tendency by regulators to impose simple, dichotomous structures on a complex world.

The research–regulatory nexus, raised in the context of Brock

Adams's call for an automotive revolution, is also disturbing. If companies are going to be reluctant to do research, because the findings will immediately be used for regulatory purposes, the research effort of the United States will suffer. The long-run consequences of technology forcing regulation for the research effort of the country definitely need to be given more serious thought than they have received so far.

NHTSA has proposed two legislative modifications to the fuel economy standards. The first is to extend the carry-forward, carry-back provisions to three years rather than the current one year. This makes good sense. It should be accompanied by the removal of the provision that makes a shortfall a violation of the law; shortfalls should simply be penalized through the fee schedule. There is a precedent for this nonviolation approach in the Energy Tax Act of 1978.[13] Section 201 of that Act establishes a schedule, starting in the 1980 model year, of "gas guzzler" taxes (completely separate from the fuel economy standards) on individual cars that fail to meet specified fuel economy targets. The seller of an automobile that falls under the limit must pay the tax. There is no violation of the law involved. The same concept could easily be applied to the overall standards themselves.

NHTSA's second legislative proposal requires slightly more explanation. Beginning with the 1980 model year, Sec. 503(b)(1) of the Energy Policy and Conservation Act requires the manufacturers to group their North American production (United States and Canada) into one pool and their imports (e.g., G.M. Opels from Germany) into a separate pool. Each pool must meet the fuel economy standards independently; they cannot be combined or averaged together. This provision was a sop to the United Auto Workers, who feared that the U.S. manufacturers might build most of their small cars abroad and then import them as a balance against their domestic production of large cars; the provision effectively required the manufacturers to build their small cars in the United States also.

But the UAW had not anticipated that Volkswagen would begin production of Rabbits in the United States. This domestic production has led to the following dilemma: If VW produces all or most of its Rabbits in the United States, its remaining imports (e.g., Porsches, Audis) will not by themselves meet the fuel economy standards. To attain the necessary fuel economy average for its import pool, VW would have to produce fewer Rabbits in the United States and import more. *That* is not what the UAW had intended. In response, NHTSA proposed that any manufacturer who established domestic production after December 22, 1975 be exempted from the requirement of separate domestic and import pools.

Section 503(b)(1) of the Act clearly represents poor public policy. It is a protectionist provision, discouraging imports (except in the case of VW!). It is analogous to the nontariff trade barriers about which the United States complains when it finds them in place in Europe and Japan. The NHTSA proposal does not make it any better. The whole provision of the Act should be dropped.

NOTES TO CHAPTER 8

[1]P.L. 94-163.

[2]*Federal Register*, June 30, 1977, pp. 33534–33570.

[3]Later amendments allow the penalty under some circumstances to be as high as $10/0.1 mpg, but under most circumstances it would be $5/0.1 mpg.

[4]See L. J. White, *The Automobile Industry Since 1945* (Cambridge, Mass.: Harvard U.P., 1971), Chapter 11.

[5]Indeed, it is clear that General Motors embarked on the planning for its first round of down-sizing of automobiles well in advance of the passage of the Act or the establishment of the fuel economy standards.

[6]This second dispute was a simple variant on a standard economics problem: the index number problem. Fuel economy was a weighted average of individual models. The procedure changes affected different models differently. And the weights—the mix of models—changed between 1975 and 1979. Thus, both sides were right. But the manufacturers could not have been expected to have remained with their 1975 fleet mix or to have anticipated EPA's procedural changes. Accordingly, I thought that the manufacturers had a valid point.

[7]General Motors, though, did require the replacement catalyst on some of the early versions of its 1980 model X cars. These cars have since been recertified so as not to require the replacement.

[8]This struck me as too high (I initially used 5% and only halfway through the exercise learned that OMB required 10%), but those were the rules by which we all had to play.

[9]If, by contrast, the regulations were considered to be designed to protect consumers (i.e., somehow, consumers were not capable of making the proper comparisons of vehicle cost and gasoline saving for themselves), then a posttax gasoline price would have been the appropriate one.

[10]B. D. McNutt, H. T. McAdams, and R. Dulla, "Comparison of EPA and Inuse Fuel Economy Results for 1974–1978 Automobiles—An Analysis of Trends," *SAE Technical Paper*, #790932, October 1–4, 1979.

[11]I had even spent a morning with some automotive experts at a consulting firm, but, again, the problems were too specific.

[12]See *The New York Times*, August 2, 1979, p. 1.

[13]P.L. 95-618.

chapter 9

Premanufacture Notification for Chemical Production

How much information should be required from chemical manufacturers prior to the production of a new chemical?

Regulation requires information, which is usually collected from the regulated industry at the latter's expense. The paperwork burden of filling out forms for the regulators (and for other government agencies) has itself become recognized as a costly aspect of regulation. The type and extent of the information required by the regulators can also have a significant influence on the industry being regulated and the products that it produces. There are ways, however, of reducing the reporting burden without appreciably lessening the effectiveness of the ultimate regulatory control, as this chapter illustrates.

BACKGROUND

The Toxic Substances Control Act,[1] passed in 1976, gives EPA the power to regulate the manufacture and use of hazardous chemicals, to require testing of chemicals, and to require reports on the tests and on the quantities, uses, and exposures involved in the manufacture and use of the chemicals. There was a strong notion that too many dangerous chemicals were being manufactured, shipped, and used and misused without adequate controls. Too many people were being exposed to health risks, and too much damage was being done to the environment. The private tort–liability system was not dealing adequately with the problem.

Section 5 of the Act deals with the reporting system that would apply to the manufacture of new chemicals or of chemicals to be used in significantly new ways. Manufacturers are required to submit to EPA a notice 90 days in advance of commencing manufacture. On January 20, 1979, EPA published in the *Federal Register* an NPRM that fleshed out the reporting requirements under Sec. 5.[2] It indicated which manufacturers must report, when, and what they must report. And it contained the proposed report forms that would be required on test results, volume of manufacture, likely uses, likely transport, environmental effects, and benefits—30 pages worth! It invited comments by March 26.

These reporting rules did not deal directly with the tests and testing procedures that would be required for these chemicals but only with the reports that would have to be filed. The tests are covered by Section 4 of the Act and would be the subject of a separate NPRM by EPA, which it had not yet announced.

The EOP realized that the reporting regulations by themselves could significantly affect the chemical industry and particularly affect innovation in the industry. OMB's Regulatory Policy division was concerned about the regulatory burden on the industry (this was one of the few times that OMB became involved directly in a regulatory rulemaking) and about the forms themselves; OMB had responsibility for approving all report forms required by other agencies, and it felt that it had not been properly consulted. COWPS was concerned about the regulatory burden. CEA was asked in early March to join in the EOP effort to reason with EPA.

THE EPA POSITION

Section 5 called for premanufacture notification so that EPA could make the necessary decisions (under other sections of the Act) as to likely risks and the necessity for regulation before manufacturing began. It was always easier to establish regulatory procedures before manufacturing and use patterns had become settled, rather than after. To estimate these risks, EPA needed complete information. It needed to know about the chemical, any tests that had been done as to exposure effects, its method of manufacture, the exposure of individuals during manufacture, its use by processors, the exposure of individuals during processing, its use by end consumers, and their exposure. Since the chemical had not yet been manufactured or used, the manufacturers would have to provide their best guesses as to this information.

EPA recognized that there were costs involved in this reporting process. But a study done for the agency by a consulting firm indicated that these reporting costs were modest, probably running only $4-5 million per year for the entire industry.[3]

EPA had considered a number of alternatives: (1) establishing no rules and letting Sec. 5 speak for itself, (2) establishing notification rules but not forms, (3) establishing notification rules and forms, (4) establishing notification rules, forms, and necessary tests, or (5) establishing notification rules, forms, tests, and EPA decision rules. Although EPA preferred the last alternative, it was not yet prepared to establish the tests and decision rules. It believed that establishing the notification rules and forms eased EPA's administrative burden and made the ground rules more readily understandable to all.

THE CEA–COWPS POSITION

We recognized that dangerous chemicals did exist and that ounces of prevention probably were worth pounds of cures (and that Congress did give EPA regulatory powers in this area). But the particular reporting scheme that EPA had chosen was excessively burdensome, inflexible, and costly, and it could well damage the international competitiveness of the chemical industry. EPA had badly underestimated the costs of the reporting scheme and had not yet addressed the question of testing and its costs. And EPA had not performed the proper marginal calculations to determine the consequences of changes in the reporting scheme.

EPA was requiring a huge amount of information for every chemical, regardless of its nature or likely use. For many harmless chemicals, this kind of reporting simply was not necessary. EPA's consultants estimated that completing the entire report would cost the manufacturers between $9,000 and $42,000 per chemical. The expected profits of most chemicals were small enough that the lower figure was likely to lead to a 50% reduction and the higher figure was likely to lead to a 90% reduction in the number of new commercial chemicals introduced each year. These percentages meant that the flow of roughly 1,000 new chemicals per year would be diminished to 500 or 100. And these estimates did not include any extra cost burden that EPA's testing regulations, yet to be announced, might require.

Further, it was far from clear that EPA had the staff capabilities to handle the massive amount of information that would be flowing in. If not, then either there would be delays or the manufacturer's efforts would have been wasted.

The Act required 90 days' notice. It also allowed EPA, for good cause, to delay for another 90 days the date on which manufacture or processing could occur. Already, then, the delay could be as much as a half year. EPA's proposed rules raised the possibility of further delay. EPA could suspend the notification period for another 30 days if there were minor problems (e.g., typographical errors that rendered the notice ambiguous). More important, EPA could declare a notice invalid if it judged that the notice contained inadequate or incorrect information. Such a declaration would force the manufacturer to start all over again. These possibilities of added delay meant added risks and added costs for the manufacturer.

The manufacturers themselves were also complaining that the rules were burdensome because they (the manufacturers) were not in a good position to estimate likely exposure during processing and final use of a chemical that had not yet been produced. But it seemed unavoidable that someone would have to estimate that exposure. EPA could have spread its net of notices and respondents much wider to include processors and end-users; but that would have been an administrative nightmare. The chemical manufacturers, who presumably had an estimate of the market for which their chemical was intended, were the logical candidates. (There need to be assurances in such regulations, however, that, if the estimates are made in good faith, the manufacturers will not subsequently be held accountable or liable for unexpected processing, uses, or exposure.)

The manufacturers were also concerned about the loss of confidentiality that could result if EPA released information (e.g., its exact chemical composition) about the new chemical. They had legitimate fears concerning competitive impacts and long-run effects on innovation as a consequence of information being made public. On the other hand, there was a clear public interest in releasing some of this information, particularly in the context of health and safety studies of the new chemical. A balancing of the two sets of concerns was necessary. EPA was aware of this need for balancing; it had devoted a substantial part of the preamble to the NPRM to the confidentiality question and had explained when it would and would not disclose information. But, we argued, EPA had not adequately explored the consequences of its disclosure rules and of possible alternatives on these two sets of concerns.

The costs that EPA attributed to the regulation were only the costs of compiling the reports for the 100 to 500 new chemicals that would continue to appear each year. EPA did not count as costs the loss to the economy of the 500 to 900 new chemicals a year that would not be developed because of the reporting burden. The value of this loss might be quite high. (EPA's initial response to this point was, "Oh, all the new chemicals are just close substitutes for existing ones. The ones that will fall by the wayside will not be much of a loss.") The costs also might drive a number of firms out of the industry (causing an increase in concentration) and raise barriers to entry. The remaining firms might collude more easily, raising prices.

Further, the international position of the chemical industry might be hurt. Although the rules applied equally to imported chemicals, they obviously did not apply to chemicals produced abroad and sold abroad. Although the rules would not discourage the domestic production of a chemical with a large expected sales, they would discourage those with small expected sales. But there is always a large band of uncertainty around the likely sales of a chemical. Some chemicals with small expected sales may turn out to be large sellers. Chemical companies abroad (in the absence of similar regulations) would not be discouraged from producing these unexpected "late bloomers" for foreign markets, whereas domestic companies would be discouraged. The former would then be in a position to market these chemicals in the United States and at that point could easily and inexpensively meet the data requirements for U.S. sales, since the foreign manufacturers would have experience and an established data base for the chemical. American chemical companies would lose ground vis-à-vis foreign companies and/or move more of their operations abroad.

Testing procedures, yet to be announced by EPA, would surely add an additional burden. It was difficult to judge the overall consequences of the notice program without having a better idea of the testing rules. And, finally, EPA simply had made no effort to determine the marginal consequences of alternative reporting requirements.

As an alternative to this inflexible program, we urged a two-stage reporting process. EPA would require a small amount of information for all new chemicals. It would then make some quick decisions based on chemical structure and likely toxicity (Is this chemical close, say, to table salt or to kepone?) and simple exposure data (Will 30 people be exposed, or 3,000?). Chemicals unlikely to be toxic and with low exposure would receive no more attention (unless something unexpected subsequently occurred); producers of chemicals likely to be highly toxic and involve wide exposure would be asked for a lot more information. Categories in between would require intermediate amounts of information. The requirements for testing could be established along the same lines. This approach would mean that EPA would have to make more decisions at earlier stages in the regulatory process. But it would reduce EPA's overall information-handling burdens.

An extension of this approach would lead EPA to develop a generic policy, in which specified classes of chemicals would be expected to receive specified responses by EPA in testing, notification, and regulatory treatment. This policy would aid the chemical industry in its planning for the development of new chemicals.

These ideas were eventually conveyed in written form to EPA on March 26 in a COWPS staff report, drafted by the COWPS staff. The COWPS staff report was a less formal document than was a COWPS filing; it was a report provided for EPA's consideration, rather than one representing the official position of COWPS. Nevertheless, it served the function of getting these ideas on the record, so that they could be the basis for post-comment period discussions.

THE OUTCOME

As of this writing, EPA has not issued a final set of regulations on this matter. It has indicated to the EOP, however, that it would try to develop a two-stage notification procedure that would be reproposed in a new NPRM.

CONCLUDING COMMENTS

EPA's initial proposal was typical of many regulatory agencies' initial approach to this kind of problem: Make as few distinctions as possible, avoid decisions that are not absolutely necessary, and require the full regulatory response from all who are covered by the regulatory mandate. It is another example of the agency's efforts to impose an overly simplified structure (with too few categories) on a complex world. We had become sensitized to this approach a few months earlier by an OSHA proposal (which received a RARG review) to deal with worker exposure to carcinogenic substances. OSHA wanted to characterize all substances with which workers were likely to have contact as either noncarcinogenic or carcinogenic. If a substance fell into the latter category, the required response was the same in all cases: Employers should reduce worker exposure to the greatest extent possible. OSHA paid no attention to potency or to exposure (and little attention was paid to costs); the world was simply divided into two categories, and the full treatment was required for all substances in the second category. The RARG report pointed out that the world was much more complex and that potency and exposure did matter in deciding which were the serious hazards that required immediate and expensive attention and which were not. It suggested a generic approach to the problem.[4] The COWPS staff report on chemical premanufacture notification was a natural extension of the generic approach.

The CEA–COWPS–OMB role in this dispute was productive. The final rules on premanufacture notification should be more flexible and

143

more sensible. Costs should drop appreciably, and the effects on innovation should not be nearly as severe, while EPA's ability to deal with really serious chemical hazards should not be diminished appreciably.

NOTES TO CHAPTER 9

[1]P.L. 94-469.

[2]*Federal Register*, January 20, 1979, pp. 2242–2313.

[3]Arthur D. Little, Inc., *Impact of TSCA Proposed Premanufacturing Notification Requirements*, prepared for U.S. Environmental Protection Agency, Office of Planning and Evaluation, Washington, D.C., December 1978.

[4]The final OSHA regulations were somewhat more flexible than the NPRM. See *Federal Register*, January 22, 1980, pp. 5001–5296.

chapter 10

Abandoned Chemical Dumps and Spills of Hazardous Substances

What should be the content of the administration's bill to deal with the problems of abandoned chemical dumps and spills of hazardous substances?

The previous chapters have focused on rulemakings and other agency actions taken under the authority of existing laws. As was indicated, these laws often prescribe or proscribe certain specific actions or criteria, which in turn put limits on the improvements in regulation that the EOP can achieve through direct pressure on the agencies. The drafting of new regulatory legislation to deal with new problems provides a rare opportunity for shaping future regulatory actions. It is far better to insert the criteria for sensible regulation directly into a law than to try to suggest them in subsequent rulemaking. This chapter provides an example of the drafting of a major piece of environmental legislation.

BACKGROUND

During the 1970s the spills of hazardous substances—primarily oil, but occasionally other chemicals—came to be recognized as a serious environmental problem. Section 311 of the Clean Water Act[1] gave EPA and the Coast Guard (located administratively within the Department of Transportation) authority to try to prevent these spills and to deal with their consequences. By 1978 both organizations had concluded that their authority was still too limited. Too many spills were still occurring, and it took too long to arrange for cleanup. Also, the two organizations were limited to spills in waterways or spills that threatened waterways. Spills on dry land were not technically covered, although EPA had been ingenious in finding threats to waterways from spills far away (but it was worried about legal challenges to its creative behavior).

In late 1978, the problem of abandoned chemical dumps attained front-page and prime-time public attention. One case in particular, that of Hooker Chemical Company's past chemical dumping in the Love Canal area of Niagra Falls, New York, attracted a great deal of public attention, although the existence of many other dump sites was soon evident. Chemicals leaking from these sites threatened public water supplies, recreation areas, and sometimes even individuals' homes. Ownership of the sites was either unknown or legally cloudy. The dumpers of the chemicals were frequently unknown. There was no one that affected parties could sue. Although EPA's responsibility under the Resource Conservation and Recovery Act of 1976[2] for dumps in operation was clear, its authority to deal with abandoned dumps and to take cleanup action was uncertain.

PRELIMINARY ACTIVITIES

In January 1979, EPA, the Coast Guard, and the Department of Justice formed a task force to study the problem of spills and abandoned dumps, the legal remedies at hand, and the possible need for new legislation. In March 1979, the Coast Guard, with administration approval, sent to Congress a proposed bill to deal with oil spills into coastal and inland waters. An annual levy of up to 3¢ per barrel (bbl) of oil refined or imported was proposed, to be used to finance any emergency response, the rapid containment and cleanup of spills, and the payment of limited amounts of financial restitution to parties damaged by the spills. The fund was not intended to replace the private tort–liability system but to hasten the remedial actions that would (presumably) occur anyway.

In April, the three-agency task force produced a report concluding that the problem of spills and dumps was serious and that new legislation was necessary. The three agencies produced a draft of an omnibus spills and abandoned dumps bill and circulated it for agency comment. A series of interagency meetings on the bill took place in early May. They were chaired by OMB and attended by staff from EPA, Coast Guard, the Departments of Justice, Commerce, Treasury, State, and Interior, the Council on Environmental Quality, COWPS, and CEA. The meetings clarified the issues and the divisions among the agencies.

THE PROPOSED BILL

The task force's bill incorporated the March Coast Guard bill and brought all spills and abandoned dumps under one regime. A "super fund" would be created, financed by a combination of general tax revenues, the annual 3¢/bbl fee on petroleum, and specific annual fees on organic chemicals (petrochemical feedstocks) and inorganic chemicals. After a few years of gradual build up, the super fund would have $500 million in annual revenues flowing into it: $100 million from general revenues, $100 million from petroleum, and $300 million from chemicals. The program had an overall limit of $6 billion, so it would run for 12 to 15 years. The super fund would be administered by EPA.

In the event of spills, if the spilling party or parties did not take rapid action to contain, clean up, and reimburse third parties for damages, the super fund could be used for these purposes. The coverage was

147

broader than that of the earlier bill, since it covered spills of all hazardous substances (not just oil) into all environments (not just water) from vehicles, as well as leaks from storage tanks. Again, it was not intended to replace the tort–liability system but to hasten its outcome. The fund was expected to recover its outlays from the liable parties and thus preserve the incentive for those parties to prevent the leaks and spills.

In the case of abandoned dumps, the fund was authorized to spend monies for emergency responses and containment. Payments for damages were not authorized, nor was cleanup or removal of the hazardous wastes unless these actions were the most cost-effective method of containment. Since, by definition, there usually was no one to sue in the case of an abandoned dump, the monies were not expected to be recovered.

THE ARGUMENTS IN FAVOR OF THE BILL

The three drafting agencies plus the Council on Environmental Quality and OMB argued that spills and abandoned dumps had become a serious enough problem to warrant a large program. There were thousands of abandoned dumps that would have to be surveyed, and EPA estimated that as many as 1,200 dumps would require containment actions. EPA also estimated that over 2,000 spills per year (involving more than 100 gallons at a time) of non-oil hazardous chemicals were occurring.

The fee on petroleum (3¢/bbl) was a tiny tax on oil selling for $20.00/bbl; the fee had not generated significant political opposition when it had been proposed a few months earlier. The public perception was that the chemical companies were responsible for the chemicals in the abandoned dumps, and hence it was proper that there should be fees on chemical products. EPA and the Coast Guard needed the funds and the authority to react quickly in the event of spills or dangerous leakages from abandoned dumps, to prevent serious damage from occurring or spreading. One could expect the agencies to be sensible in their actions and the way in which they undertook them. Further, with the threat of having to pay for the cost of an EPA or Coast Guard cleaning effort after a spill or leak, some companies would more readily carry out the cleaning task themselves, since they would expect to be able to do it more cheaply.

THE CRITIQUE OF THE BILL

CEA, COWPS, and the Treasury and Commerce departments were uneasy concerning the size and scope of the bill. We recognized that there were genuine environmental problems connected with spills and leaks and abandoned dumps. But the bill in its proposed form appeared to be a hasty overreaction.

First, the fees for the super fund were inefficient and appeared to be levied on the wrong agents. Spills occurred from vehicles, not from refineries; fees should be levied on oil and chemical transportation companies, not on refineries. Fees on chemicals would lead to distortions and inefficient substitutions of chemical inputs. And it was far from clear that the current chemical companies (except in the case of Hooker Chemical) were the sources of the chemicals in the abandoned dumps. Perhaps present or past chemical users were the sources; perhaps past chemical companies that had gone out of business were the sources. (Despite our repeated raising of this question, no one really knew the sources of the chemicals.) Also, we reminded the others, the chemical companies would likely not be the ultimate payers; rather, it was the final consumers of chemical products who would largely bear the cost. The creation of the super fund itself meant that a pot of money would come into existence, with greater pressures to spend it. Congress would scrutinize these expenditures less closely than expenditures out of general revenues. If abandoned dumps were a general social problem, appropriations from general tax revenues, without the creation of a special super fund, were the best source of funds for dealing with them.

Second, the program was too large and ambitious. A smaller program, with an early appraisal of the problems and the efficiency of the program in dealing with them, seemed more appropriate.

Third, there were no restrictions on *how much* cleanup in the event of spills, or containment in the case of abandoned dumps, should be undertaken. The bill only mentioned that these actions should be cost effective. But this only meant that shovels, not teaspoons, should be used in cleanup efforts. But should every last drop of chemical be removed from a spill site? Should containment of leakages from dumps protect against once-in-2,000-year floods? There needed to be some weighing of costs and benefits in the decisions as to how far to go in cleaning up or containing. There were estimates that it would take over $1 billion to clean up the kepone that had been spilled into the James

River by the Allied Chemical Company between 1971 and 1975. With the costs that high, cleaning up the river was probably not worthwhile. Although the bill explicitly excluded past spills from its coverage, future incidents of this nature might occur. Although the companies should certainly be penalized severely for imposing on society the costs implicit in spills, it might not be worthwhile to undertake cleanup actions or to pursue them to 100% removal. There needed to be some balancing.[3]

Fourth, the reimbursement for damages from spills appeared to be unwarranted. One could see an argument for the need for public funds for a quick response in containment and cleanup, to prevent damage from spreading while parties argued over who was really liable (e.g., as the result of a collision). But why use public funds for reimbursement of damages? That was what the private tort–liability system was for. If that system was not performing properly, it should be reformed; but circumventing it in this fashion was not good policy. A new set of administrative law judges within the super fund hierarchy would decide on the merits of claims of damages, replacing the regular court system. Maybe this system would hasten adjudications, but maybe not. Further, the reimbursement provision set a bad precedent. Congress might extend it to the dumps part of the bill, where the potential for claims was unknown but might extend to many billions of dollars. The federal treasury was simply not prepared for this burden.

SUBSEQUENT ACTIONS

Some of these criticisms were heeded and changes in the proposed bill were made early in the process. An early form of the fees on chemicals was modified to reduce (but not eliminate) the distortions that might occur. Language was inserted to force EPA to develop criteria for deciding how far to pursue cleanup and containment. But the size of the program and the fees on chemicals remained as major issues. (The fee on refineries rather than on vehicles and the reimbursement for damages were issues the fate of which was decided when the initial bill was sent to Congress in March; the administration apparently could not retreat from these positions.)

CEA and COWPS (with support from Commerce and Treasury) continued to press on these issues and proposed an overall program of $1.6 billion, phased over four years, with general revenues replacing the fees on chemicals and the fund for spills kept separate from the fund for dumps. Eventually, OMB was convinced and endorsed the idea. Isolated at this point, EPA also reluctantly agreed to it. It appeared that we had pulled the entire administration over to our side on this important point.

THE OUTCOME

In early June the President was briefed on the proposed bill and the major issues that were involved. He decided that fees on chemicals were the proper way to finance the fund for abandoned dumps. The original financing formula was reinstated, though the program was kept to four years.

On June 13 the administration announced its program on spills and dumps, and the next day the administration bill was introduced in the Congress as S. 1341. It called for a $1.6 billion program over four years, with a single super fund financed from general revenues and from fees on oil and chemicals. Reimbursement for damages from spills was included, but so was the language calling for criteria to determine the extent of cleanup and containment. The bill languished for nine months. Then, in the spring of 1980, renewed concern for the health of the residents of Love Canal sparked a renewed interest in the spills and dumps bill. As of this writing, however, the Congress had not taken any final action on the bill.

CONCLUDING COMMENTS

CEA and COWPS made a number of valuable contributions to the bill, although we ultimately lost in the effort to eliminate the excise tax on chemicals. The bill is definitely better than the initial proposal.

A serious failure on our part, however, was our lack of involvement much earlier in the development of the bill. Membership on the task force that studied the spills and dumps problem might have allowed us to shape a number of issues earlier. But apparently no one at CEA or COWPS was aware of the earlier task force or the initial drafting of the bill. This was not a case in which information was deliberately kept from us, but simply a matter of our not being part of the circle of agencies to be included automatically.

If CEA and COWPS wish to have a greater influence in similar

151

matters in the future, they will somehow have to formalize a procedure whereby they are automatically notified of such task forces and invited to join. This sounds easy. But, in fact, with a large, diverse government and small, overstretched CEA and COWPS staffs, it may be very difficult to achieve in practice.

NOTES TO CHAPTER 10

[1] 33 U.S.C. 466.

[2] P.L. 94-580.

[3] The proper criterion, of course, would be to extend cleanup only to the point at which social marginal costs equal social marginal benefits. But this was much too specific (and too controversial) for any piece of environmental legislation; thus, a less specific call for balancing and for the development of criteria to guide cleanup decisions was the best we could do.

chapter 11

Tellico Dam and the Snail Darter

Should the Tennessee Valley Authority be allowed to complete construction of the Tellico Dam and possibly cause the extinction of the snail darter fish?

Economic analysis is often thought to be antagonistic toward environmental considerations; the intangible benefits of environmental improvements are thought to escape the economist's calculus. This need not be the case. Cost-effectiveness calculations can demonstrate the least costly way of achieving environmental benefits; these calculations also show the minimum implicit value (in terms of foregone resources) that society must put on these benefits in order to find them worth pursuing. And good economic analysis—especially cost–benefit analysis, done properly—can reveal the lack of worth of some projects that might have unfavorable environmental consequences, as the Tellico Dam example discussed in this chapter demonstrates.

BACKGROUND

Construction of the Tellico Dam on the Little Tennessee River in Tennessee was first considered by the Tennessee Valley Authority in 1936 and received periodic consideration for the next 30 years. The dam, its proponents argued, would provide electricity, flood control, recreational opportunities, and industrial development opportunities. In 1966, Congress approved the initial appropriation, and construction began in 1967.

The Endangered Species Preservation Act was first passed in 1966 and was amended in 1969 and again in 1973.[1] The second amendment added Section 7, which precluded all federal agencies from authorizing, funding, or carrying out any action that might jeopardize an endangered or threatened species or its habitat.

As early as 1971 it was suspected that the snail darter, a small perchlike fish living only in the Little Tennessee River and requiring the fast-flowing river to spawn and survive, might be endangered by the completion of the Tellico Dam. The fish was eventually listed as an endangered species by the Fish and Wildlife Service of the Department of the Interior in October 1975. In February 1976 a private suit was brought to stop construction of the dam. The suit failed in the federal district court but was appealed to the sixth Circuit Court of Appeals, which issued an injunction in July preventing TVA from closing the dam (but allowing other construction to proceed). In October, DOI issued a biological opinion that the continued existence of the snail darter would be jeopardized and its critical habitat destroyed if the dam were closed. In January 1977, the Sixth Circuit reversed the district court, holding that the Endangered Species Act prevented TVA from completing the dam. The Supreme Court eventually upheld this decision in June 1978.[2] The high court's decision was greeted by much public derision and disbelief that a small, economically worthless fish could prevent the completion of a $100 million dam.

In the fall of 1978, Congress (at the principal urging of Senator Howard Baker of Tennessee) passed yet another set of amendments to the Act,[3] which established procedures for exemptions from the Act (to allow projects to be completed) and provided for special accelerated consideration of the Tellico project and one other project (the Grayrocks Dam in Wyoming, which threatened the nesting places of the whooping crane).

PROCEDURES FOR EXEMPTIONS

The 1978 amendments established a seven-member committee:

The Chairman of CEA

The Secretary of Agriculture

The Secretary of the Army

The Secretary of the Interior

The Administrator of the National Oceanic and Atmospheric Administration (within the Department of Commerce)

The Administrator of EPA

A representative from the area affected by the project

The committee could grant exemptions from the Act, allowing a project to be completed that might thereby lead to the extinction of a species, if five or more of the committee voted to do so. The criteria for granting an exemption were (1) that there were no reasonable and prudent alternatives to the proposed action, (2) that the benefits of the proposed action clearly outweighed the benefits of alternatives that would be consistent with conserving the species or its critical habitat, and (3) that the project was in the public interest.

The amendments established a special 90-day deadline for consideration of the Tellico and Grayrocks dams. Thus, the committee had only until early February 1979. If action were not taken by then, the projects would automatically gain exemptions and could be completed.

According to DOI's interpretation of the law, the committee was unique in that, unlike most other interagency task forces or committees, the principals themselves had to be at the final meeting in order to vote; they could not send deputies or convey their vote by mail or telephone. And the final meeting would be open to the public.

PRELIMINARY ACTION

DOI staff members served as staff to the committee. In December a number of staff-level meetings were held, at which the staff of the relevant agencies attended. The background, issues, and procedures were laid out and documents were distributed. DOI indicated that it would hold public hearings on the two projects. And DOI staff would develop the major analyses. The role of the remaining staff members of the committee was to contribute where we could and make sure that our principals were thoroughly briefed for the final meeting, which would be on January 23, 1979.[4]

THE CASE AGAINST THE DAM

DOI's economists, using data provided by TVA, did the main analysis of the social worth of the dam.

The dam was roughly 80% completed; about $35 million in dam construction and supporting roads and highways remained. But the gates had not been closed; the Little Tennessee still flowed over a spillway into Watts Bar Lake below. (Because the river had been channeled through the spillway, the force of the current was now too strong to allow the snail darters to migrate upstream from Watts Bar Lake into the Little Tennessee; TVA personnel had been collecting them in the lake and physically transporting them into the river.)

When the dam was completed, the gates would be closed, and the newly formed reservoir would then empty into neighboring Fort Loudon Dam. The new reservoir would allow a little more electricity to be generated at that latter dam and a little more flood control to be achieved down river at Chattanooga. There would be added recreational opportunities on the newly formed lake and possibly some good industrial sites created (since there would be a confluence of good rail, highway, and water transportation opportunities). DOI estimated the total of these benefits to be worth $6.5 million per year.

Offsetting these benefits, the closing of the gates would flood valuable farmland; it would destroy a ten-mile stretch of an exceptionally high-quality, cold-water fast-flowing river; it would flood some important Indian archeological sites; and it might lead to the extinction of the snail darter. On this last point, TVA had made an effort to transplant snail darters into the neighboring Hiwassee and Holton Rivers. The transplants appeared to be successful, but biologists claimed that another 5–15 years were necessary before the snail darters' success in these new habitats was assured. Also, a chemical spill from a railroad derailment near the Hiwassee had wiped out a large number of the transplanted fish in that river. It was hypothesized that the snail darters may have originally lived in these other rivers but that chemical spills may have wiped them out.

From a narrow economic perspective, the critical point was that the farmland had not yet been flooded. This land still counted as an opportunity cost of the dam. Its annualized value, along with the annualized value of the remaining construction costs (the construction costs already incurred were properly treated as sunk and not affecting the decision) and future repair and maintenance expenses, came to $7.5 million. Thus, even though the dam was 80% completed and the sunk costs were ignored, it still could not pass a cost–benefit test, largely because that valuable farmland had remained unflooded. The dam had clearly been a losing proposition at its conception and was still a losing proposition even now.

The best alternative appeared to be to punch a hole in the dam (which would reduce the water pressure in the existing spillway and allow the snail darter to migrate upstream by itself) and build a few of the necessary connecting roads that still needed to be built. TVA, which had begun to have second thoughts about the dam, had suggested another option, which involved punching the hole in the dam but then spending additional sums to develop the recreational potential of the river.

The Tellico Dam thus failed all three criteria necessary for exemption: There were reasonable and prudent alternatives to the project; the benefits of the project did not clearly outweigh the benefits of alternatives; and the dam did not seem to be in the public interest.

The DOI case was quite thorough and persuasive. And the case against the dam had the gratifying property that one did not have to worry about the snail darter or try to trade off snail darters against economic benefits. The dam fell of its own weighty demerits.

The CEA Chairman received a long internal CEA memo on the

issue and was briefed shortly before the meeting. Calls were made to the other staff representatives to ascertain their agencies' likely votes. Interior and EPA seemed solidly against granting an exemption for the dam; Agriculture and NOAA would probably vote against it also; only Army (the home of the Corps of Engineers) seemed in favor. No one knew how the representative from Tennessee would vote.

THE OUTCOME

The meeting of principals was held as scheduled on January 23. After a brief discussion of the project, the CEA Chairman made the motion that the dam be denied the exemption. The motion carried unanimously. Because of CEA's apparent hard-line position on other environmental issues in the past, CEA had gained a reputation among environmental groups as an inflexibly antienvironmentalist organization. Our position on the dam and the snail darter certainly helped soften that image.

The committee's decision and the justification for it did not convince everyone, however. During the 1979 session of Congress Senator Baker introduced amendments to the Endangered Species Act that would override the committee's decision and permit TVA to complete the dam. In September these amendments were passed by both Houses of Congress. The President decided to sign the bill. Shortly afterward, construction on the Tellico Dam resumed, and in November the gates were closed and the farmland behind the dam began to flood. The fate of the snail darter now depends on whether the environment in the neighboring rivers proves favorable. Whether the snail darter can survive in the neighboring rivers may not be known for a decade.

CONCLUDING REMARKS

The Tellico Dam initially appeared to be another economics vs. environment issue. At closer inspection this view proved to be incorrect. The same was the case in the Grayrocks Dam problem, decided at the same time. That dam, built for electricity and irrigation benefits, threatened the nesting sites of whooping cranes downstream on the Platte River. There are only 100–120 whooping cranes in existence, with 69 at that site. The cranes like to nest on sandbars far from vegetation. The natural spring flooding of the Platte River regularly wipes out the vegetation close to the crane's usual nesting spot. It was feared that the Grayrocks Dam would reduce the water levels, encouraging the growth of vegetation and discouraging the cranes from nesting. The solution, worked out in a compromise ahead of time, was to set up a modest trust fund to finance the mechanical (with bulldozers) removal of any threatening vegetation during the part of the year when the cranes were elsewhere. The committee's only problem was to find the best way legally within the framework of the Endangered Species Act to ratify this compromise. (There have been no legislative efforts to overturn this compromise.)

Most apparent endangered species conflicts are probably capable of being resolved in the ways indicated by the Tellico and Grayrocks examples. Either the projects will be found not to be worthwhile in the first place or there will be low-cost alternatives that will preserve the species and the project. True conflicts are unlikely. Whether the political process will allow them to be resolved in these ways, however, is a different question.

Despite the solid economic case against completing the Tellico Dam, it is nevertheless being completed. Some in Congress did not believe or understand the case; others saw the distributional consequences—giving heavy weight to those who would benefit from the dam's completion—as outweighing the efficiency considerations. This is certainly not the first time that a bad dam has been completed, and it is unlikely to be the last.

NOTES TO CHAPTER 11

[1]P.L. 89-699, P.L. 91-135, and P.L. 93-205.

[2]*Tennessee Valley Authority* v. *Hill,* 437 U.S. 153 (1978).

[3]P.L. 95-632.

[4]DOI had a reputation for being extremely (some thought excessively) concerned with procedures and with openness in government. This was borne out by my experience. One long (two-hour) staff-level meeting was devoted entirely to the procedures that would be followed at the January 23 meeting: Parliamentary procedures would be followed, there would be no staff recommendations so it would be up to one of the committee members to make a motion to take action, the table for the committee members would be arranged on the stage of the auditorium in the following manner, and so on. At one point I asked if there would be a recording of the whoop of the whooping crane before the Grayrocks Dam was discussed. "No," the DOI staff member replied with a straight face, "but we will show slides of the snail darter and the whooping crane at the meeting." And they did!

part IV

OLD-STYLE ECONOMIC REGULATION

chapter **12**

Regulation of the Maritime Industry

What should the Carter administration's policy be toward regulation of the maritime industry?

The deregulation of the airlines and of rail and truck transportation has been an important part of the Carter administration's efforts at regulatory reform. Procompetitive board members have been appointed to the Civil Aeronautics Board; the deregulation of the domestic airline industry and the partial deregulation of trucking have been achieved; the United States has adopted procompetitive positions in negotations over international airline routes; procompetitive commissioners have been appointed to the Interstate Commerce Committee; and the administration has endorsed rail deregulation legislation in Congress. The logic of these positions would seem to carry over to the deregulation of ocean shipping. As this chapter indicates, however, the Carter administration decided otherwise.

BACKGROUND

The Regulatory Regime

The maritime industry can be divided into three segments: liners, bulk carriers, and tankers. The first group, general freight carriers, carries goods that are usually shipped in less than shipload quantities—either as break bulk or, increasingly, as containerized freight.[1] In international shipping, this is the group that is subject to regulation, and this is the group for which the Carter administration had to make a major policy decision in 1979.

The international liner trade routes are served by companies that offer regularly scheduled service and by tramp steamers that offer more irregular service. On most trade routes, most of the companies offering scheduled service are organized into shipping conferences—cartels of companies that jointly set shipping rates and terms of service. This is a long-established practice, begun before the turn of the century. Most countries, with a much weaker antitrust tradition than that of the United States, have welcomed and encouraged the conferences. Between some countries, the conferences are closed (so that new companies cannot join), liner shipping is restricted to the conferences, the conference members pool their revenues, and the conferences can jointly set not only shipping rates but also shipping schedules ("rationalizing" schedules).

The U.S. attitude toward conferences has been more ambivalent. We permit them, but we regulate them. We are unique in our efforts at regulation. The Shipping Act of 1916,[2] as amended over the years, provides the basic structure for American treatment of liner shipping to and from the United States. It authorizes the Federal Maritime Commission (FMC) to regulate the conferences (consisting of American flag and foreign flag companies) that are involved in the shipment of goods to and from American ports. Conference agreements are supposed to be filed with FMC. If FMC approves them, they are exempt from the antitrust laws. FMC then has the responsibility for enforcing the agreements. There are limitations to the agreements: They cannot be unjustly discriminatory to carriers, shippers, or ports or to American exporters vis-à-vis their foreign competitors, and they cannot operate to the detriment of U.S. commerce. The conferences are to remain open; that is, anyone can join them. Also, anyone can offer service to or from American ports without joining a conference. Conferences have not been permitted jointly to allocate sailings. Generally, the legal test for agreements that has been developed by FMC and the courts is the *Svenska* test: "The proponents of an agreement must demonstrate that the agreement is necessary to accomplish a serious transportation need or public benefit, and that there is no less anticompetitive method available for accomplishing that purpose."[3]

FMC has permitted "dual-rate" contracts: contracts that give a shipper a lower rate if the shipper promises to ship only on the vessels of conference members and a higher rate if the shipper does not follow this exclusive dealing arrangement. But FMC does not allow deferred rebates: rebates for shipping only on conference lines, which are only available to a shipper after a period of time in which the shipper has demonstrated loyalty.

Although FMC could refuse to approve a conference agreement because the proposed rates were too low or too high, it almost never has. Thus, unlike other old-style economic regulatory agencies such as the CAB or the ICC, it does not make a pretense of trying to limit industry profits to a specified rate of return through price regulation. Also unlike the other agencies it does not control entry onto the transportation routes.

A large part of FMC's regulatory activity is spent trying to prevent rebating (price cutting) in one form or another. The conference members are supposed to adhere to the conference agreements, which specify shipping rates. The liner companies are free to leave the conferences, but while they are members they are supposed to adhere to the agreements and not cut prices. The FMC has the responsibility for policing the price agreements, detecting illegal rebating, and fining the transgressors.

The Industry

The American flag liner industry generally has not fared particularly well in the past two or three decades. The industry is heavily subsidized. Nine of the eleven American flag firms receive "operating differential subsidies" (administered by the Maritime Administration, located within the Department of Commerce) to allow them to be competitive vis-à-vis foreign shipping firms who pay lower wages and have lower costs. The American flag firms also receive tax subsidies. Fifty percent of all government-generated cargoes (e.g., Defense Department shipments) are supposed to be shipped in American bottoms (if available). And those companies that are also in the U.S. intercoastal trade (cabotage) are completely protected from foreign competition on those intercoastal routes.

Despite this pattern of subsidy and protection, the U.S. companies have barely managed to hold their own in the U.S. trade routes since the mid-1950s, keeping about a 30% share of the annual liner tonnage to and from the United States. And this total annual tonnage has been stagnant for 25 years, remaining in the vicinity of 50 million tons per year. In 1978, two of the American liner firms went bankrupt, and two others were up for sale.

Two liner companies—Sea-Land and U.S. Lines—were relatively healthy, however, despite their decisions to abstain from the operating differential subsidy system. Both were heavily involved in containerized shipping, which Sea-Land pioneered in the 1950s. For American firms at the leading edge of the industry's technology, the picture did not look so bad.

The companies in the industry and their employees' unions have been strong political forces in Washington. On most issues they are joined by the shipbuilding companies and their unions. The maritime lobby is a powerful one. It has pushed hard for, and often succeeded in getting, substantial economic protection and financial subsidies.

The Task Force

In the spring of 1978 the Carter administration established a task force to reexamine the federal government's regulatory and promotional (subsidy) stance toward the industry. The task force included representatives from the Departments of Commerce (MarAd), Defense, Labor, Justice (Antitrust Division), State, Treasury, and Transportation, the National Security Council, FMC, OMB, COWPS, and CEA. It was chaired by the Domestic Policy Staff. Its charge was to develop a comprehensive maritime policy for the United States and to recommend changes in the laws. Established policies were being changed in other transportation areas: air, truck, rail. It was appropriate to reexamine the maritime industry.

PRELIMINARY ACTIVITIES

Besides the industry's general unhappiness over its financial plight, it had two specific complaints with respect to the competition it faced. First, nonconference liners operated by state-owned companies from Eastern bloc countries (primarily the Soviet Union) were substantially undercutting conference rates and attracting a significant amount of traffic away from the conferences. Second, within the conferences, the American flag companies strongly suspected that the foreign flag carriers were secretly offering rebates to many customers, thus violating conference and FMC rules. But FMC's powers to subpoena records and obtain evidence from foreign flag carriers were limited by U.S. law and international sovereignty. The European governments were not at all disturbed by the rebating. Their endorsement of conferences and also of selective rebating was not contradictory; it was an expression of support for the practice of price discrimination—charging different prices to different customers. By contrast, U.S. policy in all fields has generally looked upon price discrimination as an undesirable practice that confers an unfair advantage to those who receive the lower prices.[4]

In response to these complaints, the Congress in October 1978 passed two bills. The first bill gave FMC the power to establish minimum rates for Eastern bloc nonconference liners. Thus, for the first time FMC acquired some direct rate-setting powers. The second bill strengthened FMC's power to move against foreign flag conference rebaters by strengthening its subpoena powers and giving it the power to deny access to American ports to companies that did not respond adequately to its requests for information.

CEA urged the President to veto both bills. The argument against the first was straightforward: The competition from the Eastern bloc lines was a good thing. It meant lower prices and better service for customers. The argument against the second was a bit more complicated. Rebating was not only a form of price discrimination but a form of price competition and hence should be encouraged, not discouraged. Admittedly the existing legal structure operated somewhat unfairly against American flag firms, since FMC's powers to stop them from rebating were clearly stronger than were its powers vis-à-vis the foreign flag companies. Still, it was arguable whether the even-handed administration of an unwise policy represented an improvement. And, because the American flag firms knew that they were more constrained in rebating than were their fellow (but foreign) conference members, it was probably the case that they argued within the conferences for lower conference rates. (Also the State Department was concerned about the diplomatic aspects of shutting foreign liner companies out of our ports.)

The President signed the first bill, but vetoed the second bill. The veto message, however, did not contain the strongly procompetitive language that we would have liked but instead, focused on the diplomatic problems. And it indicated that the President was asking FMC to increase its enforcement efforts under existing authority against illegal rebating. This veto message was not an encouraging sign to those of us who hoped for more competitive policies in the maritime area.

CEA became active in the workings of the task force in mid-November. By then, FMC, MarAd, and DOJ had produced long reports on the industry, and the positions of the agencies had been well established. FMC, MarAd, Defense, and Labor favored a strengthening of the conferences and a strengthening of FMC's regulatory powers. Treasury, DOJ, OMB, COWPS, and CEA favored more competition, a weakening of the conferences, and a weakening of FMC's regulatory powers. DOT and State were ambivalent.

THE PROCONFERENCE, PROREGULATION POSITION

The supporters of the conference system argued that open competition simply would not work in ocean shipping. This was an industry with high fixed costs and low marginal costs. There was always the temptation for a liner company to cut its rates to the level of its low marginal costs, so as to attract extra shipments. But this price cutting meant that rates were not sufficient to cover overhead costs. The absence of regulation would lead to destructive competition, from which only one or a few firms would emerge. The remaining firms would have monopoly–oligopoly power and would raise rates. Shippers in the long run would be worse off. Also, unlike the demand facing the airline industry, the demand for shipping services was not elastic, so the lower prices that competition would bring would not mean more shipping traffic; they would only mean lower revenues for the existing carriers.

Polls of goods shippers showed that they were not interested in price competition in shipping rates. They were primarily interested in steady, reliable service at reasonable, nondiscriminatory prices.

Further, unregulated competition meant excess capacity (over-tonnaging), which meant higher unit costs. Regulation could "rationalize" the industry—allow the lines companies to coordinate their schedules—and thus lower costs.

Finally, the American flag fleet could not survive in the competitive arena. The United States was a high-wage country. It could not compete against low-wage foreign operators. The fleet was old and inefficient. Competition would drive it out of the water. But the fleet was vital to our national and economic security. We could not and should not be entirely dependent on foreign operators for the transport of our exports and imports, even during peacetime. We could not allow the fleet to disappear by its being out-competed, even if this outcome seemed to be justified by the workings of the market.

Accordingly, the sensible policy was to strengthen the conferences. Give them stronger powers to set prices and rationalize sailings. Allow the conference members to pool revenues. Permit agreements among conferences (so as to limit competition between rival trade routes). Perhaps some conferences should be closed to new firms, so as to achieve rationalization more readily. Perhaps nonconference liners should be prevented from competing on some routes. And the program suggested by the United Nations Conference on Trade and Development (UNCTAD), to allocate shipping between any pair of countries on the basis of 40% each to the liner companies of each country and 20% to third parties, should be endorsed.

The conference supporters recognized that the potential for monopolistic abuses by the conferences would be increased by this scheme. Consequently, they favored increasing the regulatory powers of FMC. The agency would gain the power to regulate prices and conditions of service directly and would be given more legal weapons to stop rebating. A second check on the conferences would be shippers councils. These were groups of shippers who would meet with the conferences; the two groups would jointly negotiate rates. The extra bargaining power of the combined shippers would be a countervailing force to the conferences. These shippers' councils appeared to work satisfactorily in Europe.

THE ANTICONFERENCE, ANTIREGULATION POSITION

The striking aspect about the proregulation arguments was that they were virtually identical to the arguments that had been used to support regulation and oppose competition in the airline industry and were being offered to defend the regulation of trucking. (The only standard argument that did not surface was the "regulation is needed to ensure cross-subsidy" argument.) Such arguments could not withstand close scrutiny in these other industries. They did not fare any better in the maritime industry.

Competition was indeed viable in the maritime industry. Although very-short-run marginal costs might be low, over any medium term prices and capacity would adjust in this market as they did any market. The capital in this industry was exceptionally mobile. Ships could be shifted from one route to another or chartered by one firm from another, depending on where the profitable opportunities lay. Destructive competition, with monopolistic exploitation at the end, was highly unlikely. There was enough shipping capacity in the world and entry onto a route was easy enough so that no liner company could hope to exploit any monopoly power for very long. Rebating was an important part of this competitive process and should be legalized.

The demand for liner services was a good deal more elastic than most people (or, apparently, the conferences themselves) realized. The striking fact about the liner traffic to and from the United States was that it had been absolutely stagnant in terms of tonnage for 25 years! At the same time, the tonnage by dry bulk carriers—shipload quantities moving by charter (which had much lower rates than conference rates)—had almost tripled. Much of this traffic was traditional dry bulk cargo, such as grain. But some of it was shipload cargoes of items such as cars, iron and steel, paper and pulp, fertilizer, and chemicals, all of which were traditionally liner items. It appeared that as soon as shippers had shipments that were large enough to qualify as shipload quantities, they were escaping from the conferences (and their high rates) and chartering bulk carriers at much lower rates. The demand for liner shipping services was cost sensitive and elastic after all.

The over-tonnaging that one saw on liner routes was a direct consequence of the price fixing of the conferences. With price competition checked by the conferences, carriers turned to nonprice competition, notably capacity competition. Offering more frequent sailings was an obvious nonprice competitive strategy. Capacity competition acted as an equilibrating force; where there were potential excess profits, capacity competition would increase until the profits returned to normal. Thus, over-capacity was an indication that prices were higher than was necessary to sustain a lesser amount of capacity on a route and was not an indication of excessive competition. This phenomenon had been well documented for the airline industry.[5] It had equal applicability to the maritime industry. Rationalization, by reducing the number of sailings and raising the load factor of each sailing, might well reduce costs. But it meant an inferior quality of service to shippers, and it would take a perfect regulatory regime to make sure that the cost savings were passed on to shippers. The best solution was to end the conferences' price fixing and let the market determine the right price and quality combination.

Goods shippers favored conferences because they wanted uniform rates. They feared price discrimination because it conveyed advantages to those who were favored and they would have to compete among themselves to gain these favorable rates. It was much easier to have a regime that would remove this aspect of competition.

Endorsement of conferences and of the UNCTAD cargo-sharing arrangements was contrary to the American tradition of open markets and free trade. It threatened the gains we had achieved in the international airline area, where we were pushing strongly for less restrictive price and scheduling arrangements and were meeting strong resistance. In many cases, the same officials from foreign countries dealt with both maritime and air negotiations, and they did not fail to point out to our air negotiators that our maritime negotiators were endorsing quite different positions.

Shippers' councils were not a wise idea. They might provide some countervailing power. But it was a dangerous antitrust precedent to allow groups of firms to come together to talk about prices, even input prices. And the solid front of a shippers' council might prevent independent actions by individual shippers who might otherwise try to strike bargains, drive wedges between competing liner companies, and undermine the rate structure. These independent actions were an important part of the price competition process.

An increase in FMC regulatory powers would run directly contrary to the deregulation policies that the administration was pursuing in other transportation areas. Those policies were equally applicable in this area as well.

The proper policies, then, were not to strengthen the conferences and FMC but to weaken them and to encourage more competition. Rebating should be legalized. And various actions should be taken to weaken the conferences' powers of collective action; possibly, their exemption from the antitrust laws should be completely removed.

Increased competition would definitely benefit goods shippers and their ultimate customers. And it need not mean the demise of the U.S. fleet. Carriers such as Sea-Land and U.S. Lines, which had actively embraced the new container technology, had shown that American firms could survive in the international shipping market. The basic problem with ocean shipping, from the American perspective, was that it was not a high-technology industry. American firms had higher labor costs (and were over-manned, due ot union rules); in the presence of a relatively unsophisticated technology, they would surely be outcompeted. Generally, American firms had a comparative advantage in high-technology areas. This probably explained why the United States had done so well in international air transportation, despite the higher wages that U.S. airlines paid their crews and personnel compared with those paid by foreign airlines. (It also probably explained why the unsubsidized U.S. aircraft industry could compete successfully in world markets, whereas the U.S. shipbuilding industry was heavily subsidized and still could not compete very successfully.) The solution, then, for the U.S. maritime industry was to try to push the technology harder and to be at its leading edge. A more competitive atmosphere might shake the U.S. firms out of their protected lethargy. If some of them still could not survive, then the competitive process would have achieved one of its goals: the demise of inefficient firms.

Further, if there were some legitimate national security reasons for keeping alive a sizable U.S. fleet that otherwise could not survive in a competitive environment, the proper way to do so was through direct subsidies from national tax revenues rather than through protection and implicit taxes on shippers. The existing subsidy system, though, was not well designed to achieve carrier efficiency. It put too many restrictions on the firms' operations and behavior. And it was not well connected to national security needs. A better subsidy system that encouraged efficiency and met national security needs could be devised.[6]

THE CHOICES

The administration was badly split on this issue. Compromises at the agency level were unlikely. The choices would have to be presented to the President for his decision.

In December 1978, the Department of Justice's Antitrust Division provided its three options for changes in the law. All would be accomplished by improved subsidy arrangements (being developed by OMB). DOJ's first choice was to remove completely the antitrust exemptions for conferences, legalize rebating, and sunset FMC (i.e., phase out its functions over a number of years). DOJ recognized the international political problems (other countries would object to unilateral U.S. action vis-à-vis their liner companies' business practices) and the domestic political problems that this course entailed, so it did not really foster hopes that this was a realistic option. Its second choice was to forbid only the U.S. flag carriers from joining conferences. Foreign flag carriers could still form conferences, so the major international problems were alleviated, but the conferences could not have dual-rate contracts or interconference agreements. Rebating would be legalized, and FMC would be sunsetted. This was DOJ's realistic preferred option. As a third choice, and a fallback position, DOJ proposed that the conferences continue to have their antitrust exemption but that their more egregious anticompetitive aspects be clearly forbidden. Dual rate contracts, revenue pooling, and interconference agreements would be forbidden. Rebating would be legalized. And the right of a carrier within a conference to take independent pricing action would be explicitly recognized.

At the same time, FMC was developing its suggested program, which involved strengthening the conferences and strengthening FMC's regulatory role.

In an important January meeting, however, DOJ allowed itself to be outmaneuvered. DPS, as chair of the task force, decided that DOJ's first two options were totally unrealistic and could not be presented to the President. Only its last fallback option could be on the final decision memo. FMC's option would be on it. And DPS would develop a third, "middle-ground" option. In this context, then, the DOJ option was going to appear to be extreme. Had DOJ fought harder to keep its other options on the memo, its fallback option might not have appeared to be so extreme.

The task force proceeded at a desultory pace, with few meetings and little progress. Key congressional leaders began to get restive. Maritime legislation was being introduced. The President had promised that there would be an administration position. Until there was, it was difficult for representatives of departments to testify. Finally, in April 1979 DPS produced a draft of the presidential decision memo. The "middle-ground" option involved establishing by law three categories of conference practices. The first category, agreements that clearly improved efficiency (e.g., terminal sharing or equipment interchange agreements), would be presumptively legal; the second (e.g., dual-rate contrasts) would be subject to FMC hearings; the third (e.g., closed conferences) would be illegal. Shippers' councils would also be sanctioned. The President would thus be asked to choose among the DOJ procompetitive position, the FMC proregulatory position, and this "middle ground." The memo also asked for separate decisions on whether rebating should be legalized, whether cargo-sharing (market-sharing) arrangements should be pursued, and whether MarAd should be declared to be the lead administration agency on maritime matters.

All the pro-competitive agencies were unhappy with the memo and with the "middle-ground" option. We did not feel that the memo properly characterized the pro-competitive position. The proposals for reforming the subsidy system, which might make the pro-competitive option more politically palatable, had been dropped. And we did not think that the DPS option represented a true middle ground. Instead, it represented a pro-regulation step backward. The FMC would be able to achieve through regulation much of what the agency hoped to achieve through the legislative changes in its option. And shippers' councils were definitely an anticompetitive institution. If DPS were to persist with this option, CEA and COWPS believed that a fourth option, a true middle ground, should be offered to the President: a simple legal codification of the status quo, the Svenska standard, so that FMC would have less legal room to find ways of approving anticompetitive arrangements.

Meetings followed. The memo was improved slightly from our perspective, but our basic objections remained.

In early June the Congress passed a slightly revised version of the bill strengthening FMC's powers to stop rebating by foreign flag carriers. This time the President signed it.

At about the same time the final decision memo was forwarded to the President. DOJ, Treasury, OMB, COWPS, and CEA all planned to forward dissenting memos. CEA concluded that the President would not be well served by having so many separate documents and urged that the five agencies try to agree on one dissenting memo. CEA drafted a short memo, stressing the viability of competition in the maritime industry and the importance of a deregulation policy here that would be consistent with the administration's deregulation policies in other transportation areas; as a fallback, the memo urged the legal codification of the Svenska standard. The principals at Treasury, OMB, COWPS, and CEA signed it, and it was forwarded to the President; DOJ insisted on its own separate dissent.

THE OUTCOME

The President decided in favor of the "middle-ground" option. He also decided in favor of legalizing rebating, against market sharing, and for MarAd's becoming the lead agency.

On July 20, 1979, the President sent a letter as a statement of the administration's position on maritime matters to Representative John M. Murphy, who chaired the House Committee on Merchant Marine and Fisheries and was a strong defender of the maritime industry's interests. The letter endorsed the primacy of FMC in regulating ocean shipping, the three-way categorization of conference practices, and shippers' councils. It opposed cargo-sharing agreements. It was silent on rebating. And it endorsed changed subsidy procedures for the construction and operation of dry bulk cargo ships.

As of this writing, no new legislation has yet emerged from Congress.

CONCLUDING COMMENTS

The final decision represents a step backward for the administration in its transportation and regulation policies. The political pressures from the industry and the unions were clearly pointing in the direction chosen, but the same could have been said about the airlines industry before it was deregulated and about the trucking industry before its partial deregulation. The maritime decision is an unfortunate one.

NOTES TO CHAPTER 12

[1]A description of the industry and the regulatory and subsidy policies that apply to it can be found in G. R. Jantscher, *Bread Upon the Waters* (Washington, D.C.: Brookings Institution, 1975); and R. Larner, "Public Policy in the Ocean Freight Industry," in A. Phillips, ed., *Promoting Competition in Regulated Markets* (Washington, D.C.: Brookings Institution, 1975).

[2]39 Stat. 728.

[3]*Federal Maritime Commission* v. *Aktiebolaget Svenska Amerika Linien (Swedish American Line)*, 390 U.S. 238 (1968).

[4]Thus all transportation regulation has specific prohibitions against undue discrimination, and the Robinson–Patman Act contains a prohibition against unjustified price discrimination in all sectors of the economy.

[5]See G. W. Douglas and J. C. Miller, III, *Economic Regulation of Domestic Air Transport* (Washington, D.C.: Brookings Institution, 1974); and L. J. White, "Quality, Competition, and Regulation: Evidence from the Airline Industry," in R. E. Caves and M. J. Roberts, eds., *Regulating the Product* (Cambridge, Mass.: Ballinger, 1975).

[6]An improved subsidy system would require the military to specify the national security needs and would place the necessary subsidies on the military budget.

chapter 13

Electronic Mail

Should the U.S. Postal Service be permitted to enter the electronic portion of electronic mail?

Although regulation is the route that the American political system has chosen for dealing with many of the perceived problems created by business activity, it is not the only possible route. As mentioned in Chapter 3, taxes and subsidies could be used to deal with externalities. And government ownership and operation of an industry is an alternative way of achieving many of the goals sought by old-style economic regulation. This last route is one that many other countries have chosen for industries (e.g., telephone, broadcasting, railroads, airlines) that the United States has instead chosen to regulate.

A major exception to the American pattern of regulate-rather-than-nationalize is the U.S. Postal Service.[1] In principle, postal services could be provided by one or more private firms; in practice, they are legally reserved for and provided by the federal government. Prominent among the reasons cited for keeping the post office in government hands (and for retaining its legal monopoly over first-class mail) are arguments similar to those offered in defense of economic regulation: prevent private monopoly–oligopoly abuses and achieve universal service at uniform rates (which means cross-subsidy if unit costs are not roughly uniform for all customers).

This chapter provides an example of an administration debate concerning the wisdom of an extension of USPS's activities. Many of the same issues that arise in discussions of economic regulation arose in this debate. But the element of government ownership and operation added a few extra issues.

BACKGROUND

Electronic mail represents the substitution of electronic transmission and computer memory for the physical transportation and storage of pieces of paper. The simplest version of electronic mail is the old-fashioned telegram. A message is brought to the Western Union office on a piece of paper. It is then converted into an electronic message, transmitted electronically, reprinted onto a piece of paper, and hand delivered. The current MAILGRAM service offered jointly by Western Union and the U.S. Postal Service is an updated version of the telegram, with USPS doing the final physical delivery. MAILGRAMs exemplify what is called stage I electronic mail.

Stage II consists of electronic transmission from the sender to the message carrier, in addition to electronic transmission by the carrier.

For example, a large national advertiser might wish to send an advertising message to 100,000 addresses. Currently, the advertiser prepares a computer tape with the message and 100,000 addresses. The advertiser's computer then prints the message on 100,000 pieces of paper, and the advertiser puts them into the mail. USPS collects the pieces of paper, sorts them, transports them to the recipient post offices, sorts them again, and delivers them. With stage II electronic mail, the advertiser would prepare the same computer tape, but the contents of the tape would be transmitted electronically. The message would be switched to the proper receiving post office, where it would be sorted and printed in the proper sequence for physical delivery by letter carriers. Thus, there would still be physical delivery of pieces of paper from the recipient post office, but prior to that point electronic transmission would replace the physical collection and transmission of pieces of paper. (Individuals who wish to send only one or a few letters by electronic mail may be able to use facsimile scanning and transmission devices.)

Stage III electronic mail involves electronic delivery, receipt, and storage of mail. If individuals have home computers, the electronic message can simply be routed to the home and stored in computer memory. When the addressee comes home, he or she can call up the messages on a cathode ray screen, read them, and then erase them, store them, or have them printed. A nearer-term prospect is company-to-company stage III communications for invoices, billing, and payments. As James Martin has noted, most billing by large corporations is currently done by computer but is printed on paper and mailed. The information is then physically rekeyed onto the recipient company's computer, which eventually prepares the checks; they are then printed, mailed, and so on.[2] Much labor could be saved and errors avoided from having to rekeypunch the same data if stage III electronic mail could be put into effect. Electronic funds transfer systems represent the beginning of this kind of electronic mail arrangement.

THE USPS REQUEST

In December 1978 USPS approached the Carter administration and asked for its endorsement of USPS entry into stage II electronic mail. USPS had been an independent agency since 1971, and it never quite conceded its power to undertake independent action if it really wanted to. But it clearly preferred to have the support of the administration.

USPS was already participating in MAILGRAM services and was proposing to join with Western Union in a stage II service called ECOM (electronic computer originated mail). But USPS wanted to be able to develop its own stage II collection and transmission capabilities. A 1978 study done for USPS by RCA (which, curiously, is a potential competitor of USPS in the electronic portion of electronic mail) indicated that a stage II system handling 25 billion pieces of mail a year (about 33% of USPS's likely first-class mailstream) by 1990 would have average costs, exclusive of delivery, of only 2.3¢ per piece. An investment of $1.8 billion would be required. Electronic messages could be transmitted over telephone lines to USPS, but most post offices would also be equipped to receive and run tapes and would have facsimile devices. There would be a central switching and transmission network. And there would be 87 recipient post offices to sort, print, and prepare the physical messages for delivery. Only 4,000 employees would be required to run the system up to the point of physical delivery, replacing approximately 64,000 employees who currently handle the equivalent collecting, sorting, and transporting functions. USPS had labeled this system EMSS (electronic message switching system).

A task force, consisting of representatives of the Departments of Commerce (National Telecommunications and Information Administration), Justice (Antitrust Division), Agriculture, State, Labor, and Treasury, USPS, OMB, COWPS, and CEA, was formed to study the question. DPS was the chair. NTIA did much of the organizational coordination. The task force's charge was to study the impacts of EMSS on USPS, on the economy, on postal users, and on potential rivals to USPS. It would consider the overall wisdom of the EMSS concept and present a recommendation to the President or, failing agreement, present the crucial choices for decision. Final decisions were promised by late March.

INITIAL QUESTIONS

CEA was given the responsibility of examining the impact of EMSS on the overall economy (which was in keeping with the general view that CEA was primarily a macroeconomics-oriented organization). The task proved to be easy. In a $3 trillion economy in 1990, with a labor force of over 100 million people, almost nothing would be large enough to have any significant effect on the overall economy. The improvement in productivity, the job adjustment problem for 60,000 workers, the extra investment—all would be tiny in comparative magnitude, especially since the effects would occur gradually over a number of years.

The macroeconomic consequences, then, were uninteresting. Along the way, though, the displacement estimate of 60,000 employees was developed (USPS had not tried to make an estimate of employment effects), and some of USPS's cost numbers were corrected. Also, the low magnitude of the cost estimates began to be a bit troubling. The RCA estimate of 2.3¢ per message of the electronic mail portion was far below the 19¢ per message that Western Union would receive as part of the ECOM service. The latter figure included a reasonable return on investment for Western Union but did not imply huge profits. What explained the large difference between the two numbers? It did not appear to be due to the difference in the projected scales of the two services. RCA's cost estimates were not volume sensitive to this great a degree. A satisfactory explanation was never forthcoming; the possibility remained that RCA might have vastly underestimated the true costs of the EMSS system (or else that Western Union was tremendously inefficient or was somehow going to make huge windfalls on its ECOM services).

The interesting questions turned out to be more microeconomic in nature. There was no particular reason why USPS had to be an electronic carrier in a large stage II electronic mail system. One could easily imagine a system in which multiple competing private electronic carriers would carry out the collection and transmission functions, with their messages funneling into the 87 recipient post offices for physical delivery by USPS. If electronic mail were profitable, the private firms would enter; if not, they would stay out. In this version of the system, then, USPS would confine itself to its traditional role of handling pieces of paper, delivering the final hard copy. The electronics portion would be the preserve of the private sector.

Since USPS's operation of the electronics portion of the system was not technologically required, one could legitimately ask if there were any dangers to USPS operation as opposed to private operation of the electronics part. Were there costs as well as benefits to USPS entry, even if the activity were expected to be profitable for USPS? If so, where did the balance between costs and benefits lie? These questions, which were largely microeconomic in nature, were the critical ones.

THE CASE FOR USPS ENTRY

USPS (naturally) was the primary proponent for USPS entry. First, USPS argued that electronics was simply another way of collecting and transporting the mail. In the past, new technological innovations had changed the means of transporting the mail from stagecoach to rail, truck, and air. This was a natural extension, and USPS should no more be kept out of electronics than out of transporting the mail by air.

Second, the RCA study showed that the USPS electronics operations would be profitable. Thus, there was little chance that these operations would cause a net drain on USPS funds. But, if USPS were kept out, it would lose revenues as letter mail switched to electronic mail. Costs would not drop by nearly as much, so USPS would either have to raise postage rates on the remaining letter stream to astronomical heights or receive large subsidies from the federal treasury; both outcomes were politically unacceptable.

Third, throughout the debate, USPS made clear that it did not seek a monopoly on the electronic portion of the stage II system. Although it was not prepared to give up its monopoly over physical delivery of letter mail, it was prepared to be just one among a number of providers of electronic services. The entry of USPS would mean more competition in the electronics portion. (At one point, NTIA suggested that, in return for being allowed to compete in the electronic portion, USPS should be required to allow competitors into the physical delivery area; the idea was never pursued.)

Fourth, USPS did not intend to engage in cross-subsidy. The basic postal statutes made clear that each class of mail was supposed to cover its own costs. USPS intended to follow those precepts.

Fifth, USPS felt that the private sector might focus largely or exclusively on large users and fail to give proper service to small users: households and small businesses. Only the USPS, through neighborhood post offices, could provide the services to these users.

Sixth, USPS had no intention of entering stage III.

THE CASE AGAINST USPS ENTRY

NTIA became the principal opponent to USPS entry. (The Antitrust Division was also a strong opponent.) NTIA had developed a general philosophy in telecommunications of deregulating wherever possible, minimizing government intervention, and relying on private firms in competition in the marketplace to provide telecommunications services. It saw USPS's entry as running contrary to that philosophy.

First, USPS would not be just another entrant in the electronics portion of the market. It was "the Government." It would have a much deeper pocket to subsidize losses. It did not pay taxes. It did not have to show a positive return on its investment. Its presence could well deter entry by smaller firms. Thus, USPS's entry might mean less competition, not more.

Second, USPS's entry would blur the traditional distinction that had reserved telecommunications for the private sector.[3] And once USPS had entered stage II electronic mail—with all its computers and collection and transmission equipment in place—it would be natural for it to move into stage III. Then USPS would be involved in wholly electronic messages, with no paper involved at all. Entry into electronic mail was more than just a "natural" technological extension of USPS's traditional function of moving the mail by the best means possible. It would be a wholly new entry by USPS into electronic telecommunication, a complete change in established policy. This change should not be made lightly, and, indeed, it did not need to be made at all.

Third, USPS's entry meant more regulation in the electronics area. If there were only private carriers, unregulated competition was probably feasible. With USPS's entry, regulation was inevitable. The administration's policy was to encourage less regulation. Permitting USPS to enter would run contrary to that policy.

Fourth, USPS did not have a particularly good track record in its recent investments. A modern package-handling system, recently built, had become a technological and fiscal embarrassment to USPS.

Fifth, USPS might well engage in cross-subsidy, despite the legal prohibitions. There was plenty of room for "creative accounting" of joint costs (or allegedly joint costs) to cover cross-subsidy efforts. It was difficult to know *a priori*, though, whether USPS would use other operations to subsidize electronic mail, use electronic mail to subsidize other operations, or carry out cross-subsidies among electronic mail categories.

Sixth, USPS did not need entry into electronic mail to sustain itself or to avoid large price increases elsewhere. The effects would not be felt until the late 1980s in any event, and USPS was probably more flexible than it admitted. Its labor force could be reduced as mail volumes decreased. And it was not obvious, in the absence of cross-subsidy from electronic mail to other services, that electronic mail would provide the financial cushion for other services.

THE DECISION MEMO AND THE CEA–COWPS POSITION

It was quickly clear that the differences between USPS and NTIA could not be reconciled and that the major issues should go to the President for resolution. Agreement on the wording of the issues, however, proved difficult. USPS and NTIA fought over each word in a long memo. Weeks slipped by, and it was May 1979 before a draft of the decision memo was ready for agency comment and for the various agencies to indicate their positions and recommendations to the President.

My preference (embodied in a long memo to the Chairman of CEA) was to prevent USPS's entry. This position was not based on the popular image of USPS as inefficient, an image frequently based on stories of seeing postal employees standing idle or on the annual deficits that USPS runs. In any organization with over 650,000 employees there will always be employees standing idle at times; anecdotes do not count for much. And USPS is subject to an almost impossible set of political demands. It is expected simultaneously to keep postal rates low, maintain employment, avoid strikes, maintain a number of money-losing services and facilities (e.g., rural post offices), *and* avoid running a deficit.

At the same time, however, USPS's continued maintenance and defense of its legal monopoly over the delivery of first-class letter mail is one of the more serious anticompetitive elements in our economy. And the USPS record in innovation and automation has not been stellar.[4]

The important question, though, concerned the *political* economy of electronic mail. Suppose electronic mail became a popular and profitable means of communication. Where did the greater efficiency danger lie? If USPS were kept out (except for physical delivery) and saw part of its mailstream diverted, would it ask Congress for special protection, special shackles on its electronic rivals? Alternatively, if USPS entered and discovered that electronic mail was a large moneymaker that could be used to subsidize its other operations (cross-subsidy across classes) or decided that it wanted to favor certain users within the electronic mail category (cross-subsidy within the class), would USPS ask Congress for special restrictions on competition from other electronic carriers (to prevent "creamskimming," etc.)?

The latter threat seemed to be the greater (although it was still a close call). The USPS's claim that electronic mail was going to prevent large deficits or skyrocketing postal rates had an unsettling ring. USPS claimed that there were large fixed costs to maintaining the postal system and that its entry into the electronics portion of electronic mail would help to cover these costs. But there was no good evidence to support this claim. It appeared that USPS was simply hoping to be able to carry out cross-subsidies across classes.

Even worse, USPS had argued that it would probably be alone in serving small users. It had a tradition of universal service that other carriers lacked. But, if small users were profitable to serve, private carriers would serve them, through small storefront neighborhood shops similar to those established by duplicating and photocopying services firms. And, if the small users were not profitable, then USPS's service to them would mean within-class cross-subsidy, at the expense of other users. USPS's tradition of universal service was a severe liability, not an asset.

Consequently, the best policy course was to keep USPS out. But, if USPS were allowed to enter, it had to be prevented from trying to extend its monopoly on physical delivery to electronics. It had to guarantee access to all electronic carriers who wished to hook into its physical delivery system. It had to establish separate rates for full end-to-end USPS service and for physical-delivery-only service that would allow the other electronic carriers to compete and not be excluded. And it had to be prevented from seeking protection or restraints on electronic competition. (The recommendations by the COWPS staff were largely the same.)

The CEA and COWPS principals saw it differently, however. They did not believe that a potential entrant should be kept out of the market, even if it was "the Government." One more competitor simply had to be beneficial. Competition in telecommunications was likely to be so vigorous that any USPS efforts at protection or cross-subsidy would probably come to naught. But they did recognize that there were some dangers. They believed that these dangers could be handled adequately by explicit policy statements at the time of presidential approval that USPS would not be allowed to extend its monopoly, that cross-subsidy would not be sanctioned, that universal service was not to be an explicit or implicit goal of USPS electronic service, and that the administration would oppose all efforts by USPS to seek protection or inhibit competition in electronic mail. The establishment by USPS of a separate subsidiary to handle its electronic operations would reduce the possibilities of creative accounting that might mask cross-subsidies.

Accordingly, CEA and COWPS recommended that the President approve USPS entry but that he also attach the necessary restrictions on USPS's economic and political behavior.

The decision memo, with agency positions and recommendations attached, slowly went through a few more drafts. With no immediate crisis at hand, there was no need for haste. Finally, in late June the final memo was submitted.

THE OUTCOME

Only July 17, 1979, the President's decision was announced: The administration endorsed USPS's entry into stage II electronic mail (but opposed USPS's entry into stage III at any time) with the restrictions on anti-competitive behavior recommended by CEA and COWPS.

CONCLUDING COMMENTS

CEA and COWPS played a fruitful role in pointing out the microeconomic dangers of USPS entry and in structuring the safeguards that accompanied the administration's decision to approve entry. Some of these arguments were also made by NTIA and the antitrust division, but they were better articulated by CEA and COWPS. Also, unlike the spills and dumps problem discussed in Chapter 10, we were in the decision process at the beginning and could help shape the issues.

Full-scale stage II electronic mail is not likely to occur sooner than the late 1980s. But USPS's effort to establish its smaller ECOM service in conjunction with Western Union has already met with delays. The Federal Communications Commission has decided that it has authority over the pricing and terms of service of the entire service, contrary to USPS hopes that the Postal Rate Commission would have authority over the physical delivery portion.[5] Legal appeals and further delays are likely.

NOTES TO CHAPTER 13

[1]Other major exceptions are government operation of electric utilities (e.g., TVA, Los Angeles Water and Power Department), water utilities, and local transportation systems. Governments, of course, provide a much wider range of services, ranging from defense to libraries to street repair; but the "exceptions" are government-run enterprises that charge direct fees and that have private counterparts, were private at one time, or could easily be conceived to be capable of private operation.

[2]J. D. Martin, *Telecommunications and the Computer*, 2nd ed. (Englewood Cliffs, N.J.: Prentice-Hall, 1976).

[3]That distinction was blurred only once, during World War I, when the federal government briefly operated the national telephone network. See J. Brooks, *Telephone: The First Hundred Years* (New York: Harper & Row, 1975), pp. 151–159.

[4]I was reminded of this poor performance by realizing that I had never seen a cash register or even a small hand-held calculator at a post office stamp-dispensing window. When I asked the USPS staff on the task force about this absence, they replied that USPS's management studies had indicated that these devices would not be cost effective. After initial incredulity, I realized that the studies were probably right—but only because USPS did not value the waiting time of its customers and did not need to, since it was a monopoly and did not need to fear that its customers would take their business elsewhere if queues became too long. Even then, if USPS had some notion of intolerably lengthy queues—after all, there frequently is more than one service window open at a post office—it seems likely that cash registers or calculators could speed service (as could other devices, such as clerk-operated stamp-dispensing machines at the window to replace the books containing sheets of stamps from which the clerks rip individual stamps) and would be less expensive than extra personnel at extra windows. The answer did not reassure me as to USPS's cost consciousness or of its ability to satisfy consumer demands.

[5]See *The New York Times*, August 2, 1979, p. D2.

chapter 14

Retail Gasoline Margins

At what level should the Department of
Energy set retail gasoline margins?

The Department of Energy's regulation of the petroleum industry is one of the important areas of economic regulation in the current American economy. DOE's regulation does not take the traditional form associated with most other economic regulation. There is no independent regulatory commission; there are no rate-of-return criteria; and most of the decisions are made through the "informal" regulatory procedures described in Chapter 2 rather than through more formal adjudicatory procedures, such as hearings before an administrative law judge. But prices are set, industry structure is influenced, and even entry is affected (as this chapter indicates) by DOE decisions.

Most of the economists at CEA and COWPS are opposed to this regulation, on both philosophical and practical grounds. The political pressures for its continuation, however, are great. Under these circumstances much of the CEA–COWPS efforts are aimed at trying to prevent changes in DOE's regulations from making things worse. They do not always succeed, as this chapter indicates.

BACKGROUND

The petroleum industry—from the well to the gasoline pump—is the one American industry that has been subject to price controls since August 1971. Controls on most other sectors were lifted in early 1973 (although prices were again temporarily frozen in the summer of 1973), and even parts of the petroleum industry (petrochemicals, home heating oil) have been decontrolled. And in early 1979 the Carter administration decided to decontrol the price of crude oil over the following few years. But price and allocation controls on gasoline and diesel fuel beyond the well—from the refinery to the pump—remain. Despite a number of opportunities, neither the Ford nor the Carter administration has chosen to decontrol this sector.

As of early 1979, the price control regulations for gasoline were based on a "snapshot" of the economy on May 15, 1973. Prices were controlled by limiting the margin—the difference between the selling price of a product and the cost of the raw materials going into it—of each business involved in the sale of gasoline at any stage. (The margin, of course, covers labor cost, interest, rent, profits, etc.). Margins for refiners, distributors, retailers, and so on were basically frozen at the levels that existed on May 15, 1973. Each stage could pass along any increases in the costs of the raw materials it bought (e.g., crude for the refineries, wholesale gasoline for the retailer), but the margin imposed on top of those raw materials was not supposed to exceed the level that existed on that crucial (but arbitrary) date. There had been some regulatory adjustments in these margins (e.g., for increased rents and increased labor costs), but the basic principle was that of the fixed margin.

Further, any seller in the petroleum chain, from refiner to retailer, who shaved actual margins below the allowable margin was allowed to "bank" this difference; at some later time, those products could be sold at margins above the allowable levels until the bank was exhausted. There were two notions underlying this banking procedure. First, it was hoped that this procedure would allow some seasonal flexibility in prices. And, second, the procedure might encourage downward movements generally that sellers might otherwise be reluctant to undertake. (It is difficult to make good economic sense out of this second argument.)

From 1974 through the end of 1978, prices and margins throughout the gasoline chain were generally below the legal maximums. (If ever there were testimony to the largely competitive nature of the industry, surely that must be it!) Large amounts of banks had been built up.

In early 1979, in the wake of the Iran disturbances, crude oil supplies diminished and prices rose. Retail prices began to rise. Deliveries in some parts of the country began to be curtailed. By May there were long lines at gasoline stations in California and growing consumer complaints of price gouging by retailers. At the same time many retailers were complaining that the price controls were leaving them with inadequate margins in these inflationary times, especially when their volumes decreased because of curtailed deliveries.

At first glance, the cries of the consumers and the cries of the retailers might appear to be contradictory. But it might have been the case that some retailers were constrained by the regulations, while others were violating them or legally using up their banks from previous years of low margins.

It was the Department of Energy's responsibility to enforce the pricing rules. But DOE was learning that the rules were very difficult to enforce.

On June 26, 1979, DOE issued an NPRM to change the margin rules only for retailers.[1] It proposed eliminating the banks and imposing a uniform cents-per-gallon maximum margin for all gasoline stations to replace the historical margins (which were unique for each station). Retailers would be free to have lower margins, but they could not exceed the maximum margin. As alternatives to the cents-per-gallon margin, DOE raised the possibilities of a uniform national percentage margin, a uniform national price, or keeping the existing historical system but adding 3¢/gal to all allowable margins. Using provisions for accelerated procedures, it asked for comments by July 26, giving only a 30-day public comment period. A few days after the NPRM was published, DOE shortened the deadline to July 12.[2] Gasoline retailers in a number of East Coast states were threatening strikes and/or marches on Washington. From a political perspective, something had to be done quickly.

The CEA and COWPS staffs were uniformly opposed to the proposal. Although no one supported the existing system of controls—virtually all favored decontrol—we all felt that the current system, perhaps modified, was probably better than a system of uniform margins. A number of internal memos were hastily written, but the final decision was not to file comments but simply to convey our concerns orally in a meeting. The time constraints were too short for a formal filing, and it was unlikely that a filing would have any effect since DOE (with the apparent support of the President's political advisers) was determined to put through the regulatory changes. The meeting was held in the second week of July, and our concerns were conveyed.

DOE'S POSITION

DOE focused primarily on the complexity and unenforceability of the existing regulations. Consumers were complaining about price gouging. But the historical nature of the current margin rules and the banking provisions had made enforcement very difficult. Many retailers did not keep good records. A full audit to determine if a retailer was in compliance could take three person-days, yet DOE had only 50 auditors to examine all retail gasoline price complaints. With over 165,000 retailer dealers, DOE could not hope to enforce the rules. Even the elimination of the banks, but the retention of the historical margin system, would overtax DOE's enforcement capabilities. At the same time, the retailers were complaining about the complexity of the existing rules and the inadequacy of the current margins.

The solution, then, was to raise the average margin somewhat and have an easily enforceable uniform maximum margin. DOE was proposing that every retailer would be required to post on his or her gasoline pumps his or her wholesale price, the legal maximum margin, the relevant gasoline taxes, and the legal maximum price. DOE also expected the newspapers to publish this information. From these two sources, consumers could know the relevant facts and could easily spot price cheaters.

CEA–COWPS POSITION

We knew that no uniform maximum margin could be right for the entire country (unless it was so high that retailing became effectively decontrolled). Any margin that was right for a Tulsa gas-and-go self-service retailer could not be right for a Manhattan full-service retailer. There were substantial differences among retailers across the country in their overhead costs (rent, wages, etc.), in the extent of services that they provided, and in the extent of their vertical integration (e.g., did they pick up the gasoline themselves or have it delivered?). A uniform margin that was binding had to hurt the retailers in high-cost areas (e.g., central cities) and quite probably reduce the supply of gasoline in these areas, lead to reduction in services by full-service dealers, and lead to a reduction in vertical integration by dealers who had absorbed more upstream functions. It had to lead to serious inefficiencies.

We needed to find data to support our position that there was considerable diversity in margins. DOE provided a regulatory analysis only late in the process, and it never provided any data on diversity. We found the necessary data in the *Lundberg Letter*, a privately published, weekly newsletter that focuses on trends in gasoline retailing. There was, of course, a difference between the average margins of full-service and self-service dealers; by April 1979 the average difference was 2¢/gal, smaller than we had expected but still indicative of differences. What was more striking was the diversity of margins within the full-service category. As recently as March 1979, before the supply shortfalls had become a serious problem at the retail level (and thus the full competitive forces were probably still at work at the retail level), over 20% of full-service dealers had margins below 8¢/gal and almost 20% had margins above 13¢/gal. DOE had mentioned 15¢/gal as a possible regulatory margin. In March, 4.8% of retailers had margins above 15¢/gal.

By May, supply shortages were appearing in some parts of the country. The variance in margins had remained strikingly unchanged, but retail margins had increased across the board. Less than 8% of retailers now had margins below 8¢/gal, over 35% had margins above 13¢/gal, and 18% had margins above the critical 15¢/gal. Whether this increase reflected price gouging, increases up to legal margins, or the using up of banks could not be determined. But we knew that the 15¢/gal margin would be binding on quite a few retailers.

Besides the inefficiencies brought about by a binding margin, we feared that a uniform margin might become a focal point for collusion among retailers. Competition among low-cost retailers would normally keep margins below the 15¢/gal maximum, but the presence of this easily observed number might make it easier for them to collude and raise their prices and margins to this figure. (On the other hand, the gasoline retailing sector is quite competitive, so that, even with this added help, collusion might be difficult; gasoline price "wars" used to be a synonym for completely unfettered competition.) And we were sure that the uniform margin would become the focal point for future political bargaining between the retailers and DOE.

Also, the ease of enforceability of DOE's new system was highly questionable. In many cases, there was no single wholesale price that could be used as the reference point for enforcement. Prices changed, often rapidly, over time; different suppliers had different prices; it mattered if a dealer bought from a refiner, a wholesaler, or a jobber, and it mattered what services were attached to the transaction. DOE wanted to use the most recent purchase as "the wholesale price." But then dealers would buy 99% of their supplies from their normal sources and the last 1% from "Sam, the $1.50-a-gallon man." Ease of enforceability was a chimera.

With decontrol ruled out as an option, our next best choice was to retain the historical margin system (creaky as it was), eliminate the banks to make it easier to enforce, and increase DOE's enforcement resources. (Although occasional price gouging might be a legitimate expression of market forces—to which we were all sympathetic—the rules were there, and public cynicism about unenforced laws and rules was really not something that should be encouraged.) DOE did not have to audit all retailers, just enough to make others fear that they too stood a significant chance of being audited. If the May 15, 1973 date was too ancient and records that far back mostly did not exist, then DOE should use some equally arbitrary date in 1978 instead. The historical margin approach had the overwhelming advantage of being sensitive to the different costs of the different kinds of retailers.

As far as the dealer complaints were concerned, we were far from convinced that there were real problems of inadequate margins. Although volume might be down in mid-1979, over the longer term the number of retail outlets (including refiner owned) had fallen from 221,000 in May 1973 to 166,000 in May 1979; the average volume per retailer per month had risen from 30,000 gallons in May 1973 to 39,000 gallons in May 1979. But admittedly, these averages might be hiding hardship cases. So, perhaps the allowable margins might be increased by 2¢ or 3¢ per gallon. Competition (except during special short-run situations, such as the existing shortfall "panic") would be sufficient to prevent most retailers from actually exploiting those increases (as the 1974–1978 period had clearly shown), while the few hardship cases would be able to use the increase.

THE OUTCOME

On July 19, 1979, DOE published in the *Federal Register* its final rules.[3] Beginning August 1, the uniform margin would be 15.4¢/gal, to be adjusted by DOE semiannually on the basis of the GNP price deflator. This 15.4¢/gal was about 2¢/gal above the prevailing margins at the time, but the dealers were disappointed; they wanted a 25% margin on the wholesale price, which would have yielded 16¢/gal to 18¢/gal. The wholesale price to which the margins would be added was the most recent purchase (if the dealer had bought his or her last three purchases from the same source) or the weighted average of the past three purchases (if the dealer bought from different sources). Dealers were required to post the maximum legal price and the maximum legal margin (this latter requirement was later dropped). Dealers were now permitted to charge for extra services that they had previously provided free. And state governors were given the authority to increase the maximum margin by up to 10¢/gal in "hardship" cases.

CONCLUDING COMMENTS

DOE's final rules were probably slightly better than its initial proposal. The periodic adjustment of the margin allows for future inflation, the permission for the dealers to charge for services may ease the problem of full-service dealers, the wholesale price rule is not unreasonable, and giving the state governors the power to raise the margin at least gives the appearance of greater flexibility. DOE had listened to our criticisms and those of others. But these gains have been achieved at the expense of simplicity. There are more individual regulatory decisions that DOE and the state governors must make. The public is no more able to detect price violations, except in extreme cases, than it was before. Whether DOE's auditing will be easier and more effective remains to be seen. And the system is still likely to be inflexible and inefficient. Shortly after the rules went into effect, the governors of New Jersey and California turned down requests for margin increases (although the governors of Alaska, Oregon, and Arizona granted exemptions).[4] The dissatisfied dealers are likely to be back in Washington in the future, asking for larger margins.

The gasoline price controls are a mess. The historical margin system may have been bad, but the uniform margin system, even with the flexibility that DOE has added, is worse. Parenthetically, the same day that DOE announced the final rule on margins, it announced another final rule.[5] In response to dealer pressures, DOE limited the monthly gasoline allocations that refiners can provide to newly established retail stations. The rule set a maximum of 50,000 gallons a month; the minimum necessary for a new gas-and-go station to survive (these are the only kind that are currently being established) is 80,000 gallons a month. Thus, DOE has effectively stopped all new entry into the retail gasoline sector.

The sooner the federal government exits from the gasoline price regulation business, the better off the country will be. Unfortunately, political sentiment in the Congress and the country continues to run in the opposite direction, as an earlier incident illustrates. In late 1978, shortages of unleaded gasoline, particularly premium unleaded, started appearing. Owners of post-1974 cars, which had catalysts and required unleaded fuel, were increasingly using leaded and poisoning the catalysts. The refineries claimed that the price control system had not provided enough incentive to increase the production of the more expensive unleaded. EPA was justifiably concerned. But its concern focused mainly on the large price differentials (above 5¢/gal) between unleaded and leaded that were appearing in some cases. The agency was concerned that these price differentials themselves might be inducing some switching. Since only two or three tankfuls could permanently poison the catalyst, even temporary switching was serious.

Everyone agreed that the unleaded shortage was a temporary

problem. DOE was making changes in the rules that would encourage more unleaded production. But it would be two to three years before the extra production would be fully onstream. What could or should be done about the price differentials in the interim?

The obvious solution was to make adjustments in the federal excise tax on gasoline. The tax is 4¢/gal, which goes into the highway trust fund. Suppose that 2¢/gal were taken off the unleaded price and that the same amount were added to the leaded price. Then, the unleaded–leaded price differential could narrow by 4¢/gal (while the prices received by refiners remained unchanged), or the unleaded–leaded price differential received by refiners could widen by 4¢/gal (while the retail differential remained unchanged), or some combination of a narrowed retail differential and a widened refiner differential (which together summed to 4¢/gal) could occur. Thus, the price incentive for switching would be reduced and/or the price incentive to produce more unleaded would increase. Market forces would determine the final combination. If the 2¢/gal tax switch extended for a three-year period (by which time the extra unleaded capacity would be fully on line and the extra supply would keep the differential at reasonable levels), the revenues into the trust fund (which is politically sacred) would be roughly unchanged.[6]

The fundamental problem with this sensible solution was that it was politically unacceptable to Congress. Any tampering with the excise tax and the trust fund was looked upon with great suspicion. And it was argued that the decrease in the price of unleaded and increase in the price of leaded would differentially benefit rich people at the expense of poor people, since the rich tend to drive newer cars that require unleaded and the poor drive older cars that can take leaded. The excise tax adjustment was never seriously considered. Instead, at EPA's urging, DOE proposed fixing the differential at 5¢/gal.[7] Although a 5¢ limit might reduce the amount of switching due to price incentives, it offered no incentive to produce more unleaded gasoline; the switching due to shortages might even increase.

The sharp rise in gasoline prices in mid-1979 decreased demand for unleaded gasoline sufficiently so that the shortages and the switching problems apparently disappeared. DOE has not established final rules for the unleaded–leaded price differential. With luck, the issue will be forgotten. Nevertheless, as this example indicates, rather than allow a solution that would rely on tax adjustments and minimize the amount of regulatory interference, the political process tried to force DOE deeper into the regulatory morass.

DOE is not blameless in this regulatory mess; its regulations frequently make things worse. But it should not bear all of the responsibility. Congress must bear most of the blame.

NOTES TO CHAPTER 14

[1]*Federal Register*, June 26, 1979, pp. 37316–37320. The fixed margin rules for the other parts of the petroleum industry were left largely untouched.

[2]OMB's Regulatory Policy Division, responsible for enforcing the due process aspects of rulemaking, later complained about DOE's accelerated procedures in this NPRM and charged that DOE (which always claimed emergency status for its procedures) had been the worst violator of E.O. 12044's due process provisions.

[3]*Federal Register*, July 19, 1979, pp. 42541–42543.

[4]See *The New York Times*, August 10, 1979, p. B2; ibid., August 22, 1979, p. A19; and *The San Francisco Chronicle*, August 30, 1979, p. 1.

[5]*Federal Register*, July 19, 1979, pp. 42538–42541.

[6]During 1979, leaded production would be roughly 55–60% of the total, so there would be a small net increase into the fund compared with no change in the tax. In 1980, leaded would be down to 50% (more new cars would be requiring unleaded, and there would be some expansion of production), so there would be no change. In 1981, leaded would be 40–45%, so there would be a small net decrease. Over the three-year period there would be a rough balancing.

[7]*Federal Register*, April 11, 1979, pp. 21650–21654.

chapter 15

Conglomerate Mergers

Should the administration endorse a proposal to limit conglomerate mergers?

The task force, as a means of developing administration policy on major issues, has already been described in previous chapters—Chapter 10 on dumps and spills, Chapter 12 on the maritime industry, and Chapter 13 on electronic mail. Frequently, though, a policy issue is not important enough to warrant a task force, but differences within the administration must be resolved. For example, a department or agency proposes some new legislation; other agencies object; both sides feel strongly, and compromise proves impossible; eventually, the issue has to be sent to the President for a final decision.

This chapter provides an example of this type concerning a proposed amendment to the antitrust laws. As Chapter 13 indicated, antitrust policy is an alternative means of achieving some of the goals sought by economic regulation. And the proposal discussed in this chapter would have restricted large firms' behavior in much the same way as that which would have been achieved by regulation.

BACKGROUND

Section 7 of the Clayton Act,[1] as amended in 1950, is the main provision of the antitrust laws dealing with mergers. The operative part of Sec. 7 reads as follows: ". . . no corporation engaged in commerce shall acquire, directly or indirectly, . . . the whole or any part of the assets of another corporation engaged also in commerce, where in any line of commerce in any section of the country, the effect of such acquisition may be substantially to lessen competition, or to tend to create a monopoly."

Since 1950 the Act has been a potent weapon in stopping major horizontal mergers (between actual or potential competitors in particular markets) and vertical mergers (between firms in customer–supplier relationships to each other). The Justice Department's Antitrust Division and the Federal Trade Commission, the two agencies responsible for enforcing the Act, have had a very high success rate in winning the legal cases challenging these kinds of mergers. Indeed, in a dissent to a Supreme Court majority decision forbidding yet another merger, Justice Potter Stewart complained, "The sole consistency that I can find is that in litigation under Sec. 7, the Government always wins."[2]

The only kind of merger not covered by the Act is a conglomerate merger—a merger between firms that are neither actual or potential competitors nor in a customer–supplier relationship; that is, the two firms have no direct economic relationship to each other. During the middle and late 1960s there was a major wave of conglomerate mergers. A number of firms, such as ITT, LTV, Gulf & Western, and Litton Industries attained prominence as large conglomerate firms. A buoyant stock market made it easy for buying firms to offer packages of their securities in payment for the assets of firms they were purchasing. In 1969 the Federal Trade Commission issued an *Economic Report on Corporate Mergers*,[3] which warned of the economic and social dangers of the wave of conglomerate mergers. The report attracted considerable attention, but no congressional action followed. Shortly afterward, the stock market turned sour, and the number of mergers dropped precipitously. Table 15-1 shows the numbers of mergers and the values of the assets involved over these years.

Table 15-1

Mergers in Manufacturing and Mining Involving
Firms with Assets of $10 Million or More

Year	Number of Acquisitions	Assets of Acquired Firms (billions)
1960	51	$ 1.5
1961	46	2.0
1962	65	2.3
1963	54	2.5
1964	73	2.3
1965	64	3.3
1966	76	3.3
1967	138	8.3
1968	174	12.6
1969	138	11.0
1970	91	5.9
1971	59	2.5
1972	60	1.9
1973	64	3.1
1974	62	4.5
1975	59	5.0
1976	81	6.3
1977	99	8.7

Source: Federal Trade Commission, Bureau of Economics, *Statistical Report of Merger and Acquisitions*, November 1978.

During the late 1970s another conglomerate merger wave appeared to be forming. This time it was based, paradoxically, on a depressed stock market. The stock market share value of many firms fell below or close to the net book value of the assets of those firms. Cash-rich buying companies were able to acquire the assets of these firms at a bargain price, by buying them through purchases of their shares of stock. Again, there was a growing concern over the economic and social consequences of another merger wave.

In late December 1978, DOJ's Antitrust Division approached the Executive Office to try to gain general administration support for a bill that it had developed to stop large conglomerate mergers. Senator Edward Kennedy was expected shortly to introduce his own bill to halt large conglomerate mergers. The administration had to decide whether it would introduce its own bill, support the Kennedy bill, oppose all such bills, or take no public position.

THE ECONOMIC ARGUMENTS

Since, by definition, the partners in a conglomerate merger have little direct economic relationship to each other, the arguments that can be marshalled either in favor of or against the economic consequences of conglomerate mergers are not particularly powerful. Nevertheless, a number of arguments that the economic consequences are of social concern and be offered.

Pro

Mergers are a sign that efficient capital markets are working. Firms see profitable opportunities for expansion, and they take advantage of them. Capital markets are no different from other markets, and absent any evidence of monopoly–oligopoly problems (ruled out by the definition of conglomerate) or externality problems (discussed in the following paragraphs), intervention is no more warranted in this market than in any other well-functioning market. Conglomerate operation may allow firms to take advantage of economies of scale in management; the fashionable word for this concept used to be "synergism." Mergers may allow the buying firm to breathe new life into old firms or to provide vital resources to a small firm and thereby invigorate competition in a market. The fear of a hostile takeover—a merger against the wishes of management—may force otherwise sluggish corporate managers to be more efficient and more attentive to the interests of their stockholders.

Con

Large conglomerate firms may have a chilling effect on competition. If a large firm buys a small firm in an industry mostly populated by small firms, the remaining firms may fear the deep pocket of the merged entity and may be less vigorous in their competitive efforts. Large conglomerates, each with divisions in the same markets, may more readily learn patterns of mutual forbearance, of not taking aggressive actions in one market for fear of retaliation in another market. A conglomerate firm has more opportunities for reciprocal practices ("I will buy my supplies from you if you in turn will buy your supplies from me"), which could exclude competitors from markets.[4] At the same time, the merger actions of conglomerate firms may not be an indication of those firms' taking advantage of efficient opportunities but rather an expression of corporate managers' desire for growth, irrespective of efficiency or profitability. Finally, the funds used for merger acquisitions would have greater social productivity if they were used for investments in new plants and machinery and in research.[5]

The Evidence

Weak arguments are accompanied by weak evidence. There is little direct evidence on these points that make an overwhelming case either way. The academic finance research journals are filled with articles that indicate that the securities markets are quite efficient, that they process new information rapidly and efficiently. On the other hand, Dennis Mueller, in a survey[6] of the evidence on conglomerate mergers, finds that only the acquired firms' stockholders benefit from merger; the acquiring firms' stockholders do not appear to gain. From this he concludes that mergers are probably not achieving efficiency gains but are undertaken to satisfy the growth motives of corporate managers. Beyond this, one has to fall back on anecdotes, and the necessary anecdote can usually be cited to support either side. IBM did enter the photocopy business at the same time that Xerox entered the mainframe computer business; mutual forbearance did not seem to be present in their case. Some small firms have been invigorated. But some conglomerates have engaged in reciprocal buying practices, and there appear to be instances of chilled competition.[7]

THE SOCIAL ARGUMENTS

In the social area, the arguments all run in one direction: big is bad. These arguments claim that there are negative externalities from conglomerate mergers. The Jefferson–Jackson preference for small economic units over large ones, other things being equal, is still a powerful heritage in American society. Conglomerate mergers among large firms may create a problem of the concentration of social and political power in a comparatively small number of corporate hands. Larger firms may be more impersonal, less responsive to their labor forces and to the communities in which they have facilities. The purchase of a local firm by a conglomerate with headquarters in a distant city may mean the uprooting of local executives, the loss of local community leadership, and the possible disruption of the local community itself. The only argument that runs counter to these is that associations of small firms also appear to wield significant social and economic power; it is not clear which is the more powerful organization in Washington, General Motors or the Dairy Farmers' Association.

The direct evidence of the effects of corporate size on social or political power is almost nonexistent. Only one study, by Salomon and Siegfried, shows a statistically significant relationship between firm size and political gains (tax favors).[8] All the remaining direct "evidence" on the social problems of conglomerates consists of anecdotes.

AGGREGATE CONCENTRATION

Attention has also been focused on measurements of the economywide concentration of economic variables (e.g., sales or assets) in the hands of the largest firms (e.g., the largest 100, 200, or 500) as proxies for the social or economic power that would flow from that concentration. It is hard to make any judgment from a single number: for example, that the largest 100 nonfinancial corporations controlled 30% of the assets of all nonfinancial corporations in 1977. There is no economic or political theory that can tell us whether 30% is a large or a small number. But comparisons of these aggregate concentration[9] figures over time can indicate whether the trend is toward more or less concentration and hence (presumably) whether the proxied social and political problems are getting worse or better.

Measurements of aggregate concentration, however, are not easy to make. First, one has to decide on the right variable: assets, sales, employees, profits, and value added (the difference between sales revenues and the cost of material inputs) are all candidates. It is not obvious which variable is the best proxy for the underlying social and political power. Further, measurements using sales or assets cannot be extended to include the financial sector: Banks and insurance companies do not register sales in the way other companies do, and their assets (loans and mortgages) represent claims on the assets of other companies, so double counting would be involved. Value added is probably the best candidate, and in principle it could be applied to all sectors of the economy. But, in practice, value added concentration figures are only collected for the manufacturing sector. Much attention is frequently given to the data for the manufacturing sector. But manufacturing has been declining in its relative importance in the U.S. economy. It now accounts for less than 25% of the U.S. GNP. Finally, it is not clear if the foreign operations of U.S. companies should be included in the aggregate concentration measurements. Unfortunately, most companies report worldwide consolidated figures (sales, assets, employees) in their annual reports. Consequently, the numerator (e.g., the sum of the largest 100 companies' employees) of these aggregate concentration calculations frequently includes foreign operations, whereas the denominator is frequently a purely domestic figure (e.g., total U.S. employment). Thus, the ratios are often overstated.

Despite these problems, these measurements are frequently made. Table 15-2 provides a sample of the measures that were developed during the debate within the administration over DOJ's conglomerate merger proposal. A few explanatory remarks are necessary. The manufacturing sector data are the "cleanest." They include value added, and they include only domestic firms in both the numerator and the denominator. But, as noted, manufacturing constitutes less than 25% of GNP. The interesting aspect of these data is that the bulk of the increase in concentration took place before 1962, with most of it coming in the 1947–1954 period. This was due to the rapid internal growth of large companies that happened to be in rapidly growing industries at the time: autos, petroleum, aircraft manufacturing, defense, chemicals, and electrical equipment. The merger wave of the 1960s apparently did not increase aggregate concentration in manufacturing.

The remaining figures in Table 15-2 are less "clean," since the international operations of the largest companies are included in the numerators but national domestic aggregates are in the denominators. This means that the ratios in the table are higher than purely domestic

Table 15-2

Aggregate Concentration Figures

		1947	1954	1958	1963	1967	1972	1976	1977
		Manufacturing							
% Share of value added									
Largest	50	17	23	23	25	25	25	24	—
"	100	23	30	30	33	33	33	34	—
"	200	30	37	38	41	42	43	44	—
"	500	—	—	—	—	—	56	58	—
"	1,000	—	—	—	—	—	64	66	—
% Share of employment									
Largest	50	—	—	—	19	20	17	18	—
"	100	—	—	—	25	26	23	24	—
"	200	—	—	—	32	34	31	32	—
"	500	—	—	—	—	—	46	45	—
"	1,000	—	—	—	—	—	53	53	—
		Entire Private Sector							
% Share of private sector employment									
Largest	100						18	—	17
"	200						24	—	23
"	1,300						37	—	36
% Share of corporate profits after taxes									
Largest	100						47	—	46
"	200						60	—	58
"	1,300						83	—	82

Sources: U.S. Bureau of the Census, *Census of Manufactures,* various years; U.S. Bureau of Census, *1976 Annual Survey of Manufactures; Fortune,* annual "500" issues; U.S. Department of Commerce, *Survey of Current Business,* various issues; U.S. Department of Labor, Bureau of Labor Statistics, *Employment and Earnings,* various issues.

ratios would be. Whether this factor affects the comparisons over time is unknown.[10] The data again reveal that the merger wave of the 1960s apparently did not increase economywide aggregate concentration and that, at least through 1977, the latest merger wave similarly had no effect.

Because there are special problems with including the financial sector in these calculations, Table 15-3 contains separate aggregate concentration measures for the banking and life insurance sectors only. These are "clean" data, as they include only domestic operations. Again, aggregate concentration appears to be decreasing over time.

Thus, these data indicate that aggregate concentration, despite the merger waves, is not increasing and is probably decreasing. The social and political power problems, for which these measures are proxies, are probably not getting any worse.

Table 15-3

Aggregate Concentration for
Commercial Banks and Life Insurance

	1960	1965	1970	1974	1977
Commercial Banks					
Largest 50					
% Share of assets	39	39	34	37	35
% Share of deposits	38	38	32	35	32
Life Insurance Companies					
Largest 50					
%Share of assets	88	86	83	81	79
%Share of insurance in force	83	77	74	71	71

Sources: Federal Deposit Insurance Corp., American Council of Life Insurance, and *Statistical Abstract of the U.S.*

THE DOJ PROPOSAL

In response to what it perceived to be another serious merger wave, DOJ proposed a bill that contained two barriers to mergers. First, any merger in which the combined U.S. sales or assets were $2 billion and each party was larger than $100 million in U.S. sales or assets would be barred (these two figures would be adjusted upward annually by the Consumer Price Index). There were roughly 250 nonfinancial and nonutility firms in the $2 billion category in 1979 and roughly 2,000 in the $100 million category.[11] (Since financial firms and utilities are already heavily regulated as to their mergers, they have been excluded from the calculations.) Second, any firm with sales or assets of $1 billion or more (there were roughly 450 firms in this category) would be barred from acquiring a leading firm (20% of net sales) in a sizable and concentrated market (a market with $100 million or more in sales, in which the four-firm concentration ratio exceeded 75%). In either case, the merger would be permitted if the firms could prove that the preponderant effect of the merger would be to enhance competition substantially. Thus, the proposal reversed the usual burden of proof in Sec. 7 cases, in which the Government is normally required to prove that the merger may substantially lessen competition. (DOJ never did provide an adequate justification for the second barrier. Presumably, its argument was that a large firm's acquisition of a leading firm in a market might stultify competition, whereas the acquisition of a small firm—a "toe hold" acquisition—might invigorate it).

The one legal defense for a larger merger—that it would enhance competition—was unlikely to succeed in more than a very few cases; providing convincing evidence to a court *a priori* that a merger would enhance competition would surely prove very difficult. Virtually all large mergers would be halted by the proposal.

PRELIMINARY ACTIVITIES

At an initial meeting in late December that included CEA, OMB, and DPS, DOJ presented its proposal, defending it with a smattering of the economic arguments against conglomerate mergers, a smattering of populist arguments against bigness, and the recent data on mergers from 1972 through 1977 (which made it appear that the increase in merger assets was enormous; see Table 15-1). CEA expressed skepticism as to the economic arguments and pointed out that the mergers in the late 1970s thus far were still far below the levels of the peak years of the 1960s. At that point we had discovered only the data on aggregate concentration in manufacturing, but we knew that it had not been worsened by the mergers of the 1960s, so we expressed skepticism that aggregate concentration in the 1970s was getting worse. DOJ had no figures at all on aggregate concentration; it had not done its homework.

The initial meeting ended with the conclusion that we all needed to do more homework to see what could be learned about aggregate concentration. The data in Tables 15-2 and 15-3 are part of the result of that effort.

A series of meetings followed, to which the Commerce and Treasury Departments and the Federal Trade Commission were also invited. The first two agencies vehemently opposed the proposal; the last supported a modified version of it. It was generally agreed that economic arguments were not strong enough to be used to support the proposal and that the aggregate concentration data showed, at best, only a slight trend in either direction and hence also could not be used to support the proposal. Accordingly, DOJ was left with an argument of "bigness is bad and we should not let firms get any bigger through merger." DOJ supported this position with the populist arguments against bigness, but much to our surprise never attempted to survey the political science or sociology literature to see if evidence could be obtained to support these arguments.

There was one particular ironic aspect of the proposal. Hostile takeovers of large firms would be greatly restricted or eliminated. Thus, in the name of populism and "the little man" the proposal would insulate and protect a sizable number of very large firms from takeovers and the discipline of the financial markets. The largest 450 firms with over $1 billion in sales or assets would be prevented from merging with each other; since minnows rarely swallow whales, these firms were effectively protected from any takeovers. The top 2,000 firms would be protected from takeovers by the largest 250 companies. Various combinations of the 200 second-tier companies ($1–2 billion companies) and the 1,550 third-tier companies ($100 million–$1 billion companies) would also be barred. And the 20% concentration rule would protect yet more firms from takeovers by the largest 450.

The proposal also had to deal with the problem of foreign firms' merging with U.S. firms. Here, DOJ faced a dilemma. If it barred foreign firms from similar purchases, it risked the appearance of being hostile to foreign investment and thereby risked the possibility that foreign governments would retaliate against U.S. companies abroad. If it allowed foreign firms to make these purchases, it was faced with the anomaly that foreign firms could buy assets that U.S. firms could not. DOJ chose the latter route, but it is doubtful that the anomaly could have withstood political challenge in Congress. This problem alone probably would have meant the defeat of the bill.

The FTC offered a modified version of the bill, which allowed spin-offs of assets to count as a one-to-one offset to merged assets, with a carry-back, carry-forward period of a few years. This version was preferable to the DOJ proposal, but only slightly.

In early March DPS drafted and submitted a decision memo for the President, outlining the major issues.

THE OUTCOME

The President decided against endorsing DOJ's proposal. The administration would take no position on the conglomerate merger question. John Shenefield, Assistant Attorney General for Antitrust, was permitted to testify in favor of the Kennedy bill, which had been introduced in February and was broadly similar to DOJ's proposal, but he was to indicate that his views represented only those of the Antitrust Division and not necessarily those of the administration.

As of this writing, hearings have been held on the Kennedy bill, but no further action has been taken. Passage is unlikely. Senator Kennedy has also introduced a bill that would prevent only the major oil companies from conglomerate purchases. That bill stands a better chance.

CONCLUDING REMARKS

The issue involved here was not regulation in the same sense as the issues discussed in other chapters. But the DOJ proposal would have restricted the behavior of firms in capital markets in a manner very similar to that which regulation might have achieved. CEA played a valuable role here, clarifying the issues and bringing important evidence to bear.

Many people (including this author) think of themselves as Jefferson–Jackson democrats, preferring small over large when other things are equal. The proposal would have interfered with the operation of a rather efficient set of capital markets. Short of a showing that there were general social dangers at hand, the proposal should have been defeated. It did not represent good public policy.

NOTES TO CHAPTER 15

[1]15 U.S.C. 12.

[2]*U.S.* v. *Von's Grocery Company*, 384 U.S. 270 (1966).

[3]U.S. Federal Trade Commission, *Economic Report on Corporate Mergers.* (Washington, D.C.: FTC, 1969).

[4]Reciprocity is more accurately described as a form of price discrimination. If firm A makes the "I will buy from you if you buy from me" offer to firm B and would not otherwise buy from B, then presumably A is foregoing a better purchasing opportunity elsewhere. By nevertheless buying from B, firm A is effectively receiving a lower price on the net transaction with B than it receives on sales to other customers.

[5]For this last argument to be complete, one would have to know what the firms would otherwise do with the funds used for conglomerate mergers. Would they be used for physical investments? Or would they be paid out as dividends? What would the stockholders do with the funds? And what do the stockholders of the acquired firm do with the funds they receive?

[6]D. C. Mueller, "The Effects of Conglomerate Mergers: A Survey of the Empirical Evidence," *Journal of Banking and Finance*, 1 (December 1977): 315–348.

[7]See U.S. FTC, op cit., Chapter 6.

[8]L. M. Salomon and J. J. Siegfried, "Economic Power and Political Influence: The Impact of Industry Structure on Public Policy," *American Political Science Review*, 67 (September 1977): 1026–1043.

[9]The term "aggregate concentration" has been used by economists to differentiate this economywide concentration concept from concentration in individual markets, such as autos, steel, or computers.

[10]This factor would only affect comparisons over time if the foreign operations of the largest firms were expanding at a rate different from that of their domestic operations.

[11]These are slight overstatements, since the foreign sales and assets of firms have been included in arriving at the size classification figures.

part V

CONCLUSIONS

chapter 16

Conclusions

The previous chapters have provided a number of case studies of regulatory actions and the Executive Office's efforts to deal with them. This chapter will try to distill the lessons that can be learned from these experiences. First, the characteristics of the regulators and the regulatory process that have important consequences for the development of sensible regulation—primarily social regulation—will be summarized. Next, the strengths and achievements and also the weaknesses of the Executive Office's efforts to deal with regulation will be described. Finally, after a review of recent regulatory reform proposals, some recommendations for future public policy will be offered. The primary focus of this chapter will be on social regulation.

THE REGULATORY PROCESS

Dichotomizing the World

Perhaps the most salient characteristic of the regulatory process is that regulators (and the legislators who created the regulation) are looking for simple decisions, for certainty, for a dichotomous world in which yes-no answers can be given to problems that in reality are very complex and uncertain. They are uncomfortable with uncertainty, with probability distributions, with a world that is continuous rather than dichotomous.

The case studies have illustrated a number of the regulatory efforts to dichotomize the world. The national ambient air quality standard system (Chapter 4) is based on a threshold concept: air quality levels below the standard are "safe"; air quality levels above the standard are "unsafe." Thus, the regulatory task is to determine this safe level and then institute the proper controls so that this safe level is achieved. This kind of process has obvious political appeal. But it is worth reemphasizing that, if the real world does not contain these safe–unsafe critical points, this appearance of complete safety will be a chimera, and the pursuit of it represents misguided public policy that will likely have excessive net social costs.

The continuous nature of the real world may express itself through four paths. First, there may not be any thresholds for individuals. Even small doses of pollutants may have their effects on the wear and tear on humans, increasing slightly the probability of illness and/or shortening slightly the expected lifetimes of individuals. Individuals may vary in susceptibility, but there is no safe dose for anyone. As we noted in

Chapter 4, this is the present model of carcinogenic pollutants that EPA and other regulatory agencies have adopted. It may well be that further research on other pollutants, with more precise measurement methods, will lead to the same conclusion.

Second, even if there are thresholds for individuals (one could hypothesize a repair mechanism within humans that eventually becomes overwhelmed by an excessively large dose of a pollutant), these thresholds are likely to vary widely across different individuals. There will almost always be individuals (the young, the old, the otherwise sick, the allergic) whose thresholds will be very close to a zero dose of the pollutant. Thus, despite the existence of individual thresholds, the world becomes continuous in terms of the aggregate dose–response relationship across the entire population. There is no safe threshold (short of zero) that applies to everyone.

Third, even if there is a safe threshold that applies to everyone, the stochastic nature of meteorological events implies that there can never be complete certainty that the threshold will not be breached. Even if pollutant emissions are kept to low (but nonzero) levels, so that the average level of pollutants in the ambient air is below the threshold level, there is always the possibility that particular meteorological conditions will create high ambient air pollutant levels that will exceed the threshold, at least in some localities. The lower the average level in the ambient air, the less likely this is to occur, but the probability is always present. Thus, instead of a dichotomous safe–unsafe world, the world becomes one of a continuous set of probabilities that unsafe levels will be reached.

Finally, as long as pollutant emissions (even at comparatively low levels) occur in relatively concentrated doses at the point of emission, there will always be small local areas that will exceed the threshold. Place the monitor close enough to the emission point, before the pollutants have had a chance to disperse, and high readings will surely occur. Someone will be at risk. EPA cited local carbon monoxide problems as its justification for idle standards on trucks (Chapter 6) and high roadside particulate levels as part of its justification for tight controls on diesel particulates (Chapter 7). Again, the world loses its dichotomy. Less emissions mean fewer people at risk in the immediate vicinity of the emission point; more emissions imply the opposite.

EPA acknowledged the existence of the first three arguments for continuity in its approach to setting the NAAQS for ozone (Chapter 4). But it never truly integrated these factors into its decision. The Clean Air Act (the title itself suggests something about Congress' dichotomous view of the world!) forced it into the charade of finding a safe threshold.

Another area in which regulators try to dichotomize the world is in the setting of specific control standards on firms. The regulators want only to know whether specific standards will or will not be achieved by a specific date. They tend to impose an over-simplified engineering view on the world: Technology either will or will not be available. They are not interested in the *probabilities* that technologies will or will not be available or the *likelihoods* that in-use problems will develop even if the technology is "available." Indeed, the enabling regulatory legislation in virtually all cases uses terms such as "practicable," "feasible," "available," or "achievable." The legislation does not include terms such as "reasonable probability." EPA's decision on heavy-duty truck emission standards (Chapter 6) and on diesel particulate standards (Chapter 7) and NHTSA's decision on fuel economy standards (Chapter 8) were all couched in terms of certain availability.

Third, most regulatory standards are in terms of "achieve this level or else. . . ." A near miss is no better than complete failure; over-achievement is no better than just meeting the standard. This kind of regulatory standard meshes nicely, of course, with the view that there are safe–unsafe critical points in the world. Only recently, and only on a few standards, have penalties begun to replace "do it or else . . ." standards.

A fourth area in which regulators tend to dichotomize is the treatment of hazardous chemicals, especially carcinogens. In the view of many regulators, either chemicals are safe or they are not safe. If they are not safe, the full regulatory treatment should be applied. No considerations of potency or exposure are introduced to modify the required response. As mentioned in Chapter 9, OSHA's initial proposal on worker exposure to carcinogens embodied this approach. The Delaney Amendment's response to carcinogenic food additives exemplifies it. And the initial draft of the dumps and spills bill (Chapter 10) was written in the same way: EPA had the power to undertake complete containment and cleanup actions irrespective of the degree of hazard involved. An even simpler version of this theme was EPA's initial effort in the chemical premanufacturing notice case (Chapter 9): Make no distinctions at all and require complete information on all chemicals. (There is one encouraging exception to this pattern, however: EPA's proposal with respect to regulation of airborne carcinogens, in which potency and exposure are explicitly taken into account.[1] EPA's scientists' linear dose–response model for exposure to carcinogens, mentioned in Chapter 4, appears to have played an important role in developing this regulation.)

The desire for dichotomous decisions is understandable. The decisions do become simpler. The decision makers do not have to worry about explicit, complex trade-offs. They can reassure themselves and their constituencies that complete safety has been achieved, that regulatory controls will certainly be put in place at the required time. It is a pity that the world is more complex and that these reassurances are almost certainly false.

Regulatory Treatment of Costs

Congress has largely shied away from asking for regulatory agencies explicitly to weigh costs and benefits in their regulations. Instead, Congress frequently specifies in legislation only that the necessary technology be "practicable," "feasible," "available," or "achievable." Even when costs are explicitly mentioned, the legislation at best will indicate only that costs are to be taken into account. The regulatory agencies have interpreted these words (feasible, etc.) as permitting any standards that the industry "can afford." The usual test of what is feasible, for example, is a level of technology (e.g., to achieve emission controls or fuel economy standards or safer work environments) that will financially push the industry to the point at which some of its members are close to financial failure or (for a multiproduct firm) would decide not to produce that product. Thus, there is no consideration of costs until factories are on the brink of closing or jobs are being lost; at that point the process stops. To paraphrase Winston Churchill, this might be described as "squeezing industry until the pips speak." NHTSA's legal philosophy underlying the fuel economy standards (Chapter 8) embodies this approach, as does OSHA's policy on worker exposure to carcinogens and EPA's approach to water pollution under the Clean Water Act. It used to be fondly hoped that somehow these costs would be borne by "business." There is now a much wider recognition that regulatory costs are usually going to be passed on to consumers in higher product prices (and it is the higher prices and reduced consumer demand that may lead to the demise of a company or a product).

This "what the industry can afford" criterion is quite different from the criterion that an economist would choose: increase the stringency of regulation until the marginal social benefits are equal to the marginal social costs. The former criterion might lead to the same regulatory outcome as the latter only if (1) the marginal benefits from the regulatory

217

action are very high over the full range of possible stringency (in which case, why stop when one or two companies are forced to fold?) or (2) the social distributional weights are such that those who receive the benefits from the regulatory action are weighted heavily in the social calculus while those who bear the costs are weighted lightly or not at all. If neither of these conditions is met, the affordability criterion will lead to different (usually greater) levels of stringency than would the cost–benefit criterion; if (as most economists would argue) the cost–benefit criterion is the proper one, then society's resources are being misallocated and/or wasted.

Further, the regulatory agencies consistently underestimate the prospective costs of their regulations. They want to minimize the apparent costs that they are imposing on the regulated industries. Since the regulated industries can be expected to overstate the costs, the disparity between the regulatory agencies' estimates and the industries' estimates does not automatically throw public doubt on the accuracy and credibility of the former. There are no accounting audits or penalties for agency understatement. There have been no follow-ups or retrospective surveys of cost estimates. The agencies have no incentives to change their ways.

A problem with which neither the Congress nor the regulatory agencies have yet come to grips is that the regulators cannot all simultaneously impose a "what the industry can afford" set of regulations on the same industry. A single industry may have to meet air pollution, water pollution, solid waste disposal, *and* workplace safety standards. Even if one accepted the philosophy that there is a certain sum that can be exacted out of an industry's hide (beyond which closures occur, etc.), this sum would still have to be allocated among the regulatory areas. There currently is no means of making this allocation. A real risk exists that each regulatory agency will ignore or underestimate the costs that are being imposed by other agencies and assume that the sum available to finance its requirements is far larger than actually is the case. The simultaneous imposition of all these requirements could well have much more serious consequences for the industry than expected. The Regulatory Council (see Chapter 2) is expected to investigate this problem.

Technology Forcing

Many of the regulations are designed to be "technology forcing"; that is, the regulators try to force the industry to develop technologies (that otherwise would not be developed) to meet the regulations. They estimate the feasible level of technology (if it is suitably forced) at some future date and set the standards accordingly. Frequently, the regulators use as evidence technologies that are in the research stage but that (they claim) can be brought to production by the requisite date. The EPA diesel particulate standard (Chapter 7), the EPA heavy-duty truck testing and enforcement procedures (Chapter 6), and the NHTSA fuel economy standards (Chapter 8) embody this approach. The technology forcing approach, especially when coupled with standards that have the form of "meet the standard or else we will close you down," may encourage delay and inefficiency; important firms in regulated industries may delay the development of practicable technology and then, in effect, "dare" the regulators to close them down.[2] The fuel economy standards case brings out a somewhat different, longer-run consideration. Companies may be reluctant to undertake research if they fear that any findings that they report will shortly be thrown back at them as stiffer regulatory requirements for a few years hence. If firms in supplier industries (who hope to get the supply contracts when the stiffer regulations are imposed) are the only ones doing research in a number of areas, the research effort and consequent technological progress in these areas may well slacken. Ironically, technology forcing regulation may contain the seeds of its own undoing.

Admittedly, this is an oligopolistic view of the world. The firms in a competitive industry confronting a regulator would each hope to discover the new technology on which the regulators would then base standards, since the firm would hope to gain in market share by being able to meet the standards when some of its competitors could not (or it could hope to earn large royalties from licensing the technology to its competitors). But there are enough oligopolies in regulated areas, in which firms are likely to take the industry view rather than the competitive view of the consequences of regulatory-relevant research, that these consequences should be given more serious examination.

Risk Aversion

In the health–safety–environment area, regulators are likely to opt for risk-averse, politically safe regulatory strategies. This approach is likely to mean extra degrees of safety and of controls required for industry. Regulators are most likely to be politically embarrassed and raked over congressional hearing coals when accidents happen, as in the Three Mile Island nuclear reactor incident in March 1979 or the American Airlines DC-10 crash in May 1979. The extra costs imposed on

219

industry and ultimately on consumers by tighter regulations, even if they are ultimately more socially costly, are less likely to generate the specific and focused political criticisms of a major crash, accident, disaster, or epidemic that might have been avoided by tighter regulation.

The aftermath of the May 1979 DC-10 crash provided a good example. Following the crash, the Federal Aviation Administration delayed grounding all DC-10s until it had enough information to suggest that there might be a general problem with all DC-10s. In the congressional hearings that followed, FAA was severely criticized for not grounding the DC-10s sooner, despite FAA's protestations that its decisions at the various times were appropriate in the light of the information available at those times. It is likely that FAA will be quicker to ground planes after crashes in the future, despite the inconveniences imposed as travelers.

One might ask, How can traveler inconvenience be compared with the risk of lost lives in a crash? But, as was pointed out in Chapter 3, we as a society apparently consider that the inconvenience of a 45 mph speed limit more than offsets the lives that would be saved from the fewer and less serious crashes at that speed. We have declined to build pedestrian underpasses at every busy intersection, and we do not station an ambulance on every block.

This last point brings out another aspect of the political environment in which regulation operates: Chronic, low-level social costs, even deaths, do not attract the same political attention (and heat on regulators) as do occasional but more noteworthy accidents. An annual traffic toll of over 50,000 deaths attracts comparatively little political attention, because it occurs in isolated bits and dabs; a plane crash that kills 300 people attracts much more attention. A colleague at CEA calculated that the coal mined for burning in electric utilities is accompanied by roughly 90 deaths of miners per year in mine accidents.[3] These losses attract little attention; a nuclear reactor accident that kills no one attracts much more.[4]

THE EXECUTIVE OFFICE'S EFFORTS

The Achievements

The Executive Office's efforts at the reform and better management of social regulation—E.O. 12044, the Regulatory Analysis Review Group's filings, the COWPS filings, CEA's and COWPS's scrutiny of regulations—have had an effect in improving the quality of the regulations that have been proposed and promulgated. The agencies now know that their major proposals will receive close scrutiny by CEA and COWPS. The RARG and COWPS filings have received attention in the press. No agency likes to receive public criticisms that make it appear misguided or foolish. The agencies are preparing their regulations more carefully, providing better analyses, scrutinizing costs and consequences more carefully. Cost-effectiveness is becoming a more accepted concept, as is the wisdom of performance standards over design standards. There is now general recognition that consumers will ultimately pay for the costs of regulation.

These are generalities, of course, and there are still many exceptions. The millennium certainly has not arrived. CEA and COWPS cannot claim victory and retire from the field. But progress has definitely been achieved.

The pressures from the EOP are also strengthening the groups within the agencies that are interested in more sensible regulations. Mirroring the divisions concerning regulatory policy across the federal government are the divisions within the agencies or departments themselves. The agencies almost always have an office with responsibility for policy evaluation (as compared with the offices with direct operating responsibility for proposing and enforcing regulations), and the staff in these offices are frequently more inclined to take a balanced view of specific regulations. If their criticisms of operating divisions' proposals are subsequently supported by the EOP, their ability to influence the shape of future regulations must be enhanced.

Evidence for these effects is found in the general slackening in the pace of new regulatory proposals and promulgations. Agencies are taking more time in the preparation and analysis of proposals. As the basis for setting ambient air quality standards, EPA's criteria documents for pollutants, for example, are far more comprehensive than they were a decade ago, and EPA's overall level of documentation is much more impressive and careful. Preparation times are lengthening, as are the times between proposal dates and final promulgation dates. Indeed, one major regulatory agency, the Occupational Safety and Health Administration, did not promulgate a major final rule in the 14 months between November 1978 and January 1980 and did not propose a major new regulation during an even longer period.[5] There was a six-month period, in the spring and summer of 1979, in which many people thought that RARG had ceased functioning. But the "problem" was simply that there were few new major regulations to review.

Also, legal deadlines are being missed more frequently as agencies discover that they simply cannot develop an adequate basis for the required regulations in the time Congress has allowed. As noted in Chapter 7, despite the Clean Air Act's requirement of particulate standards for all vehicles for the 1981 model year, EPA is applying its light-duty diesel particulate rules only to the 1982 model-year vehicles, and it had earlier announced that particulate standards for heavy-duty trucks would not be required until the 1983 model year. EPA's heavy-duty truck emissions standards for hydrocarbons and carbon monoxide (Chapter 6) were originally supposed to apply to the 1983 model year; the final rule delayed application until the 1984 model year. In the future Congress will have to allow more time for the development of regulations.

Further evidence is found in the ozone episode (Chapter 4). EPA, through its own processes, did propose an ozone NAAQS that was less stringent than the existing one and subsequently, again largely through its own processes (though the EOP's sentiments were clear by then), did promulgate a final standard that was yet less stringent. The agency may not have gone as far as many would have liked, but similar behavior, even as recently as three or four years ago, would have been highly unlikely.

As another example, EPA in July 1979 issued an NPRM for HC and CO emissions for light-duty trucks for 1983.[6] Its provisions are virtually identical to those in the heavy-duty truck proposal (Chapter 6). An earlier version of the light-duty truck proposal, however, also contained a provision that would have tightened NO_x emissions in 1983, two years earlier than required by the Clean Air Act. EPA's internal forces—without any intervention by the EOP—succeeded in excising that provision.

Finally, regulatory analyses accompanying major regulations now routinely acknowledge that the costs of regulation will be passed on to consumers in the form of higher product prices. At the news conference following the announcement of the administration's spills and dumps bill (Chapter 10), EPA indicated quite explicitly that it expected the excise taxes on chemicals to be borne ultimately by the consumers of chemicals.

Again, the millennium has not arrived. There are still too many cost-ineffective regulations; design standards still appear; there are too many claims of "the regulations pay for themselves, therefore they are costless"; the regulators almost always understate the costs of regulation; too many regulators are reluctant to quantify the benefits; and all the problems described in the first part of this chapter still persist. Further, some of the agencies' improved performance is probably due to legal reversals in the courts when their evidence and support for regulations were not adequate. Nevertheless, the EOP's efforts are definitely having an effect.

The Strengths and Weaknesses

The EOP's greatest strength is clearly in the area of cost-effectiveness. CEA and COWPS economists can analyze overall regulatory packages and suggest alternative ways of achieving the same effects at lower costs to society. The corporate averaging proposal for diesel particulates (Chapter 7) and the selective information proposal for chemical premanufacture notification (Chapter 9) are examples.

Further, CEA and COWPS can serve to check the more extreme regulatory proposals: the standards that offer virtually no benefits (although some argued that EPA's final ozone standard, even at 0.12 ppm, was an example of a standard with virtually no benefits), the cost estimates that are badly understated, the legislative proposals that will have serious distorting effects on the economy. Even here, CEA and COWPS cannot check or stop all, but they can have some effect on most of the proposals.

Finally, they can support and reinforce the individuals who do perform solid analyses within the regulatory agencies. The snail darter case (Chapter 11) is an example of this.

The glaring weaknesses of CEA and COWPS is their staffs' comparatively small size and lack of complete detailed technical knowledge (e.g., engineering data, cost data) on many issues. Even with the help of the Office of Science and Technology Policy, they will always be at a great disadvantage vis-à-vis the regulatory agencies in arguing over details. The staffs are simply too small and cannot hope to acquire a mastery over the details of all the regulatory issues with which they must deal. Inevitably, they are going to be caught between regulatory agency engineers saying "The technology is available, it's easily applied, and it's low cost" and industry engineers saying "The technology is unproven, it has high risks, and it's horrendously expensive." This conflict was most apparent in the Ohio local coal dispute (Chapter 5) and the fuel economy standards dispute (Chapter 8). The EOP can focus the discussion and narrow the range of disagreement, and occasionally a staff member will have special expertise on the basis of which he or she can provide independent estimates. But in many cases the EOP will be caught in the middle, with no arbitrator to which it can turn.

Unfortunately, it is these details on which the marginal decisions on regulatory standards hinge. Whether to have a somewhat more lenient or a more stringent standard will usually depend crucially on these estimates of costs and effectiveness. Thus, although the EOP may be able to deter the grossly misspecified standards, it will be at its weakest in the discussions and negotiations over marginal changes. The same principle applies, of course, to the details on technical issues such as testing procedures, as in the heavy-duty truck emissions case (Chapter 6).

The regulatory agencies could well decide to exploit this weakness. If they conclude that the final levels of standards are going to be the outcome of a bargaining process with the EOP, they may initially propose standards that are more stringent than the agency would otherwise find satisfactory and then compromise to their desired level. The EOP will have "prevented" the more egregious standards from being established but will then have lost on the details. Also, the agencies may try to achieve more through tightening the technical procedures surrounding standards (e.g., testing procedures, averaging times, durability requirements), while leaving the standards unchanged. Finally, to avoid the scrutiny of the RARG process and the application of E.O. 12044, agencies may break their regulations into smaller pieces that fall below the $100 million tripping point.[7]

The preceding paragraph has described what might be called an adversary or collective-bargaining model of the determination of final regulations: The parties start far apart, knowing that each expects the other to compromise toward a middle ground. The description earlier in this chapter of the achievements of the EOP was characterizing an accommodation model: Agencies do not like to be mauled in public or to lose face by being pushed to positions they have opposed. The process of EOP review and management of regulation is still new enough that it is difficult to predict which model will prevail. It is possible that aspects of both will coexist: The agencies could well decide to accommodate the EOP on cost-effectiveness issues but adopt the collective-bargaining model on the levels of standards.

A similar failing, which had definitely been exploited by the regulatory agencies, was the EOP's weakness on another set of technical details—the legal ones. The regulatory agencies were able to say, "Our hands are tied; the law *requires* us to do the things we have proposed," relying on legal opinions by their general counsel offices. Lacking legal expertise, the economists in CEA and COWPS were not able to offer a suitable rebuttal. As noted in Chapter 5, however, by March 1979 this situation had changed, with the appointment of a new General Counsel of COWPS, who has effectively become the general counsel to the EOP's regulatory management effort.

RECENT PROPOSALS AND SOME RECOMMENDATIONS ON REGULATORY REFORM

Before offering some recommendations with respect to the regulatory management effort, it is worth reviewing the major proposals for dealing with the regulation "problem" (often ill defined) that have surfaced in the past few years. They fall into four groups.

Reform the Regulatory Procedures

Usually suggested by lawyers, this approach usually entails changes in rules for public representation at hearings during the public comment period, providing more time for public comments, improving notification procedures, requiring various kinds of impact statements by the agency, changing the standards for review by the courts, and so on. Its proponents believe that somehow the "public interest" will prevail if only the right procedures are found. This is reminiscent of the Ash Report of a decade ago,[8] which concluded that the major problems in economic regulation were largely those of procedures and the personnel of the agencies. The Ash Report was mistaken,[9] and so are those who believe that procedural changes will solve the problems of social regulation. If—as much of this book has argued—the problem is mainly that there are too many instances of regulations that generate large social costs without commensurate social benefits, procedural reforms will have little or no effect. The procedural reforms may help maintain a public sense of fairness and legitimacy in the regulatory process, and so they should not be discouraged.[10] But one should not expect much from them either.

225

Sunset

This proposal, embodied in former Senator Edmund S. Muskie's S. 2 bill in the 95th Congress, would require regulatory agencies periodically to review their regulations and programs; presumably, the agencies would "sunset" (rescind) those that are ineffective or excessively costly. Unfortunately, like the previous proposal, it wholly misses the mark. To the extent that the personnel of the regulatory agencies genuinely believe in the value of their regulations (and have strong constituency support), sunset will achieve little. As with zero-base budgeting, which was popular a few years ago, this concept appears to be fine in principle but will fall far short of target in the real world. It is noteworthy that the debate in the Senate on S. 2 was almost entirely in terms of generalities—"sunset will mean the demise of programs that do not work, that have grown unresponsive and ineffective"—with virtually no specific programs mentioned. Only the Civil Defense Agency (with an annual budget of only $90 million!) was named specifically.[11]

Reexamination of programs should certainly not be discouraged. Occasionally some improvements may occur, as in the ozone case (Chapter 4). But one should not expect wholesale improvements in regulatory results from sunset proposals.

Regulatory Budget

This proposal, first suggested by the Department of Commerce and embodied in Senator Lloyd Bentsen's S. 3550 in the 95th Congress, would establish an annual budget for the costs that the regulatory agencies impose on society.[12] It uses the analogy of the federal budget. The executive branch would propose and the Congress would pass annually a budget limiting the costs that regulatory agencies could impose on the sectors they regulate, in a fashion similar to the way in which Congress currently limits the amounts that regulatory agencies can spend. (The regulatory budget focuses solely on costs and ignores benefits, but so does the current federal budget.)

The proposal has the advantages of forcing the regulatory agencies to internalize the social costs of regulation. The agencies would have to allocate their regulations carefully and would have a strong incentive to minimize the regulatory costs involved in achieving their goals. The federal government as a whole would be in a far better position to consider the total social costs of all regulatory proposals in setting the annual regulatory agenda. Also, the concept recognizes that, even if regulation is beneficial, its costs should be controlled and allocated over a number of years. Again, the federal budget analogy is useful. Although Congress believes that its spending programs are useful, it does not try to cram all construction projects, for example, into one year but instead spreads them over a number of years.

Unfortunately, the regulatory budget would mean a large increase in the administrative burden of the Executive Office and in the legislative burden of the Congress. An entirely new budget process, almost as large as the current one, would have to be established, with a new or expanded OMB and new congressional committees. Further, the cost figures themselves would be very difficult to establish. Unlike the current fiscal budget, in which the dollar figures themselves are largely indisputable, the regulatory budgets' dollar figures would be subject to very wide ranges of judgment, even if a standardized methodology were imposed on all agencies. The regulatory agencies would have an even stronger incentive to underestimate the costs that they impose on the economy. The monitoring burden of OMB would be substantial.[13]

Legislative Veto

This proposal would require congressional approval for major regulations. One version, embodied in S. 2011 in the 95th Congress (sponsored by 6 senators), would require that major regulatory rules (e.g., those with impacts of over $100 million per year) receive concurrent resolutions of approval from both Houses of Congress within 60 days of promulgation before becoming effective and that other regulatory rules would be rendered inoperative if either House passed a resolution of disapproval within 60 days of promulgation. Other versions would not require explicit approval but would render major regulations inoperative if one or both Houses passed resolutions of disapproval within 60 days of promulgation.

This approach would put Congress squarely into the middle of the regulatory process.[14] It would greatly increase the oversight burden of Congress. It would mean a major shift of the power over the content of regulations to Congress and away from the executive branch. Further, the Carter administration has argued that the legislative veto provisions are unconstitutional.[15] In essence, they provide Congress with a way of achieving outcomes by majority vote that are not subject to presidential veto; that is, Congress could repeatedly reject (by majority vote) proposed regulations until it got the one it wanted. Under the normal constitutional legislative process, a two-thirds majority is required to override a presidential veto and hence to achieve outcomes independently of the President. (Despite this opposition, the legislative veto currently exists in a few laws; it is not, however, a widespread practice.)

Not one of these four proposals is likely to have much effect on regulation in the next few years. The first two simply will have little effect, even if the necessary laws are passed; the last two are too radically different from current procedures and are, in any case, unlikely to be put into effect on a broad basis in the near future.

Accordingly, it is worth considering some less global but probably more constructive suggestions for improving the regulatory management effort begun by the Carter administration. Again, these deal mainly with social regulation.

Legal Input

The process begun in March 1979 whereby the COWPS General Counsel serves as legal counsel to the EOP's regulatory effort must be expanded and strengthened. This expanded legal input means that there will be more interagency legal disputes that the Department of Justice will have to arbitrate, as it did in the Ohio coal case (Chapter 5). It will probably also mean more conflicts within the EOP. The COWPS lawyers will undoubtedly want to do more to affect the substance of regulatory management policy than just write briefs; the economists will undoubtedly resent this. Unfortunately, the history of conflict between lawyers and economists in Washington is far longer than the history of their cooperation. Nevertheless, from this economist's vantage point, this probable conflict is a price worth paying. The regulatory agencies' frequent cries of "our hands are tied by the law" cannot be allowed always to go unrefuted.

Task Forces

CEA and COWPS must make sure that they are represented on all interagency task forces, even those that ostensibly are dealing only with "technical" matters. There are few government policies that do not have microeconomic implications. The task forces that deal with them should have a voice of sensible microeconomics represented on them. The absence of CEA and COWPS on the initial task force to study dumps and spills (Chapter 10) was a failing that should not be repeated. OMB and DPS, as the coordinators of administration policies, must ensure this representation.

Pre-NPRM Activity

CEA and COWPS must involve themselves to a much greater extent in the shaping of proposed regulations *before* they reach the stage of the notice of proposed rulemaking. By the time regulations have reached the NPRM stage, they are largely shaped and the levels set. The agency has put its face and prestige on the line; the proposal and its numbers begin to take on lives of their own. Changes become more difficult to effect.

Regularizing pre-NPRM involvement by the EOP will not be easy. Occasionally, we heard from regulatory agencies, in response to EOP critiques of NPRMs, the comments, "Where were you when we were formulating it?" The fuel economy standards case (Chapter 8) was basically a pre-NPRM effort in which EOP involvement was not resisted. But more often we heard, in response to efforts to involve ourselves in pre-NPRM proposal formulation, "Stay out! Let us make our own decisions." The regulatory agencies will surely resist any *regularized* EOP involvement. Although currently there are frequent opportunities for informal EOP contributions, these are sporadic. And, given the heavy "fire-fighting" duties of the CEA and COWPS economists in dealing with current "crises" with short deadlines, it is difficult for them to find the time to initiate involvement in the longer-range development of regulations when crises are not involved and there are no short deadlines. Regularizing this involvement (i.e., making it a generally understood responsibility of the EOP) would effectively force the EOP staff to find the time.

It is not clear how this involvement could be regularized. One possibility would be to extend the OMB clearance and coordination process (see Chapter 2) to NPRMs. If general administration agreement is advisable when agencies make public statements through legislative proposals and testimony in congressional hearings, why not also require it when agencies make public statements through the publication of NPRMs? This clearance procedure would give CEA and COWPS an opportunity to review the NPRMs before they are published (in the same way in which they currently review agency legislative proposals and testimony). The clearance procedure would not necessarily regularize EOP involvement yet earlier in the process, which is vital, but it would be a start.

Reviewing Appeal Briefs to the Supreme Court

Regulations are increasingly likely to be appealed to the courts by the affected parties. The important cases are, of course, appealed to the Supreme Court. The Justice Department serves as lawyer for the agencies in appeals and, in coordination with the agencies' general counsel offices, develops the briefs for the Supreme Court. The content of those briefs can help to determine not only the decisions in the specific cases, but sometimes also the general legal interpretation of broad regulatory issues. For example, OSHA, in its appeal of the Fifth Circuit's reversal of its regulations on worker exposure to benzene (see note 4), wanted to argue that regulatory agencies generally should not be required to specify the benefits of their regulation. The EOP, though not sympathetic to the specific OSHA regulation at issue, did recognize the legitimacy of OSHA's right to appeal the case and to resolve legal uncertainties surrounding its regulations, since other circuits had ruled in OSHA's favor on other regulations. But the EOP wanted the argument narrowed as much as possible and not generalized. The EOP became aware of the appeal brief comparatively late in its development but was able to effect some changes; earlier involvement would have been better.[16]

Regularized EOP review of appeal briefs on regulatory issues to the Supreme Court would be desirable. Again, an OMB clearance process seems appropriate. The Justice Department would undoubtedly object, arguing that these are technical questions and that an OMB clearance procedure would "politicize" the process of writing briefs. But, again, these briefs are to some extent statements of an administration's intended policies. They should not be left solely to the lawyers of the affected agency and DOJ. They deserve review.

EOP Manpower

The size of the EOP staff devoted to regulatory management is inadequate. The day-to-day work is mainly borne by the CEA and COWPS staffs, with only occasional help from the other agencies within the EOP. A dozen economists and two or three lawyers at COWPS (which also has responsibility for filings on the public record of independent regulatory agencies) and three economists at CEA are not enough. They cannot properly deal with the full panoply of regulation that they now confront. If any of the previous four suggestions are heeded, the workload will increase measurably. An increase of both the COWPS and CEA staffs devoted to regulation would not be amiss, and OMB must become more involved in regulatory management issues.

Clarifying the Role of the EOP

The legitimacy of the EOP's efforts to manage executive branch regulation must be clarified. If the President is to be held responsible for the regulatory activities of his administration, he and his advisers must have the clear power to manage that regulation and influence the decisions. When conflicting national goals (e.g., environment, energy, inflation, employment) are involved, as they inevitably will be in any major regulation, there must be someone to coordinate and to decide on the relevant trade-offs that are to be made. If multiple regulations all affect the same industry or sector, someone must decide how hard each regulation will bite. The EOP should play this role. Many in Congress may object that Congress is the proper body for determining the trade-offs and priorities. But Congress has shown little awareness in the past of the need to make these choices, and a legislative body is unlikely to have the flexibility and capabilities to sustain a management effort. At its base, though, this is an argument over how the power of control over regulation should be divided between the executive and legislative branches. Inevitably, this power must be shared. Congress passes the necessary laws and directs specific actions, but the EOP must have the power to take advantage of the flexibility inherent in most legislation.

This EOP management role must imply extensive post-comment period activity by the EOP in rulemakings. Again, EOP activity here must be acknowledged and legitimized. If court decisions rule otherwise, new legislation must be sought. The possibility of a President who is held responsible for his administration's decisions but who cannot affect those decisions (except through the extreme action of dismissals) is an anomaly that should not be allowed to persist.

The previous six suggestions have been aimed at strengthening the particular procedures of the Carter administration's regulatory management effort. There are also broader policy measures that should be pursued.

Noncompliance Fees

As a substitute for "meet the standard or else we will shut you down" regulations, noncompliance fees should be sought wherever possible. The flexibility they provide is invaluable, and, as indicated in Chapter 6, they also provide the right incentive for the regulatory agencies to estimate accurately the costs of regulation. Where these fees are currently in the law but have not been implemented, as was originally the case in heavy-duty truck emissions (Chapter 6), the EOP must press hard for their implementation; where they are in the law but anyone taking advantage of them technically violates the law, as in the fuel economy standards (Chapter 8), the law violation aspect must be removed; and where they are absent from the laws, the EOP should press hard for amendments to include them.

Amending Legislation

Even the best regulatory management effort can achieve only limited results if legislation instructs or encourages regulatory agencies to ignore costs and benefits. If legal interpretations that this is the intent of the legislation (e.g., important parts of the Clean Air Act, the Occupational Safety and Health Act, the Clean Water Act, the Energy Policy and Conservation Act) persist, the EOP must eventually press for amendments to these acts that would call for consideration of both costs and benefits and for a balancing of the two. These amendments need not call for universal cost–benefit analysis (although this author, for one, would not shy away from such a call). But legislation that encourages the opposite is clearly bad public policy and will ultimately stand in the way of effective regulatory reform. It will not be politically easy to propose amendments that may lead to more dirt and less safety. But the social costs of doing otherwise appear too high.

Economic Regulation

Little space has been devoted to recommendations for dealing with economic regulation, because the proper policy is clear: deregulate. The securities, banking, trucking, and airline industries represent a welcomed start that should not be allowed to lose momentum. The maritime industry decision (Chapter 12), unfortunately, was in the opposite direction. It will be difficult for the Carter administration to reverse itself; a reversal may have to wait for a new administration. But rail transportation is certainly a prime candidate for deregulation, as is most of telecommunications. Further deregulation of trucking should be pursued. Natural gas at the wellhead and crude petroleum are currently scheduled to be completely decontrolled by the mid-1980s. Deregulation of the remainder of the petroleum–gasoline industry should be pursued even sooner; the costs of the Department of Energy's price and allocation regulations (Chapter 14) are too high now and are likely to grow. Regulation of the agricultural sector by the Department of Agriculture is another important target.

CONCLUDING COMMENTS

Regulatory reform and management are still comparatively new concepts. There have been inconsistencies in the Carter administration's efforts, and mistakes have been made, especially in the energy area. There are still glaring weaknesses. The reform efforts could be strengthened, or they could wither. It would be a pity if the latter were to occur. Both economic regulation and social regulation play such important roles in the American economy that their reform and management should not be neglected; the social costs of ill-conceived or badly structured regulation are too high. The reform efforts should be strengthened.

NOTES TO CHAPTER 16

[1]*Federal Register*, October 10, 1979, pp. 58624–58661.

[2]See the references in Chapter 3, note 5.

[3]In addition, there are injuries to miners and shortened lifespans because of mining-induced illnesses such as black lung disease.

[4]The radioactive emissions from Three Mile Island may have longer-term mortality and morbidity consequences. But so do the particulates and sulfates emitted from coal-burning electric utilities.

[5]Part of the reason for the hiatus may have been OSHA's desire to wait and see how its regulation on worker exposure to benzene fared in the Supreme Court. The regulation had been overturned by the Fifth Circuit Court of Appeals in October 1968. See *American Petroleum Institute et al. v. OSHA*, 581 F. 2d. 493 (1978).

[6]*Federal Register*, July 12, 1979, pp. 40784–40795.

[7]There was some suspicion within the EOP that this was one of the reasons why EPA chose to issue separate regulations on toxic water pollutants over the 1979–1981 period for each industry covered.

CONCLUSIONS

[8]The President's Advisory Council on Executive Organization, *A New Regulatory Framework: Report on Selected Independent Regulatory Agencies* (Washington, D.C.: G.P.O., 1971).

[9]See R. G. Noll, *Reforming Regulation* (Washington, D.C.: Brookings Institution, 1971).

[10]The Carter administration's regulatory reform bill, S. 755, consists largely of procedural reforms, plus the enactment of E.O. 12044 into law and its extension to the independent agencies. Giving E.O. 12044 the force of law should strengthen it, and its extension to the independent agencies is surely a step in the right direction.

[11]See *Congressional Record—Senate*, October 11, 1978, pp. S18166–S18220.

[12]See C. C. DeMuth, R. H. Shackson, E. O. Stork, and A. W. Wright, "The Regulatory Budget as a Management Tool," commissioned by the Joint Economic Committee, U.S. Congress, 96th Congress, 2nd session, May 29, 1979; C. C. DeMuth, "Constraining Regulatory Costs—Part II: The Regulatory Budget," *Regulation*, 4 (March–April 1980): 29–44; and R. Litan and W. D. Nordhaus, *The Regulatory Budget* (Washington, D.C.: Brookings Institution, forthcoming).

[13]As noted in Chapter 6, however, if noncompliance fees at marginal cost were instituted, and if the regulatory agency would prefer compliance, then the agency would no longer have an incentive to understate costs.

[14]See A. Scalia, "The Legislative Veto: A False Remedy for System Overload," *Regulation*, 3 (November–December 1979): 19–26.

[15]See the testimony of John W. Harmon on S. 2011 before the Subcommittee on Administrative Practice and Procedure, Committee on the Judiciary, U.S. Senate, 95th Congress, 2nd session, September 13, 1978.

[16]EOP intervention in the writing of DOJ briefs has occurred in other administrations. See W. Safire, *Before the Fall* (New York: Ballantine, 1977), p. 726.

Index

INDEX

Arizona, 194
Antitrust Division (see Justice
   Department)
Army Corps of Engineers, 155, 158
Arthur D. Little, Inc., 144
Ash Report, 225
Assembly of Life Sciences, 117
Automobiles and automobile industry
   (see Diesel particulate
   emissions, Fuel economy
   standards, Heavy-duty truck
   emissions, Motor vehicle and
   motor vehicle industry,
   Ozone)
Automotive Environmental Systems,
   Inc., 70
Automotive Testing Laboratories,
   Inc., 95

Bailey, Martin J., 44
Baker, Howard, 155, 158
Banking industry, 19, 29–31, 204,
   206, 232
Bator, F. M., 43
Benefits of regulation, 4, 39, 43, 223,
   232 (see also individual
   regulatory issues)
Bentsen, Lloyd, 226
Briggs, T., 118
Brooks, J., 187
Bruff, H. H., 26
Bubble concept, 114
Bureau of Alcohol, Tobacco and
   Firearms, 36
Bureau of Land Management (BLM),
   36
Bureau of the Budget (see Office of
   Management and Budget)
Bureau of the Census, 110, 205

California, 43, 133, 190, 195
Canada, 134

Cancer (see Carcinogens)
Carbon monoxide (CO), 9, 48, 68,
   101, 112
   diesel vehicles, 104, 112
   heavy-duty truck emissions, 86–96,
   222
   light-duty truck emissions, 222
Carcinogens, 68–69, 98–100, 106,
   115, 215–216
Carlson, R., 70
Carroll, R. E., 70
Carter, James C., 19, 21, 34 (see also
   President)
Catalysts, 89–90, 93, 97, 128, 136
Caves, R. E., 176
Chemical industry, 137–152, 204
Chrysler Corp., 99
Churchill, Winston, 217
Cincinnati Gas & Electric Co., 77, 84
Civil Aeronautics Board (CAB), 9, 19,
   21, 30–32, 164–165
Civil Defense Agency, 226
Clayton Act, 199
Clean Air Act, 8, 17, 43–44, 215, 222,
   232
   diesel particulate emissions, 99,
   102, 105, 115
   fuel economy standards, 120
   heavy-duty truck emissions, 86, 89,
   91
   Ohio coal, 72
   ozone, 48, 53, 56, 61, 63–64, 67–76
Clean Water Act, 146, 232
Cleveland Electric Illuminating Co.,
   77, 81, 83
   Ohio Coal, 77, 81, 83
Coal (see Ohio coal)
Coast Guard, 36, 146–148
Columbus & Southern Ohio Electric
   Co., 77, 81
Commerce Department, 38, 102, 147,
   149, 150, 155, 166–167, 180,
   205, 208, 226 (see also
   Maritime Administration,
   National Oceanic and

236